ANNOTATED GUIDE TO THE

Contract Management Body of Knowledge
(CMBOK)

2ND EDITION

Annotated Guide to the Contract Management Body of Knowledge
Second Edition

©2006 National Contract Management Association
All rights reserved. Published 2006.
Printed in the United States of America.
ISBN-13: 978-0-9700897-4-8

Preface to the Annotated Edition			i
Section 1	**The Contract Management Profession**		
Chapter 1	Introduction		2
	1.1	Purpose of This Guide to the CMBOK	2
	1.2	What Is a Contract?	3
	1.3	What Is Contract Management?	3
	1.4	The Contract Management Profession	4
	1.5	About NCMA	5
	1.6	Professional Certification	8
	1.7	Competencies for Contract Management	9
	1.8	The CMBOK Structure	9
Chapter 2	The CMBOK: An Overview		10
	2.1	Contract Life Cycle	10
	2.2	Contract Stakeholders	10
	2.3	Organizational Influences	11
	2.4	General Business Competencies	11
	2.5	General Contracting Competencies	14
Section 2	**The Contract Management Knowledge Areas**		
Chapter 3	Acquisition Strategy Competencies		22
	3.1	Acquisition Planning	22
	3.2	Market Research	22
	3.3	Contract Methods and Methodology	25
	3.4	Contract Types	26
	3.5	Contract Incentives	28
	3.6	Other Types of Contracts, Agreements, and Arrangements	29
	3.7	Contract Financing	30
	3.8	Intellectual Property	30
Chapter 4	Pre-award Contract Competencies		31
	4.1	Requirements Preparation	31
	4.2	Publicity	35
	4.3	Proposal Evaluation	36
	4.4	Source Selection	39
	4.5	Negotiations	41
Chapter 5	Contract Award Competencies		46
	5.1	Award	46
	5.2	Notification	48
Chapter 6	Post-award Competencies		48
	6.1	Contract Administration	48
	6.2	Subcontract Administration	50
	6.3	Changes and Modifications	51
	6.4	Property	52

	6.5	Transportation	53
	6.6	Disputes	54
	6.7	Termination	56
	6.8	Contract Closeout	56
Chapter 7		Specialized Knowledge Competencies	57
	7.1	Research and Development	57
	7.2	Architect, Engineering, and Construction Services	59
	7.3	Information Technology	60
	7.4	Service Contracts	61
	7.5	Contracting with State and Local Governments	61
	7.6	Supply-Chain Management	62
	7.7	International Contracting	63
Chapter 8		Unique Commercial Contracting Competencies	64
	8.1	Commercial Contract Law Basics	64
Chapter 9		Unique Federal Contracting Competencies	69
	9.1	Government Contract Law Basics	69
	9.2	Operational Practices Unique to Federal Contracting	71
Section 3		**Contract Management Body of Knowledge**	
Chapter 10		NCMA Certification Examinations	82
	10.1	The Anatomy of A Multiple-Choice Question	83
	10.2	How to Study	83
	10.3	Test Specifications for Certification Examination	83
	10.4	How to Approach the Certification Examination	83
Section 4		**The CMBOK Lexicon**	
		Federal Contracting	86
		Commercial Contracting	101
Bibliography			**114**
Appendix A		**The UCC Table of Contents**	**118**
Appendix B		**The FAR Table of Contents**	**132**

preface

This work builds upon the National Contract Management Association's *Guide to the Contract Management Body of Knowledge (CMBOK)*, second edition, 2004, authored by Marlys Norby, Emmalyn Smith, and Ronald Smith.

This annotated edition of the CMBOK expands, refines, and reorganizes the information presented in previous editions. It provides further definition of the field of contract management, the framework for the BOK, the practices outlined, the definitions, and the processes of contract management. This edition defines the contract and provides a step-by-step explanation of its life cycle, from its planning and administration to its closeout or termination. The guide provides procedural steps that apply to the contract management process in general, and discusses in Section 4 those processes that are unique to commercial or federal contracting. This section will be expanded upon in future editions of this guide.

This annotated edition of the CMBOK was compiled, written, and edited by Stratecon LLC. Stratecon is a management consulting company that specializes in acquisition services. The effort was lead by Catherine Z. Remley and Robert A. Ludvik of Stratecon. Additional editing was performed by Steve Boshears, Paula Cushman, Lyle Easley, Marlys Norby, Marge Rumbaugh, Gloria Sochon, Dr. Ronald Straight, and Diane Whitmoyer.

This *Guide to the Contract Management Body of Knowledge* will continue to be expanded to provide the contract management professional with a comprehensive source for information on the competencies required to succeed in the profession.

The Contract Management Profession

section one

Introduction **Chapter 1**

The CMBOK: An Overview **Chapter 2**

Chapter 1
Introduction

NCMA, with the assistance of many practitioners at all levels of performance, has developed an inclusive term and a document that describes the sum knowledge required for the practitioner in the contract management and procurement profession. This document is called the Contract Management Body of Knowledge (CMBOK).

In 1996, Frank Meneely defined the body of knowledge as:

> ...a conceptual framework that is systematized about a central theme and formulated through the process of definition, classification, and analysis with reference to the discovery of general concepts, theories, laws, and/or principles. The (body of knowledge) is the keystone of a profession and provides the baseline for the development of education and training materials, and certification requirements for its membership. It encompasses both theory and practice.

Building on Meneely's definition, the CMBOK Committee outlined the following encompassing definition:

> The CMBOK is an inclusive term that describes the sum of knowledge for the profession of contract management. The complete body of knowledge concerning contract management resides both with the practitioners and those who, like academicians and governing bodies, apply and advance contract management. This body of knowledge includes both the generally accepted practices (such as business and finance) that are widely applied, as well as state-of-the-art practices (such as e-commerce and catalog aggregation).

The CMBOK will always be a work in progress and consistent with NCMA's vision statement "...that enterprises will succeed through improved buyer–seller relationships based on common values, practices, and professional standards..." (for the complete vision statement, see page 7).

In 1996, the CMBOK was revised and reorganized to make it more relevant and useful to the contract management profession. In 2001, the Contract Management Certification and Accreditation Board (CMCAB) appointed a CMBOK Committee. This committee was charged with investigating, and subsequently updating, the CMBOK. The primary function of this document is to serve as the foundation for NCMA's professional education and certification programs. The original committee was responsible for the publication of the first edition of the *Guide to the CMBOK* (2002). Another committee added commercial content, and ongoing committee activities continually monitor the profession for changes to this primary document.

The second edition of the CMBOK (2004) included an updated lexicon of contracting terms for both federal and commercial areas. A series of charts patterned on a work breakdown structure (WBS) helped the reader understand the relationship among the elements of the CMBOK, as well as the similarities and differences among competencies associated with federal and commercial contract management. The dictionary complemented the charts and defined the terms used. The definitions take the guesswork out of discerning the meaning ascribed to each term.

This annotated edition of the CMBOK further refines and reorganizes the information presented in previous editions. The basic WBS pattern was retained, and the content was reordered into a series of chapters. Each chapter discusses a grouping of competencies essential for successful practice. The chapters are arranged from the general to the specific, and also attempt to stress the similarities between federal and commercial contracting, as well as unique aspects of each.

1.1 Purpose of this Guide to the CMBOK

Contract management is a mature profession, but still growing. The purpose of this guide is to provide a common understanding of the terms used in the profession. As a basic reference, this document is neither comprehensive nor all inclusive, but rather it seeks to provide a tutorial of the contract management process in commercial as well as federal contracting.

This document is also used by the National Contract Management Association as a basic reference about contract management knowledge and practices for its professional development programs, including NCMA's revised certification program.

1.2 What Is a Contract?

A contract is an agreement between two or more parties, especially one that is written and enforceable by law. For a contract to be valid, both parties must indicate that they agree to the terms. This is accomplished when one party submits an offer that the other accepts within a reasonable time or a stipulated period. If the terms of the acceptance vary from those of the offer, that acceptance legally constitutes a counteroffer; the original offering party may then accept it or reject it. At any time prior to acceptance, the offer may be rescinded upon notice unless the offering party is bound by a separate option contract not to withdraw. Only those terms expressed in the contract can be enforced; secret intentions are not recognized. For a contract to be binding, it must not have an immoral or criminal purpose or intent or be contrary to public policy. Since a contract is an agreement, it may be made only by parties with the capacity to reach an understanding.

Most contracts are bilateral, consisting of reciprocal promises. Under bilateral contracts, each party has made a promise, has an obligation to perform, and has expectations that the other party will perform. An example is a contract where one party promises to provide services and the other party promises to pay an agreed-up amount of money.

There are unilateral contracts where only one party has made a promise and is obligated to perform. An example of this may be a contract that promises monetary reward to find a missing purse. No one is obligated by that contract to search for that purse, but if the purse is found, the party who promised the reward is obligated to pay a reward.

An express contract is one in which the terms of the contract are stated in words, either written or spoken, and assented to by both parties. An implied contract, sometimes called "implied in fact," is one in which the terms of the contract are wholly or partly inferred from conduct or surrounding circumstance. Quasi contracts, sometimes called "implied in law," are obligations imposed by law to prevent the unjust enrichment of one person at another's expense.

A legally binding contract must:

- Involve two or more parties that have the capacity to contract;
- Show agreement, including offer, acceptance and mutual assent;
- Show something of value changing hands between the parties to a contract, or other inducement that leads a person to make a promise;
- Be for a legal purpose, and;
- Be in the correct form.

A contract can be partially or totally unenforceable. If a party to the contract does not have the capacity to contract, such as youth or mental infirmity, a contract is unenforceable. An illegal contract violates public policy or statutes. A court will not intervene in the case of illegal contracts, however, the court may divide the contract into legal and illegal portions and consider only the illegal portions void. A contract also can be unenforceable in cases of misrepresentation, duress, undue influence, lack of written evidence of the terms of certain business-related contracts, and in some cases, mistakes.

A contract is executed when all the parties have fully performed their contractual duties.

Commercial contracting refers to a contract between two or more commercial (non-governmental) entities. Government contracting refers to a contract between two or more entities, at least one being a government entity.

1.3 What Is Contract Management?

Contract management is the process of managing contracts, deliverables, deadlines, contract terms, and conditions, while ensuring customer satisfaction. Public agencies and private companies know that the purchasing process doesn't end when the contract is awarded. Effective post-award contract management is essential to the seamless acceptance of supplies and services. Contract management affects many areas within an organization and can significantly influence its budget, operations, customer service, and public image.

Procurement and contract management are actually mirror images of each other. Both professions describe the broader process of sales or acquisition between two parties. Some objectives of buyers and sellers are distinctly different, while others are surprisingly similar. A mutually beneficial contract often can be challenging to craft. Buyers want the lowest price, whereas sellers want to maximize it. Both, however, should strive to meet the quality, delivery, and performance expectations of each other. Working together, they form a group of professionals under the "acquisition" umbrella.

Procurement consists of evaluation and selection of suppliers based on availability, reliability, and price to obtain the highest quality products at the lowest price. Buyers attend trade shows and conferences and they visit suppliers' plants to examine products and stay abreast of industry trends. They must develop a working technical knowledge of the goods or services they buy. Often, they forge a strong working relationship with their supplier counterparts—the contract managers—to optimize the outcome for both parties.

The mission of a contract management organization may read as follows:

> …The…contract management organization's mission is to provide vision, leadership, and professional expertise within the total business team necessary to ensure, at the lowest cost consistent with the significance of the issue or matter, that:
>
> 1.) …Contracts with its customers are negotiated, managed, and communicated in a manner that satisfies customers' needs and requirements;
>
> 2.) Working with program and business management functions, the (organization) complies with contractual terms and conditions and applicable laws and regulations;
>
> 3.) Contractual issues and risks are anticipated, avoided, or mitigated if possible, and appreciated in making business decisions; and
>
> 4.) Opportunities to advance or protect the (organization)'s legitimate interests are identified and appropriately pursued.

To be fully effective, contract management services are best developed and provided through full integration and active participation in the business team from the first moment of the business process.

1.4 The Contract Management Profession

What constitutes a profession? Although individual responses to this question may differ, the Department of Labor has held that a profession has at least five distinct characteristics: a professional organization, a code of ethics, a body of knowledge, research activities, and a credentialing arm. The contract management profession has all five of these characteristics: a professional organization (National Contract Management Association, with news of the profession being published in *Contract Management* magazine and monthly electronic newsletters); a code of ethics for the profession; a body of knowledge, which is updated continuously; a research publication (*Journal of Contract Management*); a research arm (The Contract Management Institute); and a viable and highly visible credentialing program.

Contract management is a niche within the business profession, but it has a very broad perspective in terms of the responsibilities assigned to a contract manager. The job scope ranges from the administrative skills of managing, organizing, and planning, to the excitement and challenge of negotiating a major contract. Both procurement and contract management demand competence in such areas as contract law, administration, accounting, psychology, management, and planning.

The Contract Management Institute (CMI) commissioned two studies on the contract management profession in 1999 and 2001. The first study, conducted by PriceWaterhouseCoopers, analyzed the implications of current and future business requirements on contract and business management professionals. An important objective of this research was to reach conclusions gleaned from the insights of active and inactive contract management professionals and others, such as educators, consultants, lawyers, and those working in various related disciplines. Some notable findings of the study were as follows:

1. Essential core activities of contract managers include structuring business arrangements, managing contract formation and execution, pursuing innovative contracting or business approaches, making decisions, and building strategic relations.

2. More than 80 percent of CMI's respondents believe that the contract professional's role is more time-sensitive, involves more responsibility, is

more team-oriented and more strategic than in the past. In the future, contract managers will have an increasingly important role to play in cross-functional or integrated process teams.

3. In the future, business-related performance metrics must be used to assess practitioner effectiveness.

4. Almost 93 percent of CMI's respondents agreed or strongly agreed that a specialized undergraduate degree in contracting or purchasing is the most desirable educational background. However, effective written and verbal communication skills are the most important current and future professional requirements. Analysis and negotiation skills are highly prized in the short term, but will be superseded by computer literacy and problem-solving skills. Business judgment is a highly valued competency regardless of the time period.

5. With respect to education and training opportunities, contract and business managers largely are responsible for guiding their own career development.

6. The results showed a high correlation between salary levels and education.

The purpose of a second study commissioned by CMI, conducted by Stratecon, was to provide a better understanding of the performance metrics and performance evaluation systems by which organizations measure the performance of contract managers and purchasing professionals today, as well as what standards might be appropriate to use in the future.

The study showed that the contract management profession was evolving. Seventy-five percent of survey respondents agreed or strongly agreed that the contract management or purchasing function in their organizations was evolving into a strategic function that interacts with most aspects of an organization's business to include: (1) building strategic relationships internally and externally; (2) strategic planning and sourcing; (3) collaborating on acquisition planning; (4) participating in cross-functional or integrated process teams; (5) pursuing innovative contracting or business approaches; and (6) increasing decision-making authority.

The top 10 metrics chosen by the overall population to evaluate the performance of contract management and purchasing professionals included: responsiveness, integrity, and adherence to ethical standards; timeliness; written and verbal communication; human relations and interpersonal skills; problem-solving ability; education; internal customer service; and strong business judgment.

The top 10 metrics recommended for use in the future to evaluate the performance of contract management and purchasing professionals included: integrity and adherence to ethical standards, human relations and interpersonal skills, business judgment, decision-making ability, external customer service, written communication, negotiation skills, customer focus, problem-solving ability, and responsiveness.

As a premier research organization in contract management, CMI strives to further the contract management profession by conducting research in areas where there has been little or no known previous research. One important value of the research is that it provides a sharing of information among contract management and purchasing organizations through which the contract management and purchasing professions can be strengthened.

1.5 About NCMA

NCMA is devoted to education and training, to research and study, and to a certification program that reflects the highest standards of professional achievement. Guided by a code of ethics, the association is committed to develop and provide programs, products, and services that nurture and enhance contract management competencies through leadership and business management partnering.

Thousands of professionals enhance their knowledge and leverage opportunities in purchasing, procurement, project management, and contract management with NCMA. Comprised of individual members and professional groups from nonprofit, industry, and government, NCMA provides unique resources for the contracting community.

For more than 45 years, members have taken advantage of NCMA membership benefits to advance their careers. Practical, proven survival techniques and industry news help members stay informed of current contract management events.

NCMA continues to provide vital information about the field through the association's prestigious publications, educational materials, and professional resources.

Over the next five years, unimagined technological changes will produce a new realm for virtually instantaneous business transactions. And over the next decade, what now seems far-fetched in electronic commerce will become commonplace. Even the most vivid imaginations cannot predict what may occur and affect the contract management profession, NCMA, and its membership. To help prepare for the vagaries of an uncertain future, NCMA continues to monitor the contract management profession and reflect the changing character of that profession in its certification program.

NCMA was formed in 1959 to foster the professional growth and educational advancement of its members. NCMA is a membership-based, professional society, whose leadership is composed of volunteer officers.

The NCMA office has a full-time staff to support its members' needs. The NCMA staff directory provides information about the NCMA office departments responsible for different services. NCMA is located at 8260 Greensboro Drive, Suite 200, McLean, Virginia 22102. The NCMA office is open between the hours of 8:30am and 5:00pm ET.

To further describe NCMA's commitment to the contract management profession, provided below and continued on page 7 is NCMA's Code of Ethics and Standard of Conduct.

NCMA Code of Ethics

Each member of the National Contract Management Association accepts the obligation to uphold the purposes of the organization as set forth in the NCMA Bylaws, to strive for the increase of knowledge in job performance in the field of contract management, and to abide by the letter and spirit of the ethical standards of the association.

As prescribed in Article XIX of the bylaws, this code of ethics establishes for the member a foundation of professional conduct. However, ethical conduct may require more than merely abiding by the letter of the code. It is therefore incumbent upon each member of the association to make a commitment to honorable behavior in all aspects of work and professional activity.

Each member of NCMA shall:

1. Strive to attain the highest professional standard of job performance, to exercise diligence in carrying out the duties of his or her employer, and to serve that employer to the best of one's ability.
2. Keep informed of acquisition developments, through academic course work and attendance at symposia, in order to increase knowledge, skill, and thoroughness of work preparation
3. Respect the confidence and trust reposed in the member by one's employer.
4. Conduct oneself in such a manner as to bring credit upon the association, as well as to maintain trust and confidence in the integrity of the acquisition process.
5. Avoid engagement in any transaction that might conflict with the proper discharge of one's employment duties by reason of a financial interest, family relationship, or any other circumstance causing a breach of confidence in the acquisition process.
6. Not knowingly influence others to commit any act that would constitute a violation of this code.

NCMA Standard of Conduct

I. Our Vision

NCMA will lead and represent the contract management profession. Our vision is that enterprises will succeed through improved buyer–seller relationships based on common values, practices, and professional standards.

II. Our Mission

NCMA exists to enable the workforce to grow professionally, assess individual and organizational competency against professional standards, establish values, develop best practices, and provide access to skilled individuals, enabling enterprises to improve their buyer–seller relationships.

III. Our Value Propositions

We enable our members to develop professionally by offering access to a diverse contract management community of practice, a sanctioned code of ethics, an organized body of knowledge, and an accredited certification program. Through its international chapter network, publications, programs, and activities, NCMA provides the tools, resources, and leadership opportunities to enhance each member's professional career and gain recognition for their voluntary accomplishments.

We enable our chapters to successfully establish an organized local presence, sustain a voice in the professional community, and advance the objectives of the association by providing a national infrastructure, organizational support, strong branding, and access to training and marketing resources. Chapters, in turn, provide a local venue and distribution system to support the national brand, attract new members, retain current members, and generate revenue to advance the goals of the local and national organization.

We enable organizations that employ members of our community of practice to advance their organizational goals by facilitating ready access to skilled human capital, learning resources, and best practices, standards, and metrics of the profession. We uphold the professional standing of our members to improve contract management performance and bring strategic value to those organizations.

We enable other external customers, such as researchers, consultants, trainers, recruiters, and universities, to gain broad access to defined segments of our community of practice and our body of knowledge for the purpose of advancing the profession and fulfilling their individual goals.

IV. Our Values

We are committed to:

- Principled professional conduct and achievement, as dictated by our code of ethics;
- An open exchange of ideas in a neutral forum;
- A culturally and professionally diverse membership;
- Excellence in everything we do, especially our service to our members and the contract management community;
- Continuing education, training, and leadership opportunities through a network of local chapters;
- Remaining the preeminent source of professional development for contract professionals;
- Growing the association to serve the widest possible constituency in the field of contract management;
- Recognizing and rewarding professional excellence and superior individual achievement in support of the contract management profession;
- Demonstrated professional achievement through certification;
- Quality volunteer leadership; and
- Members' independence of purpose, freedom of action, and responsibility to the people and organizations they serve.

1.6 Professional Certification

NCMA's first professional certification designation, the certified professional contracts manager (CPCM), was established in 1974. NCMA's leadership, understanding that NCMA needed to establish a method of recognizing professional achievement, worked closely with industry and government professionals to develop a comprehensive program. The CPCM represents a hallmark of professional achievement in the field of contract management.

The first CPCM exams were held across the country in 1976, with 23 successful candidates receiving the CPCM designation. Based on a set of stringent educational criteria and years of experience and service, some senior professionals were given a one-time opportunity to receive the CPCM designation without sitting for the examination.

The certified associate contracts manager (CACM) designation was added in 1980 to certify the mastery of the fundamentals of federal government contracting. In 2002, the CACM designation was renamed the certified federal contracts manager (CFCM) to more accurately describe its content and focus. All those who were awarded the CACM have been automatically redesignated as CFCMs.

Although the CPCM and CACM designations were originally developed as methods of recognizing professional achievement among peers, both have evolved to be much more. Today, NCMA's professional designations and the standards behind them are widely recognized by both government and industry as a consistent measure of the skills and experience needed by successful contract managers. Across the nation, employment requisitions and advertisements are stating, "NCMA designation preferred."

Government agencies are recognizing the value of certification when making promotion decisions. NCMA's designations are seen as a standardized hallmark of excellence across the contract management community.

NCMA's Revised Certification Program

At the start of the new millennium, NCMA began to seriously consider revising and revitalizing its certification programs. In July 2001, at the West Coast Conference, NCMA leadership voted in favor of a Contract Management Certification and Accreditation Board (CMCAB) to direct this effort. The CMCAB, which comprises nine contract management leaders from the upper echelons of government and industry, has been extremely active. NCMA is proud to announce a certification program that is presented in modules, delivered at Thomson Prometric centers around the country, and available on a continual basis, five days a week, at least 51 weeks of the year.

The certification program has three modules: (1) a general business knowledge module; (2) a federal knowledge module; and (3) a commercial knowledge module. Each module consists of approximately 100 multiple-choice questions. All candidates must take and pass the general business module, which provides a common thread among the certifications and with the business community. If candidates also take and pass the federal knowledge module, they will be awarded the CFCM designation. If candidates take and pass the commercial knowledge module, in addition to the general business knowledge module, they will be awarded the Certified Commercial Contracts Manager (CCCM) designation. The CPCM candidate must have earned the CFCM and CCCM designations as a prerequisite to application and must, as part of the application process, provide a self-authored statement of professional qualifications.

Eligibility Requirements

Eligibility requirements for the CFCM and the CCCM are nearly identical. Candidates must have a degree at the bachelor's level from a regionally accredited college or university, with at least 24 hours of course work in business management topics; two years of contract management experience; and 120 hours of continuing education in the business management area. Candidates for the CFCM need to have at least 40 of those continuing education hours specific to federal contract management, while candidates for the CCCM need to have 40 hours specific to commercial contract management. Eligibility requirements for the CPCM include, in addition to the designations for CFCM and CCCM, a degree above the bachelor's level, five years of experience, and a self-authored statement of professional qualifications (500-800 words).

Waivers of these degree criteria are possible, if the candidate has at least 10 years of experience and can provide a letter of support from a supervisor.

Applications, as well as more information on the programs, can be found on the NCMA Web site at www.ncmahq.org or by calling NCMA at 800-344-8096.

1.7 Competencies for Contract Management

A contract manager's skills are developed through continuing education and practice. A successful contract manager has developed skills in three main areas: technical, conceptual, and human relations.

Technical skills are demonstrated by competently performing the tasks required, such as preparing and issuing solicitations, preparing bids and proposals, preparing or analyzing terms and conditions, or analyzing procurement requirements and supplier capabilities. Training for these skills can be accomplished in degree, certificate, professional continuing education, or specialized programs.

Conceptual skills relate to the manner in which the contract manager visualizes the contract's organization in terms of the agency's or company's goals. These skills involve the ability to see and use the "big picture" for greater organizational and personal success.

Human relations skills focus on the "people" aspect of contract management. Effective performance requires the cooperation of many others over whom the contract manager has little or no organizational control. Dealing with government and contractor representatives from a diverse range of disciplines requires strong relational and communication skills. Many contract managers consider competency in human relations to be the most important skill for the future of their jobs and careers.

1.8 The CMBOK Structure

The CMBOK is organized in three major components; foundational (or core) competencies, subject matter competencies, and job or task-level skills. The same structure applies to both federal and commercial contract management.

The illustration below presents a graphic depiction of the CMBOK. This part of the guide concentrates on the general and specific contract management competencies for practice in both the federal government and commercial environments. NCMA's certification program comprises three examination modules that address both the commonalities and differences between federal and commercial practice.

Specialized Knowledge	General Business	General Contracting
Post-award	CMBOK Outline of Competencies	Acquisition Strategy
Award		Pre-award

Chapter 2
The CMBOK: An Overview

2.1 Contract Life Cycle

Contracts have a defined beginning and end. The contract life cycle defines these parameters. The contract life cycle is broken down into several contract phases. The phases during the total life cycle can be categorized as acquisition planning, pre-award, contract award, and post-award. There is also consideration of special competencies required based on the requirement, contract type, and processes employed in the contract life cycle.

The contract life cycle begins with acquisition planning. Planning is an essential preliminary component to the successful completion of virtually any effort. Acquisition planning is a critical first step in the contract life cycle. Such competencies as conducting market research, selecting the proper contract type and formulating the acquisition strategy are all part of this phase.

Once the planning is completed, the next phase is pre-award. This involves all of the work that leads up to an awarded contract. Some acquisitions are very simple, others exceedingly complex, and the majority fall somewhere in the middle. The pre-award phase includes preparing requirements, evaluating proposals, conducting negotiations, and completing source selection.

The award phase is a transitional phase that goes from signing a contract to notifying unsuccessful vendors. The elements of the contract award phase include awarding the contract, debriefing unsuccessful offers, and addressing any mistakes in proposals or any protests or litigation.

Once the award phase is completed, the post-award phase begins. This involves all of the contract management functions known as contract administration. The contract administration functions will vary greatly, depending on the complexity of the contract. However, the basic premise remains the same. Is the seller delivering what was contracted for to the buyer? The post-award phase includes the necessary contract administration activities to ensure performance and bring the contract to a successful conclusion. This includes executing contract modifications, addressing any issues arising during contract performance, and, upon completion of performance, invoicing, payment, and closing out the contract.

2.2 Contract Stakeholders

A contract is an agreement between two parties. Therefore, contract stakeholders are on both sides of the agreement (contract). The party with the requirement, usually the initiating party in the contractual process, has several stakeholders who are directly affected by the contracting process.

The stakeholders begin with the organization that has the requirement for which a contract will ultimately be executed. This stakeholder is generally the end-user of the item or service provided under the contract. There is also a program office that is responsible for defining the requirement in a manner that can be readily identifiable, clear, and concise enough to allow for consistent understanding for all parties involved in the contracting process. The program office may be part of the end-user's organization, but does not have to be.

There is a finance office, which may be part of the program office that is responsible for identifying the funding to be used to buy the supply or service. Then there is the contracting officer, who is responsible for executing the contracting process, and ensuring and enforcing contract terms and conditions, including performance or delivery.

The second set of stakeholders is part of the organization receiving the contract and tasked with providing the goods and/or services to the requiring organization. Those stakeholders include the company or organization receiving the contract, including the group within tasked with providing the goods or services. The organization may not have the internal capability to provide the total requirements of the contract. In that case, some of the effort would be subcontracted and those subcontractors would become contract stakeholders.

The organization providing the goods or services must have the financial capability to perform contractual requirements prior to delivering and receiving payment. That source of funding, whether internal or through creditors, is also a stakeholder in the contract process.

2.3 Organizational Influences

Organizational influences have a profound effect on the contracting process. These influences can be internal or external to the organization. Senior management in an organization directly influences the initiation of requirements that are ultimately fulfilled through the contracting process. This influence takes place in several ways.

For example, senior management may adjust or change company focus through strategic planning. This change in focus will commonly result in changing business processes and procedures. This results in new requirements for software, hardware, and can even cause a change in the qualifications of people working for the organization. These changing requirements are generally fulfilled or supported through the contracting process.

Evolving technology has a profound influence on an organization. It affects business processes, which ultimately can affect organizational structure and enhance organizational performance. To take advantage of evolving technology and its benefits, an efficient and effective contracting process must be in place.

Competition in the marketplace is a strong organizational influence. This involves maintaining awareness of industry best practices and, where possible, developing best practices rather than continually implementing those already developed. Again, an efficient and effective contracting process is required to be an industry leader.

2.4 General Business Competencies

The duties and responsibilities of a contracting professional extend well beyond the specialized set of knowledge and experience unique to the profession. Current business and government organizational models are rapidly and continuously changing in pursuit of increased efficiency and decreased cost. Given the current environment of rightsizing, outsourcing, lean management, six sigma, continuous process improvement, balanced scorecards, transformation, and reinvention, one would have difficulty arguing that the people who function in this environment have no need to change as well.

Contracting professionals, as well as other professionals in business and government, can no longer perform effectively in the neatly insulated isolation of specialized knowledge and experience. Most organizations rely, to greater or lesser degrees, on various forms of matrix-managed functions, project or program teams, permanent or temporary process improvement groups, and similar types of collaborative entities. These relatively new structures exist primarily to bring more attention to the idea that each segment of an organization, whether public or private, needs to make a positive contribution to the business of the business or the mission of the agency.

The team approach to the operation of business and government often results in a smaller and necessarily more proficient and agile staff. The knowledge required to be an effective contracting professional today extends beyond the complex and dynamic contracting environment. A contracting professional must also be a business professional. One must have a clear understanding of the general functions of business and government and how those functions combine with and complement each other to achieve organizational goals.

The following brief descriptions discuss some of the key general business competencies that contracting professionals might reasonably be expected to possess. While no one person will be an expert in all of these areas, a seasoned contracting professional should at least have a basic understanding of each general business competency.

Marketing	Management	Operations Management
Information Technology + Systems	General Business Competencies	Accounting
Finance	Economics	Budgeting

These competencies include management, operations management, accounting, budgeting, economies, finance, information technology and systems, and marketing.

2.4.1 Management

The ability to manage is essential for successful contract management because this will determine the success or failure of a contract. Management consists of the processes used to accomplish the goals of a contract organization. The basic and commonly accepted functions of contract management include: (1) planning, (2) organizing, (3) directing, and (4) controlling. The size of an organization and the complexity of its business normally dictate the size of the contract management staff. A small business may have only one person in charge of all contract organization management activities. A large corporation or government agency may have hundreds, or even thousands of managers, with each being responsible for some segment of the contract organization's activities. Regardless of the entity's size and business purpose, the four key functions of management noted earlier are essential at all levels within the contract management organization team.

Managerial Skills and Competencies

In addition to the four basic functions of management discussed earlier, there are a number of other direct and indirect (hard and soft) skills that are most valuable in ensuring managerial effectiveness.

Technical skills: Although it may seem intuitively obvious, the need for managers to be technically competent cannot be overemphasized. It is imperative that managers possess the knowledge required to perform the work they require of their subordinates. Though it is likely that a manager will be less proficient than his or her subordinates in actually performing the work on a day-to-day basis, the ability to manage well has a direct relationship to the manager's level of technical knowledge.

Communication skills: The ability to effectively communicate is essential for successful management. Effective communication is a two-way street and has multiple facets, including the ability to speak clearly and concisely to individuals, small groups, and large groups; the ability to listen and understand others at all levels within an organization; the ability to plan, conduct, and control formal and informal meetings; and the ability to convey written information in a format and at a level appropriate to the intended recipient.

Human relations skills: Effective managers must be able to work with a wide variety of individuals and groups with differing social, educational, and experiential backgrounds and varying capabilities to ensure that goals are accomplished. These human relations skills, often more art than science, are of increasing importance as the workforce of most organizations continues to become more diverse.

Time management skills: Time is one resource that most managers wish they had more of. For a manager to succeed, it is vital that he or she have the ability to structure his or her time in a hierarchical manner; to know what is important now and what can be deferred; to recognize "time-wasting" activity masquerading as productive effort; to be accessible when needed and alone when required; to organize, plan, and execute the expenditure of time; and to know when to modify the plans.

Technology skills: Continuing advancements in information technology and communications technology provide significant opportunities for managers to increase their effectiveness. It is important that all managers, particularly those who were educated and began their careers before such technology was widely available, become familiar with and appropriately incorporate the use of technological advances into their arsenal of skills.

2.4.2 Operations Management

Operations management is a subset of management activity that is primarily concerned with actions related to the directing and controlling functions of management. Operations management is attuned to ensuring

- That each function has the correct quantity of necessary inputs (such as materials, labor, etc.) required to perform the desired tasks;

- The success of the transformation process—the way or system in which inputs are changed into something of desired value (e.g. an accounting report);

- Outputs are what were in fact desired initially, and that they conform to the quality and quantity originally planned for; and

- Appropriate feedback occurs, whether it is:
  - Informational feedback—a two-way exchange between management and workers to seek clarification, discuss improvements, and share status;

- Corrective feedback—an exchange from the manager to workers to point out mistakes and redirect effort toward improvement; or
- Reinforced feedback—an exchange from the manager that includes praise for a job well done or for exceeding standards to promote continued improvement.

2.4.3 Accounting

Accounting is a body of principles and conventions, as well as an established process for capturing financial information related to an organization's resources, and using that information to meet the organization's goals.

Contract professionals need to consider the accounting function very early in the acquisition planning process. The pricing structure of the resultant contract, payment terms and provisions, and an understanding of overhead rates are key accounting issues that will have a direct effect on successful contract performance.

2.4.4 Budgeting

Budgeting is the process of generating a quantitative plan of operations that identifies the resources needed to accomplish the organization's goals and objectives. It can include both financial and nonfinancial aspects.

Contracting professionals need to interact with budgeting personnel throughout the contracting life cycle to ensure that sufficient funding exists for the resultant contract.

2.4.5 Economics

Economics is the social science that studies how a society solves the human issues of unlimited wants and limited resources. Economics makes distinctions between needs, those things that are required and wants, those things that are desired but in excess of a need. Economics also recognizes that resources are scarce to the extent that there are never enough resources to completely satisfy all wants. The issue of scarce resources forces individuals, organizations, governments and society at large to study the relationships among needs, wants, and resources; to prioritize how needs and wants might be satisfied; and to make economic trade-offs and choices to maximize the use of scarce resources.

Contracting professionals need to conserve scarce resources by ensuring maximum competition on each contracting action. They must also understand the basic principles of supply and demand, inflation, and the effect of government policies on general business conditions.

2.4.6 Finance

Corporate or business finance relates to the methodology employed to allocate financial resources with financial value in such a manner as to optimize their benefits to the organization or agency.

Contracting professionals need to have a basic understanding of how finance interacts with the other business competencies in their organization.

2.4.7 Information Technology

Information technology is the study, design, development, implementation, support, and management of computer-based information systems, particularly software applications and computer hardware.[1]

While the contracting professional is not expected to be an expert in information technology, a basic understanding of the field is highly desirable in today's contracting environment. In addition, contracting professionals that are involved in acquiring and/or administering information technology contracts need to have a good working knowledge of information technology.

2.4.8 Marketing

Marketing relates to the business process that develops, prices, places, and promotes goods, ideas, or services to enhance exchanges between buyers and sellers. This also relates to the process of planning and executing the conception, pricing, promotion, and distribution of ideas, goods, and services to create exchanges that satisfy individual and organizational goals.

The contracting professional may interact with marketing professionals during the acquisition planning and pre-award phases of the contract life cycle. Marketing professionals are identifying business opportunities during these phases. It is important for the contracting professional to give equal treatment to each vendor during the acquisition planning and pre-award phases to ensure the integrity of the procurement process.

---

1. Information Technology Association of America.

2.5 General Contracting Competencies

Section 2.4 presented an overview of general business competencies that are relevant to the contracting profession. Section 2.5 narrows the focus somewhat and provides an overview of some general contracting competencies.

[Diagram: General Contracting Competencies — Ethics, Laws and Regulations, Standards of Conduct]

2.5.1 Laws and Regulations

At its core, the contracting profession is about the knowledge and application of laws and regulations. Contracts are legal documents of agreement, whose terms and conditions are legally binding and enforceable in various courts of law and other administrative bodies. As such, it is important for the contracting professional to have a good working knowledge of the laws, regulations, and other sources of guidance that define—to a large extent—the environment in which the contracting professional operates. These sources of law and guidance include

- The *Uniform Commercial Code* (*UCC*)
- The *Federal Acquisition Regulation* (*FAR*)
- Laws related to international contracting

2.5.1.1 The *Uniform Commercial Code* (*UCC*)

The *UCC* is a comprehensive set of laws governing commercial goods transactions within the United States. The fundamental intent of the *UCC* is to provide a framework in which commercial organizations can conduct business across state or other jurisdictional boundaries with reasonable assurance that the same or similar rules apply. This concept of mutual understanding of commercial terms and practices is essential to an organization's ability to contract effectively. It is important to note that the *UCC*, as a uniform law, must be adopted as law by each state separately. As a result, there are differences in the *UCC* from state to state.

The *UCC* was created as the result of a joint effort by the National Conference of Commissioners on Uniform State Laws and the American Law Institute.

The National Conference of Commissioners on Uniform State Laws is a nonprofit association founded in 1892. Its membership consists of attorneys from all 50 states, the District of Columbia, the Commonwealth of Puerto Rico, and the U.S. Virgin Islands. Each jurisdiction determines how appointments are made. The national conference is the combined membership of the various state commissions of uniform laws. The principal purpose of the national conference is to study and review state laws to determine which laws should be uniform. The national conference also drafts and proposes specific statutes when uniformity is advantageous.

The American Law Institute was organized and created in 1923. Its elected membership consists of attorneys, judges, and law professors from all areas of the United States as well as some foreign countries. The institute was created "to promote the clarification and simplification of the law and its better adaptation to social needs, to secure the better administration of justice, and to encourage and carry on scholarly and scientific legal work."[2] In addition to its collaboration with the national conference on the *UCC*, the institute also collaborates with the American Bar Association in a national program of continuing legal education.

The *UCC* has been enacted in 49 states; Louisiana being the exception. Louisiana has enacted most of the *UCC*, but differences in state law resulting from Louisiana civil law and the Napoleonic Code, make complete adoption of the *UCC* difficult.

---

2. The American Law Institute, www.ali.org, "Creation of the Institute."

The *UCC* consists of nine articles, most with multiple parts:

The *Uniform Commercial Code* Articles	
Article 1	General Provisions
Article 2	Sales
Article 2A	Leases
Article 3	Negotiable Instruments
Article 4	Bank Deposit
Article 4A	Funds Transfers
Article 5	Letters of Credit
Article 6	Bulk Transfers and Bulk Sales
Article 7	Warehouse Receipts, Bills of Lading, and Other Documents of Title
Article 8	Investment Securities
Article 9	Secured Transactions

The *UCC* has long been a primary source of agreement and guidance in the commercial contracting community. The *UCC*, as with any body of law, is undergoing continual review, refinement, and revision to keep pace with changes in the business environment and technological advancements. Further, as the government contracting community continues to expand its use of commercial contracting practices, government contracting professionals should expand their knowledge base to include the *UCC* and its effect on contracting policy, procedures, and commonly accepted practices.

A more detailed table of contents for the *UCC* is provided in Appendix A.

2.5.1.2 The *Federal Acquisition Regulation* (FAR)

The *FAR* is the principal source of contracting guidance within the federal government. The *FAR* was established, as part of the Federal Acquisition System, to codify and publish uniform policies and procedures for acquisition by all executive agencies. In addition to the *FAR*, the Federal Acquisition System also contains agency acquisition regulations that supplement the *FAR*; e.g., The *Defense Federal Acquisition Regulation Supplement* (DFARS); as well as others.

The *FAR* is prepared, issued, and maintained through the coordinated efforts of two councils: the *Defense Acquisition Regulation* (DAR) Council and the Civilian Agency Acquisition (CAA) Council. The two councils must agree to all revisions proposed by either council.

The *DAR* Council chair is appointed by the secretary of defense. Remaining council membership includes representatives from the military departments, the Defense Logistics Agency, and the National Aeronautics and Space Administration.

The CAA Council chair is appointed by the administrator of general services. Remaining council membership includes representatives from the Departments of Agriculture, Commerce, Energy, Health and Human Services, Homeland Security, Interior, Labor, State, Transportation, and Treasury, and from the Environmental Protection Agency, Social Security Administration, Small Business Administration, and the Department of Veterans Affairs.

The *FAR* is printed, published, and distributed by the *FAR* Secretariat, which is controlled by the General Services Administration.

The *FAR* is organized in eight subchapters totaling 53 parts.

Federal Acquisition Regulation

Subchapter	Title
A	**General**
Part 1	Federal Acquisition Regulations System
Part 2	Definitions of Words and Terms
Part 3	Improper Business Practices and Personal Conflicts of Interest
Part 4	Administrative Matters

Subchapter	Title
B	**Competition and Acquisition Planning**
Part 5	Publicizing Contract Actions
Part 6	Competition Requirements
Part 7	Acquisition Planning
Part 8	Required Sources of Supplies and Services
Part 9	Contractor Qualifications
Part 10	Market Research
Part 11	Describing Agency Needs
Part 12	Acquisition of Commercial Items

Subchapter	Title
C	**Contracting Methods and Contract Types**
Part 13	Simplified Acquisition Procedures
Part 14	Sealed Bidding
Part 15	Contracting by Negotiation
Part 16	Types of Contracts
Part 17	Special Contracting Methods
Part 18	Emergency Acquisitions

Subchapter	Title
D	**Socioeconomic Programs**
Part 19	Small Business Programs
Part 20	Reserved
Part 21	Reserved
Part 22	Application of Labor Laws to Government Acquisitions
Part 23	Environment, Energy and Water Efficiency, Renewable Energy Technologies, Occupational Safety, and Drug-free Workplace
Part 24	Protection of Privacy and Freedom of Information
Part 25	Foreign Acquisition
Part 26	Other Socioeconomic Programs

Subchapter	Title
E	**General Contracting Requirements**
Part 27	Patents, Data and Copyrights
Part 28	Bonds and Insurance
Part 29	Taxes
Part 30	Cost Accounting Standards Administration
Part 31	Contract Cost Principles and Procedures
Part 32	Contract Financing
Part 33	Protests, Disputes, and Appeals

Subchapter	Title
F	**Special Categories of Contracting**
Part 34	Major Systems Acquisition
Part 35	Research and Development Contracting
Part 36	Construction and Architect–Engineer Contracts
Part 37	Service Contracting
Part 38	Federal Supply Schedule Contracting
Part 39	Acquisition of Information Technology
Part 40	Reserved
Part 41	Acquisition of Utility Services

Subchapter	Title
G	**Contract Management**
Part 42	Contract Administration and Audit Services
Part 43	Contract Modifications
Part 44	Subcontracting Policies and Procedures
Part 45	Government Property
Part 46	Quality Assurance
Part 47	Transportation
Part 48	Value Engineering
Part 49	Termination of Contracts
Part 50	Extraordinary Contractual Actions
Part 51	Use of Government Sources by Contractors

Subchapter	Title
H	**Clauses and Forms**
Part 52	Solicitation Provisions and Contract Clauses
Part 53	Forms

A more detailed table of contents for the *FAR* is provided in Appendix B.

2.5.1.3 Laws Related to International Contracting

When contracting beyond the governmental limits of the United States, with foreign governments or foreign corporations, contracting professionals must exercise great care to ensure a complete understanding of the legal, regulatory, political, and social consequences of their actions. Some of the more significant issues regarding international contracting include:

The Foreign Corrupt Practices Act (FCPA)

The FCPA is primarily concerned with the issues of bribery and other corrupt payments, as well as record-keeping and accounting provisions to facilitate the review or audit of international transactions. The FCPA prohibits the payment or promise of payment of money or other items of value to foreign officials to influence or attempt to influence obtaining business, retaining business, or directing business to anyone. The record-keeping and accounting provisions require that reasonable record systems and accounting controls be present to ensure that all transactions and the disposition of assets are reflected. These requirements apply to domestic as well as foreign operations.

Export Regulations

The Bureau of Export Administration (BXA), a federal bureau in the Department of Commerce, is charged with enforcing the *Export Administration Regulation* (*EAR*). The *EAR* governs the export of commercial goods and data, and the BXA controls such exports by issuing general and specific export licenses. Violations of these regulations can result in civil and criminal penalties for the entire organization, and loss of the organization's exporting privileges in the future. It can also result in debarment from government contracting. It is important to be aware of the applicable *EAR* requirements when entering into a contract.

International Traffic in Arms Regulations (ITAR)

The State Department's Office of Defense Trade Controls (DTC) controls all exports of defense articles, related technical data, and services by issuing licenses and approvals. The U.S. Munitions List, located in Part 121 of the *ITAR* details the items subject to DTC control. The *ITAR* also provides instructions on the procedures and types of licenses required. Violations of the *ITAR* can result in substantial civil fines, and willful violations can result in criminal penalties including up to ten years of imprisonment and fines up to $1 million. U.S. exporters need to be aware of the ITAR status before entering into a contract.

Anti-Boycott Regulations

The U.S. Department of Commerce and the U.S. Department of Treasury both enforce regulatory requirements to prevent U.S. companies from entering into foreign transactions that could be construed as supporting a foreign boycott against a country that is friendly to the United States. Violations can result in fines, imprisonment, and loss of their privilege to export.

Foreign Laws and Customs

In addition to ensuring compliance with applicable U.S. laws and regulations, U.S. firms pursuing or contemplating international contracting need to become knowledgeable regarding the myriad of foreign laws, regulations, customs, and practices that may impact their ability or desire to conduct business in foreign countries. Particular care is required when dealing with or in foreign countries whose legal, political, business, and social systems are vastly different from our own.

2.5.2 Standards of Conduct

There are many federal, state, and local laws; regulations; and ordinances that provide the legal framework in which many activities, including the operation of government and business in general, as well as the contracting profession in particular, are conducted. In addition to the legal framework, there are other procedural or policy documents that exist to formalize basic concepts and guide employers and employees in the performance of their functions. These documents are commonly referred to as standards of conduct, codes of ethics, statements of professional responsibility, standards of ethical conduct, and similar terms. Regardless of the title used to identify them, these documents normally

- Are formal, written statements that act as a guide for how people in the organization should act to make ethical decisions.
- Can be issued by government agencies at various levels, individual business entities, business associations, professional organizations, and similar groups.

- Address issues related to
  - Conflict of interest
  - Behavior toward competitors
  - Privacy of information
  - Gift giving and receiving
  - Making and receiving political contributions
  - Levels of dedication and work effort required
  - Encouraged behavior
  - Discouraged or prohibited behavior

Though standards of conduct can sometimes be codified as law when issued by a government agency, and can sometimes be issued by corporations as a requirement of the law, they are also sometimes issued as a matter of policy or preference, or to promote an organization's values to the general public. More than 90 percent of the Fortune 500 firms, over 50 percent of all other firms, and virtually all government entities have published standards of conduct or ethical codes.

A sampling of standards of conduct and ethical codes is included as Appendix C.

2.5.3 Ethics

Laws, regulations, and policy documents, such as standards of conduct, provide an authoritative, formalized, written set of guidance that requires certain actions, prohibits others, and defines broad goals or desired traits relative to the proper way to conduct business. A logical next step in discussion of competencies related to the contracting profession is ethics—an environment of structures, people, concepts, and values that enables an organization and its individuals to operate in a manner that conforms to the basic norms of society and business.

An excellent working definition of ethics was provided in the April 2004 issue of *Contract Management* magazine.

> Ethics are standards by which one should act based on values. Values are core beliefs such as duty, honor, and integrity that motivate attitudes and actions. Not all values are ethical principles…. Ethical principles are values that relate to what is right and wrong and thus take precedence over non-ethical values when making ethical decisions.[3]

Though ethical conduct can be viewed as both the means and the end, there is also a practical application and benefit associated with high ethical standards and conduct; ethics is good for business and government. Business flourishes in an environment of profitability and sustainability. The government functions best in an environment of efficient and honest service to the governed. Good ethical conduct is a critical component to both commercial and federal government models.

In commercial and federal government business practices, formal as well as informal methods are commonly used to instill a sense of ethics and ethical behavior. Typical components of ethical systems may include

- The formalized, written document that presents the standards of conduct or code of ethics;
- An ethics compliance office or manager to monitor and enforce the written standards. The ethics compliance officer or manager is frequently a senior staff executive, with direct access to the senior executive in the organization;
- A formal training program for employees to provide recurring refresher training in ethics issues;
- An internal information system to respond to general questions and provide specific guidance to employees; and
- A complaint system to receive, investigate, and respond to actual or perceived issues of non-ethical behavior. Some of these complaint systems also provide, either internally or externally, information regarding the resolution of ethics complaints. They may also include information about specific actions taken with regards to confirmed ethics violations, though the identities of violators are sometimes not revealed for legal reasons.

Government and business organizations generally recognize that ethics-related issues can have a positive or negative effect both internally and externally. They also realize that internal and external influences can have positive as well as adverse impacts on the best-planned ethics compliance system. Therefore, organizations that take ethics seriously seek to instill and influence high ethical standards in their own employees and with other firms and organizations with which they do business. Additionally,

---

3. "Ethical Decision-Making: Issues for Contract Managers and Educators," Margaret G. Rumbaugh, *Contract Management* (April 2004): 34–35.

they seek to make their clients or customers, as well as the general public, aware of the significant role that ethics play as a means to foster goodwill and a positive image.

The issue of personal ethics, as opposed to the issue of organizational ethics presented earlier, is naturally more philosophical than fact-based. Though an organization can implement and maintain a very aggressive and far-reaching ethics function or program, the value of such a program can be easily diminished or severely damaged by the action or inaction of individuals throughout the organization. Personal ethics—knowing the "right" thing to do and doing it—is therefore a significant issue. Personal ethics is of particular significance in the contracting profession, due to the fiduciary nature of the contracting function, the requirement to build good working relationships both internally and externally, and the effect that contracting can have on an organization's "bottom line" and public image.

Contracting professionals are people first, professionals second. One's sense of personal ethics is in no small part defined by one's life experiences. Though one is not bound exclusively to one's past, what has occurred before often influences what may occur in the future. It is important that as individuals we clearly understand the ethical challenges that our profession sometimes presents to us, and that we clearly understand corporate or agency requirements or policy related to such challenges. We must then bring our life experiences, as well as societal norms, into the equation to determine if a particular course of action is right or wrong. In some cases, these decisions are so simple that they are made automatically. In other cases, they can be the source of great anxiety and turmoil. Regardless, true professionalism requires that we continuously verify the "true north" of our "ethical compass" and that our words and deeds proceed in the right ethical direction.

The Contract Management Knowledge Areas

section two

Acquisition Strategy Competencies **Chapter 3**

Pre-award Contract Competencies **Chapter 4**

Contract Award Competencies **Chapter 5**

Post-award Competencies **Chapter 6**

Specialized Knowledge Competencies **Chapter 7**

Unique Commercial Contracting Competencies **Chapter 8**

Unique Federal Contracting Competencies **Chapter 9**

Chapter 3
Acquisition Strategy Competencies

This chapter provides a discussion of specific competencies desirable for successful performance as a contracting professional. Pertinent topics include:

Acquisition Strategy Competencies

- Acquisition Planning
- Market Research
- The Acquisition Plan
- Contract Methods + Methodology
- Contract Types
- Contract Incentives
- Other Types of Contracts, etc.
- Contract Financing
- Intellectual Property

3.1 Acquisition Planning

Planning is an essential preliminary component to the successful completion of virtually any effort. In the government and business environment, planning is required to focus the application of usually scarce resources to the goal-directed activity necessary to accomplish the mission or functions of the organization. As it relates to the contracting profession, acquisition planning in particular was a function that was often thought to begin at the point where a customer expressed a need for goods or services, or delivered a requirement to the contracting office. The April 2004 NCMA *Guide to the Contract Management Body of Knowledge* (*CMBOK*) defined acquisition planning in the public sector as

> The process by which efforts of all personnel responsible for an acquisition are coordinated and integrated through a comprehensive plan for fulfilling the agency need in a timely manner at a reasonable cost. It includes developing the overall strategy for managing the acquisition. (FAR 2.101)

The guide further defined the term, as it relates to the private sector, as

> Activities and events required for both buyers and sellers to prepare for, negotiate and form a binding contractual agreement.

Though both definitions may be somewhat accurate, they both imply that the need for planning occurs once a need or requirement has been identified.

The contracting function, as well as other administrative, staff, or overhead functions frequently operated adjacent to, but often not directly with each other, or with line components that performed the core functions of the organization. This historical concept of technical specialization has been challenged in recent years by many factors, including technological advancements in communications and information exchange, an aging workforce, competitive pressures on businesses to enhance profitability, political pressures on government to reduce the cost of providing services, and many others. A new reality has emerged that requires both public and private sector organizations to be leaner, agile, more productive, less expensive, and as a result, more collaborative. Recent literature in the contracting profession has defined and described the need for the contracting professional to expand beyond the historical boundaries of the contracting office, and become a business professional or business broker, and part of the multidisciplinary management team. As a result of this new environment, changes are required in the way that contracting professionals perform acquisition planning. Acquisition planning should be viewed as a team effort, requiring the talents and input of many individuals other than the contracting professional, including the customer, budget or finance experts, various technical experts (IT, logistics), legal counsel, and other direct or indirect stakeholders. The planning process should begin before the traditional first customer contact, and should have an inward, as well as outward, focus; particularly as it relates to an important acquisition planning tool—market research.

3.2 Market Research

In the expanded role of a business professional, the contracting professional should consider an expanded concept of market research. Not only should contracting professionals determine the degree to which external sources could meet requirements, they should also look within the organization for information that might be of value in anticipating future requirements. It is within this context that market research can be viewed as having internal and external components.

3.2.1 Internal Market Research

For contracting professionals to be of maximum value to the management team and the overall organization, they must be knowledgeable in the business of the business or the mission of the government agency. The contracting professional needs to know about the products or services generated by each segment of the organization, how these products or services are generated, the organization's customers, the organization's goals, and what structures, processes, and procedures are in place to accomplish the goals. Fundamentally, the contracting professional needs to become immersed in the organization's activities and plans to the maximum extent possible. This level of involvement can usually be accomplished by activities such as

- Reviewing historical information on prior acquisitions for internal customers;
- Attending regular management meetings of all internal customers;
- Receiving detailed briefings on the functions and processes of internal customers;
- Dividing short-term assignments into customer work units;
- Reading pertinent customer-oriented professional publications;
- Serving on cross-functional process improvement teams, or similar ad hoc teams, addressing issues that may have little or nothing to do with contracting; and
- Sharing information on contracting issues and trends with other managers.

The basic goal of internal market research is to learn as much as possible about the organization, how it does business, and how it has used goods and services acquired in the past. A secondary goal of internal market research is to develop good working relationships with the customer base.

3.2.2 External Market Research

External market research, as the definitions previously provided illustrate, normally pertains to research activities undertaken once a requirement has been either defined or at least conceptualized. However, generalized external market research, undertaken in the absence of a requirement, can also be of value to the contracting professional, particularly when one has also engaged in some level of internal market research. Whether it is used in response to a specific need or not, the external market research effort seeks to gain useful information about capabilities and limitations inherent in the commercial marketplace. The basic intent of external market research is to gain knowledge that will be used in determining the best method to obtain required goods and services consistent with pertinent law, regulation, and/or corporate policy. Just as the contracting professional can use internal market research to better understand and anticipate the actual and potential needs of the customer, external market research should be used to better understand the actual and potential capabilities of external sources of supply. Standard external market research techniques include:

- Reviewing historical information on similar prior acquisitions for related market research information;
- Reviewing pertinent professional news, trade, association, or industry publications;
- Contacting knowledgeable third-party sources of unbiased information regarding potential sources;
- Attending trade or professional association shows and exhibits;
- Contacting customers of potential sources for past performance information;
- Reviewing catalogs and other printed or electronic information published by potential sources;
- Contacting potential sources for specific capabilities information or briefings; and
- Joining pertinent professional organizations and attending their meetings.

Though the amount of external market research conducted will vary according to the complexity of the anticipated effort and other issues, the results should be formally documented for current and future use.

3.2.3 The Acquisition Plan

The acquisition plan should reflect a collaborative effort involving significant stakeholders. The level of detail provided in the acquisition plan will vary depending on the anticipated dollar value, level of complexity, degree of significance, and other appropriate factors. A written plan may not be required for simple, straightforward, low-dollar value purchases. In the absence of a written plan, the contracting professional should ensure that there is a common understanding and consensus among the stakeholders regarding the course of action to be taken. When required, written acquisition plans should clearly explain all pertinent issues relating to the acquisition, including:

- A description of the need to be satisfied. The description should be concise, yet complete enough to explain what the need is, how it came to be needed at the current time, any pertinent history of related prior acquisitions, and how they were acquired;

- An explanation of conditions or constraints that relate to the proposed acquisition. These conditions or constraints might include the need for compatibility with existing or future equipment or systems; implementation constraints caused by space, personnel, or other limitations; budget constraints, particularly as they relate to lease vs. purchase decisions; and other known constraints that could influence cost, schedule, capability, or performance issues;

- The established cost targets for the acquisition with sufficient explanation to support the targets. This section should include discussions of the following issues as appropriate: the make-or-buy decision, estimated life-cycle costs, design-to-cost, should-cost analysis, and other cost issues determined to be of significance;

- The required capabilities or performance to be acquired. This section should address such issues as speed, accuracy, reliability, ease of use, and other pertinent performance characteristics when acquiring goods. When acquiring services, the required performance standards or knowledge requirements that are required to provide the services should be discussed. This section should also explain how the goods or services being acquired relate to, and will satisfy the need;

- Delivery or performance period requirements. This section should provide the required delivery date(s) or the required period of performance, as well as an explanation for why the dates or periods were selected. If an emergency or urgent condition exists that has influence on the delivery or performance requirements, explain that relationship, as well as the incremental impact that the emergency may have on cost considerations;

- Trade-offs related to the previously defined plans for cost, technical performance, capability, and schedule requirements. Explain what trade-off issues are likely to occur, the degree to which a trade-off decision may impact other plan components, and how trade-offs may impact the overall acquisition plan;

- A discussion of the level of risk associated with the technical, cost, schedule, and other pertinent aspects of the plan. This discussion should clearly define the anticipated risks; the strategies or actions planned or taken to eliminate, reduce, or mitigate risk to an acceptable level; and the likely consequences that might result from failure to achieve goals; and

- The contracting plan of action. Taking into consideration all of the pertinent plan components mentioned earlier, the contracting plan of action should address issues such as

  - Proposed sources that can provide the required goods or services;
  - The degree to which the acquisition will be subject to competition;
  - The contract type(s) proposed for use;
  - The source selection process, including an explanation of how the evaluation factors relate to the achievement of the goals of the acquisition;
  - How the contract will be administered after issuance;
  - Milestones or target dates for completion; and
  - Any other pertinent issues of concern. (See FAR 7.105)

The need for acquisition plans differs in the federal and commercial contracting areas. In the federal sector, such plans are normally required for significant or complex acquisitions. In the commercial sector, such plans may be created as the result of corporate policy or as a matter of professionalism or convenience. Regardless of whether they are required or desired, acquisition plans provide valuable information regarding the initial intent of a proposed acquisition and a basic roadmap to check progress during the acquisition cycle.

3.3 Contract Methods and Methodology

Contract methods and methodology are terms that refer to the processes employed and the means used to solicit, request, or invite offers that will normally result in issuing a contract.

3.3.1 Sealed Bidding

Sealed bidding is a method that involves the unrestricted solicitation of bids, a public opening of the bids, and award of a contract to the lowest responsive and responsible bidder. Sealed bidding may be used to obtain goods and services, including construction. Sealed bidding requires complete specifications, requirements, or descriptions since the contract award decision is anticipated to be based only on price and price-related factors. The solicitation tool normally used for sealed bidding is the invitation for bids (IFBs). (See FAR Part 14)

3.3.2 Two-Step Sealed Bidding

Two-step sealed bidding combines two competitive methods and is sometimes used to obtain the benefits of sealed bidding when adequate specifications, requirements, or descriptions are not available. The first step consists of the solicitation for the submission of technical proposals, which are evaluated on technical merits only. The second step involves the submission of sealed price bids only by those bidders who submitted acceptable technical proposals in the first step. The solicitation tool normally used for two-step sealed bidding is the request for technical proposal (RFTP). RFTPs are used to prequalify bidders relative to their technical capacity to perform. (See FAR Subpart 14.5)

3.3.3 Negotiation

Negotiation is a method of contracting that can be used to solicit proposals, either competitively or noncompetitively, and usually includes discussions. Negotiation is a flexible process that includes the receipt of proposals from offerors, permits bargaining, and often affords offerors an opportunity to revise their offers before final evaluation and award of a contract. A contract issued by any method other than sealed bidding is normally considered to be a negotiated contract. The solicitation tool normally used for negotiation is the request for proposal (RFP). The RFTP can also be used in negotiation when the intent is to conduct a two-step negotiation in a manner similar to the intent of two-step sealed bidding. (See FAR Part 15)

3.3.4 Simplified Acquisition

Simplified acquisition is a less rigorous method for entering into relatively low-dollar threshold contracts. Simplified acquisition usually occurs without the elaborate and formal solicitation techniques required by sealed bidding and negotiation. Very small purchases may be made using simplified acquisition tools such as charge cards. (See FAR Part 13)

3.3.5 Federal Supply Schedules

The Federal Supply Schedules (FSS) is a program directed and managed by the General Services Administration (GSA). The FSS program provides federal agencies, as well as some state and local governmental agencies, with a streamlined process for obtaining commonly used commercial goods and services. Fundamentally, the supply schedules are a series of pre-negotiated, awarded contracts that can be used by authorized sources to issue delivery orders for required goods or services. (See FAR Part 8)

3.3.6 Electronic Commerce (E-Commerce)

Electronic commerce refers to a group of automated processes that can be used to accomplish business transactions. Electronic commerce includes processes such as electronic mail (e-mail) or messaging, Internet technology, electronic bulletin boards, electronic funds transfer, electronic data interchange, and similar tools. [See FAR 5.102 for Government-wide Point of Entry (GPE).] The contracting officer must make available through the GPE solicitations synopsized through the GPE, including specifications and other pertinent information determined necessary by the contracting officer. Transmissions to the GPE must be in accordance with the interface description available through the Internet at **www.fedbizopps.gov**. (See FAR 32.11 for electronic funds transfer)

3.3.7 Modular Contracting

Modular contracting refers to the use of one (but usually more than one) contract to acquire major information technology (IT) systems in successive, interoperable increments. The intent of modular contracting is to divide the acquisition of complex, major IT systems into a series of related smaller, related contracts that are easier to issue and mange than a single all-inclusive contract. (See FAR 39.103)

3.3.8 Auctions

Auctions are sales transactions in which usually goods, but also services are offered and sold to the highest bidder. Reverse auctions are purchase transactions in which usually goods, but also services are required and are purchased from the lowest bidder.

3.3.9 Request for Quotation (RFQ)

The RFQ is a solicitation document used in negotiated procurements to request information and quotes. The RFQ differs from the RFP in that an RFQ is fundamentally a request for information. Quotes received in response to an RFQ are not offers. They are usually counteroffers, and include the seller's terms and conditions.

3.3.10 Request for Information (RFI)

An RFI is a tool sometimes used as part of market research to gather information from vendors in the marketplace. RFIs are sometimes issued to determine the availability of products and services, and to gather market information on capabilities to perform when less intrusive forms of market research do not produce the desired results.

3.3.11 Unsolicited Proposal

An unsolicited proposal is a proposal from a prospective contractor to provide goods or services without a prior formal or informal solicitation from a contracting office. (See FAR 15.6)

3.3.12 Point-of-Sale Transactions

A point of sale transaction is a business transaction in which the entire business arrangement between the parties is executed in a single event.

3.3.13 Master Agreements

A master agreement is a business arrangement in which the parties determine the underlying commercial parameters governing the relationship, such as terms and conditions, but defer negotiation of specific elements of the contract, such as price or delivery requirements, to a later date based on the occurrence of specific events or transactions.

3.3.14 Sales Contract

A sales contract is a business arrangement in which all elements of the transaction are determined and defined between the parties at the time of contract formation, including mutual assent, exchange of consideration, capacity to contract, and legal purpose.

3.3.15 Framework Pricing Arrangement

A framework pricing arrangement is a contract that is definitive in all respects except pricing. The agreement or contract specifies a predetermined index, formula, algorithm, or method (the framework) for the calculation of price at the point of sale.

3.3.16 Performance-Based Contract

A performance-based contract is a contract that is structured around the purpose of the work to be performed, or the goal to be achieved, as opposed to either the manner in which the work is to be performed or a broad, imprecise statement of work. The requirements for performance-based contracts should be clear, complete, and objective with measurable outcomes. (See FAR 37.6 for performance-based contracting)

3.3.17 Single-Source Negotiation

Single source negotiation, also known as sole-source negotiation, refers to contracting with a single provider in lieu of competitive contracting. Single-source or sole-source negotiation usually occurs because the provider is the only source of the product or service required or the business relationship with the provider is of strategic importance to the buying organization, and is normally based on a long-term relationship built on mutual trust.

3.3.18 Gap Fillers

Gap fillers are other sources of pertinent information that may be used to "fill a gap" when a contract fails to adequately address an issue of concern. The *Uniform Commercial Code (UCC)* is frequently used as a gap filler, as are memoranda of understanding, letter contracts, and other agreements when appropriate.

3.3.19 Prequalification

Prequalification refers to a buyer's announcement of interest, including criteria for selecting proposals, and selecting the further participation of all offerors capable of meeting requirements. (See FAR 9.2)

3.4 Contract Types

There are three basic types or groups of contract pricing most commonly used in commercial and federal contracting. They are fixed-price, cost-reimbursement, and time-and-materials.

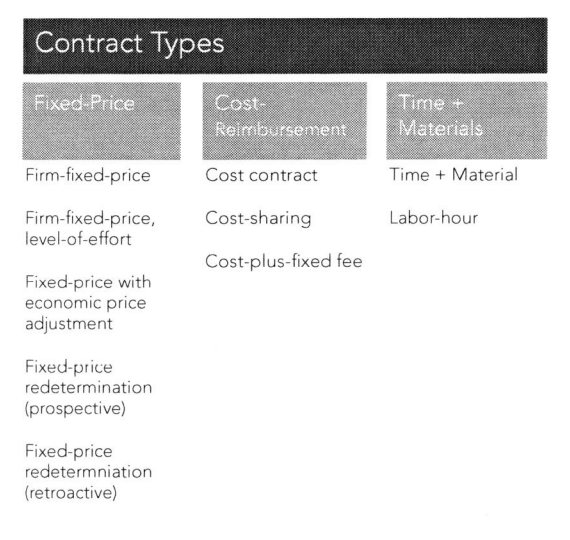

Contract Types

Fixed-Price	Cost-Reimbursement	Time + Materials
Firm-fixed-price	Cost contract	Time + Material
Firm-fixed-price, level-of-effort	Cost-sharing	Labor-hour
Fixed-price with economic price adjustment	Cost-plus-fixed fee	
Fixed-price redetermination (prospective)		
Fixed-price redetermniation (retroactive)		

3.4.1 Fixed-Price Contracts

A type or group of contracts that provide for a firm pricing arrangement established by the parties at the time of contracting. Fixed-price contracts typically include firm-fixed-price; firm-fixed-price, level-of-effort; fixed-price with economic price adjustment; and fixed-price redetermination. (See FAR 16.2)

Firm-Fixed-Price Contracts

As the name implies, firm-fixed-price contracts provide for a price that is not subject to any adjustment on the basis of the contractor's cost experience in performing the contract. This contract type places the maximum performance risk on the contractor as well as full responsibility for all costs and the resulting profit or loss. It provides strong incentives for the contractor to control costs and perform effectively, and imposes a minimum administrative burden on the contracting parties. The level of risk assumed by the contractor is often reflected in the contract price. (See FAR 16.202)

Firm-Fixed-Price, Level-of-Effort Contracts

This type of contract requires the contractor to provide a specified level of effort, over a stated period of time, on work that can be stated only in general terms. In return for the specified level of effort the contractor is paid a fixed-dollar amount. (See FAR 16.207)

Fixed-Price with Economic Price Adjustment Contracts

Fixed-price with economic price adjustment contracts provide for upward and downward revision of the stated contract price on the occurrence of specified contingencies. There are three general economic price adjustments.

- **Adjustments based on established prices.** The price adjustments are based on increases or decreases from an agreed-upon level in published or otherwise established prices of specific items or contract end items.

- **Adjustments based on actual costs of labor or material.** The price adjustments are based on increases or decreases in specified costs of labor or material that the contractor actually experiences during contract performance.

- **Adjustments based on cost indexes of labor or material.** The price adjustments are based on increases or decreases in labor or material cost standards or indexes that are specifically identified in the contract. (See FAR 16.203)

Fixed-Price Redetermination (Prospective) Contracts

These types of fixed-price contracts combine a firm-fixed price for an initial period of deliveries or performance, and a prospective redetermination, at a stated time or times during performance, of the price for subsequent periods of performance. (See FAR 16.205)

Fixed-Price Redetermination (Retroactive) Contracts

These types of fixed-price contracts combine a fixed-ceiling price and a retroactive price redetermination after completion of the contract. The redetermined price cannot exceed the original ceiling price. (See FAR 16.206)

3.4.2 Cost-Reimbursement Contracts

Cost-reimbursement contracts provide for the payment of allowable, allocable, and reasonable costs incurred in the performance of a contract to the extent that such costs are prescribed or permitted by the contract. Cost-reimbursement contracts typically include cost contracts, cost-sharing, and cost-plus-fixed fee. (See FAR 16.3)

Cost Contract

Cost contracts are the least complicated type of cost-reimbursement contract. They provide for reimbursement of appropriate costs with no allowances for profit or fees.

Cost-Sharing Contracts

Cost-sharing contracts provide for the partial reimbursement of the contractor's allowable costs with no allowances for profit or fees. Both the buyer and the seller share the costs. Cost-sharing contracts are used when both the buyer and the seller will derive some benefit from the contracted effort, and that benefit is sufficient enough that both parties are willing to share the costs and benefits. (See FAR 16.302)

Cost-Plus-Fixed-Fee (CPFF) Contracts

Cost-plus-fixed-fee contracts provide for the reimbursement of appropriate costs associated with contract performance, plus payment of a fixed fee that is negotiated at the inception of the contract. The fixed fee does not vary with actual cost, but may be adjusted as a result of changes made in the work to be performed under the contract. (See FAR 16.306)

3.4.3 Time-and-Materials Contracts

Time-and-materials contracts are a means of acquiring goods or services based on direct labor hours and the cost of materials required for contract performance. The labor-hour rates are negotiated between the parties for each type or category of labor required. Each fixed hourly labor rate is a composite rate that includes wages, overhead, general and administrative expense, and profit. Time required to complete a requirement is difficult to accurately estimate. Time-and-materials contracts that do not require the contractor to provide materials are also referred to as labor-hour contracts. (See FAR 16.601)

3.5 Contract Incentives

Contracts containing various forms of incentives may be appropriate when there is a desire or need to provide additional motivation to a contractor to obtain specific acquisition objectives that would likely not be possible without the incentives. Such objectives might be improved delivery, improved technical performance, cost consciousness, or some other significant parameter. Incentives generally fall into four categories:

3.5.1 Cost Incentives

Cost incentives normally take the form of a profit or fee adjustment based on a formula. Cost incentives are intended to motivate the contractor to effectively manage costs. Generally, cost incentives are a requirement for the inclusion of other types of incentives in a contract. (See FAR 16.402-1)

3.5.2 Performance or Quality Incentives

Performance or quality incentives may be appropriate when a level of performance or quality in excess of the requirement is attainable by the contractor and provides a desirable enhanced benefit to the buyer. These incentives should be designed to relate profit or fee to results achieved by the contractor compared to specified targets. (See FAR 16.402-2)

3.5.3 Delivery Incentives

Delivery incentives should be considered when improvement from the specified delivery schedule provides a tangible benefit that exceeds the value of the incentive. (See FAR 16.402-3)

3.5.4 Multiple Incentives

Multiple incentives may be included in a contract when there is sufficient justification to motivate the contractor to strive for outstanding results in multiple areas simultaneously. Multiple incentives sometime require the contractor to make trade-off decisions among the incentives to achieve the maximum beneficial result. The buyer should be aware of the potential problems inherent in providing multiple incentives, and closely monitor these situations to ensure that the primary goals of the acquisition are not compromised. (See FAR 16.402-4)

Contract incentives can be used in both fixed-price and cost-reimbursement contracts, including:

3.5.5 Fixed-Price Incentive (FPI) Contracts

A fixed-price incentive contract provides for an initial fixed price, and also allows for adjusting profit, and establishing the final contract price by use of a formula that compares the relationship of total final negotiated cost to total target cost. The final price is subject to a price ceiling, which is negotiated at the outset. There are two basic forms of fixed-price incentive contracts: (See FAR 16.403)

3.5.6 Fixed-Price Incentive (Firm Target) Contracts

An FPI (firm target) contract specifies a target cost, a target profit, a price ceiling, and a profit adjustment formula. (See FAR 16.403-1)

3.5.7 Fixed-Price Incentive (Successive Targets) Contracts

An FPI (successive targets) contact provides for an initial target cost, an initial target profit, and an initial profit adjustment formula. The targets and the formula are used to establish the firm target profit, including a ceiling and floor for the firm target profit, the production point at which the firm target cost and firm target profit will be renegotiated, and a ceiling price that is the maximum that may be paid to the contractor. (See FAR 16.403-2)

3.5.8 Fixed-Price Contracts with Award Fees

A fixed-price contract with award fees is sometimes used when it is difficult to include other incentives because contractor performance cannot be measured objectively. A fixed-price contract with award fees establishes a fixed price, including normal profit that will be paid for satisfactory contract performance. It also establishes an award fee that can be earned by the contractor in addition to the fixed price, based on the results of periodic evaluations of the contractor's performance against an award fee plan. (See FAR 16.404)

3.5.9 Cost-Plus-Incentive-Fee Contracts

A cost-plus-incentive-fee contract is a cost-reimbursement contract that also provides for an initially negotiated fee that can be adjusted later by using a formula based on the relationship of total allowable costs to target costs. (See FAR 16.405-1)

3.5.10 Cost-Plus-Award-Fee Contracts

A cost-plus-award-fee contract is a cost-reimbursement contract that also provides for an award fee pool that the contractor may earn in whole or in part during performance, based on the results of periodic evaluations of the contractor's performance against an award-fee plan. (See FAR 16.405-2)

3.6 Other Types of Contracts, Agreements, and Arrangements

In addition to the contract types and incentive options indicated earlier, there are a number of other contracts, agreements and arrangements commonly used by contract professionals.

3.6.1 Basic Agreements

A basic agreement is a written instrument of understanding, negotiated between a buyer and a seller, that contains terms and conditions that will apply to future contracts between the parties during the term of the agreement. A basic agreement contemplates separate future contracts that will incorporate, by reference or attachment, the appropriate terms and conditions negotiated in the basic agreement. A basic agreement itself is not a contract. (See FAR 17.702)

3.6.2 Basic Ordering Agreements

A basic ordering agreement is similar to a basic agreement, but may also include terms and conditions intended to describe the types of goods and services that may be ordered in the future, to define pricing methods that will apply or to define ordering or delivery procedures. A basic ordering agreement itself is not a contract. (See FAR 16.703)

3.6.3 Letter Contracts

A letter contract is normally a brief, written preliminary contractual instrument that authorizes a contractor to begin performance immediately. Letter contracts are used to initiate performance when performance is required, but there is insufficient time to negotiate a more formal, complete contract. (See FAR 16.603)

3.6.4 Indefinite Delivery/Indefinite Quantity Contracts (IDIQ)

IDIQ contracts provide for the purchase of an indefinite quantity of goods or services for a fixed period of time. The indefinite quantity provisions sometimes include a guaranteed minimum quantity and normally include a maximum quantity. Deliveries or performance is scheduled by placing orders with the contractor. Examples of variations of IDIQ of contracts include delivery order, task order, definite quantity, and requirements.

Delivery-order contracts are IDIQ contracts generally

used to purchase goods. Task-order contracts are IDIQ contracts generally used to purchase services. Definite quantity contracts are IDIQ contracts generally used to purchase a definite quantity of goods or services with an indefinite schedule for deliveries or performance. Requirements contracts are IDIQ contracts that are generally used to purchase all required quantities of specified goods or services needed by a buying organization for a specified period of time. Delivery or performance is accomplished by placing orders with the contractor. (See FAR 16.504)

Governmentwide agency contracts (GWACs) are federal contracts for goods or services issued by one federal contracting entity, but available for use by many or all federal contracting entities.

3.7 Contract Financing

Contract financing issues are important in both the commercial and federal contracting environments.

3.7.1 Commercial Contract Financing

Financing in commercial contracting may include obtaining loans and lines of credit from financial institutions, obtaining advance funding of accounts receivable or funding of purchase orders from private firms, or obtaining funds from venture capitalists. It may include negotiating favorable payment clauses such as a sizable down payment or milestone payments as the work progresses. (See FAR 32.2)

3.7.2 Government Contract Financing

In some cases, successfully completing a government contract may require government assistance with some form of contract financing. One example where contract financing might be appropriate could be a multimillion dollar contract for goods that would require the contractor to make substantial initial investments in labor, materials, and production costs. In cases where the government determines that some type of contract financing is appropriate, it usually takes one of two forms.

Contract financing could include methods such as advance payments in anticipation of complete performance, progress payments based on costs incurred, progress payments based on a percentage of work completed, payments for a portion of the goods or services received and accepted, performance-based payments, and loan guarantees designed to enable contractors to obtain private financing for national defense items. (See FAR 32.1)

Commercial contract financing could include methods such as: commercial advance payments made before performance has started, commercial interim payments made after some work has been done, and delivery payments made after receiving and accepting a portion of the total work to be performed.

3.8 Intellectual Property

Intellectual property is sometimes referred to as the kind of property that results from the fruits of mental labor. Contracting professionals should be aware of the various forms of intellectual property, the need for intellectual property that may be part of contract requirements, and limitations on the use of intellectual property imposed by law. Typical examples of intellectual property include
the following:

3.8.1 Patent

A patent is a government grant of exclusive rights, issued by the U.S. Patent and Trademark Office, to an inventor that prohibits others from making, using, or selling the invention for a specified period of time. The patent holder has legal remedies available to those who infringe on a patent.

3.8.2 Copyright

A copyright is the exclusive right to reproduce, translate, publish, use, and dispose of various forms of written or recorded material or data, and to authorize others to do so. Copyright is of particular interest to contacting professionals as it relates to the appropriate purchase and/or use of computer software.

3.8.3 Trademark

A trademark is a distinctive mark of authenticity. It can include words, symbols, devices, or designs affixed to or placed on an article or its container to identify an article offered for sale. The term can also include "service marks," which designate particular manners or modes of service delivery protected as intellectual property.

3.8.4 Data

Date is recorded information, regardless of the form or media on which it may be recorded. Rights to use technical data developed by a contractor may vary depending on the source of funds used to develop the item, component, process, software, or software documentation.

3.8.5 Licensing

Licensing is the sale of permission by the owner to use forms of intellectual property, including computer software, to another. A license normally includes terms and conditions specifying the manner in which the intellectual property may be used, may contain specific uses that are prohibited, and often has time limitations.

3.8.6 Royalties

Royalties include costs or fees that may be charged by the owner of various forms of intellectual property to permit others to use the intellectual property for specified purposes.

3.8.7 Trade Secrets

Trade secrets refer to information, processes, or procedures used in business that may give the owner some advantage over its competitors in the marketplace.

3.8.8 Shop Rights

Shop rights are the right of an employer to use, without payment of royalties, an invention conceived by an employee in the course of employment or through the use of the employer's facilities if the employee was not hired to perform such work.

3.8.9 Nondisclosure Agreement

A nondisclosure agreement is a legally binding document setting forth the conditions under which proprietary information is offered, received, used, and protected between two or more parties.

Chapter 4
Pre-award Contract Competencies

In Chapter 3, a discussion of acquisition planning and strategy competencies was presented. In this chapter, those competencies, as well as the more general competencies presented in Chapters 1 and 2, are used in a discussion of activities often required in various pre-award functions.

Acquisition Planning	Market Research	The Acquisition Plan
Contract Methods + Methodology	**Pre-award Competencies**	Contract Incentives

4.1 Requirements Preparation

The preparation of the requirements, also referred to as solicitation preparation, is arguably the single most important function in the acquisition cycle. Although the acquisition planning activities presented in Chapter 3 also have a significant impact on the success or failure of the proposed acquisition, requirements preparation usually provides the last major opportunity for the contracting professional to influence the solicitation package before it leaves the organization. It is therefore important that the contracting professional, in collaboration with the customer and required internal sources of specific expertise, craft a solicitation package that accurately reflects the customer's needs and communicates those needs and other related information clearly and concisely to potential offerors. The end goal should always be to satisfy the customer's need, at a fair price, with the minimum acceptable level of risk.

Some acquisitions are very simple, others exceedingly complex, and the majority usually fall somewhere in between. The format and content of solicitation packages and the resulting contracts are often mandated by law, regulation, or corporate policy, such as the use of the Uniform Contract Format for government contracting professionals. Regardless of the complexity, the solicitation package normally provides the following information:

Requirements Preparation

Statement of Work	Evaluation Procedures
Contract Type + Method	Proposal Preparation + Submission
Terms + Conditions	Other Considerations

4.1.1 Statement of Work (SOW)

The statement of work is likely the single most important document in the solicitation package. The SOW is the document that describes the goods or services required in sufficient detail so as to provide potential offerors with a complete understanding of the requirement. Generally, there are three basic types of SOWs—design, performance, and functional. The differences among them relate to the degree to which the requirement is defined and explained—from specific to general. Each type of SOW has its own advantages and disadvantages, and SOWs often reflect elements of all three basic types in order to completely describe the requirement.

Design SOW

A design SOW is most often used when the buyer requires a specific manufactured good. Design SOWs are extremely detailed, and usually define all required materials, production processes, and specifications such as size, shape, color, tolerances, etc. Design SOWs also frequently provide specific requirements related to quality, inspection, packaging, and related needs. The basic intent of a design SOW is to document the requirement with such specificity as to permit any competent seller to be able to provide the product, and that the end product will be exactly what the buyer required. The degree of precision inherent in design SOWs also presents challenges for the contracting professional. Design SOWs may restrict the competitive process by imposing too many specifications that result in no-bid decisions from sellers that might otherwise be willing to provide the product. Design SOWs may also result in higher costs, since the seller may have to use materials and processes that are different from those used in the normal course of business. Additionally, the buyer assumes virtually total performance risk when contracting with design SOWs, since the seller is performing based on the buyer's design and specification requirements. As a result of these drawbacks, the use of design SOWs is commonly discouraged whenever a less restrictive type of SOW can be reasonably expected to provide the results required.

Performance SOW

Performance SOWs are less restrictive than design SOWs. Performance SOWs define requirements in terms that relate to minimum acceptable standards or ranges of acceptable performance. A performance SOW may require a particular approach or a particular type of product, but it leaves most of the "how" decisions to the contractor. Performance SOWs are normally considered to enhance competition because they enable a contractor to utilize their inherent strengths and creativity to satisfy the requirement.

Functional SOWs

The functional SOW is the least restrictive of the three basic SOW types. Functional SOWs describe requirements in terms of the end purpose, expected result, or final objective rather than in terms of how the work effort is to be performed. Though the functional SOW may include needed quality standards or minimum essential characteristics, it focuses primarily on the "what" aspects of the requirement. Functional SOWs provide the contractor with the maximum degree of flexibility and innovation in determining how best to satisfy the buying organization's needs. It is for this reason that functional SOWs are currently the most preferred type of SOW in most government and commercial contracting organizations.

In practice, SOWs rarely fall neatly into one of the three types discussed above. Most SOWs reflect characteristics of at least two, if not all three, SOW types in order to adequately describe the requirement. Regardless of which type or types are used, SOWs normally contain at least some of the following elements:

Objective

An objective is a brief statement of the goal to be achieved, the end product desired, or the basic purpose of the requirement.

Scope

The scope is a general statement defining the parameters or boundaries of expected actions, required performance, or products required. Scope statements can be viewed as the "fenced-in area" in which the contractor performs.

Description of Work Required

The description is a sufficiently detailed explanation of what is required. The description often contains an explanation of interfaces that will affect the work effort, a history of how the required effort came to be needed, required place of performance, issues and problems that require resolution, and other pertinent information. To the maximum extent possible, the description should be outcome focused, providing the contractor as much flexibility as possible for determining how to accomplish the work required to achieve the objective, within the defined scope. When necessary, specific performance elements can be prescribed, but they should be kept to a minimum.

Performance Standards and Reporting Requirements

Performance Standards and Reporting Requirements are an explanation of how the contractor's work effort will be evaluated, in terms of quantity, quality, frequency, or other appropriate measures. The performance standards should define clearly the expected, required, or acceptable level of performance from the contractor. The standards need to be achievable and measurable. Reporting requirements should explain how often and in what format any required progress or performance reports will be provided. Both performance standards and reporting requirements should be limited to the minimum necessary to achieve effective and efficient contract administration.

Staffing Requirements

If personnel with certain specific qualifications are required to perform the work, (e.g., electrical engineer, certified public accountant, etc.,) these qualifications should be included. However, in most cases, the contractor should have the option to propose staffing levels and composition to accomplish the required work.

Resources to Be Provided

Specify any space, equipment, materials, services, information, or other resources that will be provided to the contractor.

Appropriate Reference Documents

Provide a list of any pertinent reference documents that may have been discussed in the SOW, or that may be required by the contractor to ensure adequate performance or clarify contract requirements.

As previously mentioned, statements of work may be of varying lengths and levels of complexity, depending on the needs of the buying organization. While not all SOWs will necessarily contain all the elements noted earlier, each SOW should be constructed so as to provide a complete, clear, and concise description of the requirement. Well-constructed SOWs reduce risk, enhance competition and help achieve organizational goals.

4.1.2 Contract Type and Method

The solicitation package should also define the contract type and method that the acquisition will use. An explanation of commonly used contract types and method was presented in Chapter 3. As it relates to the solicitation package, the contract type and method should complement the degree of complexity and risk associated with the overall statement of work. The use of certain contract types and methods for specific types of acquisitions is sometimes required by law, regulation, or corporate policy. In other cases, the contract type and method used is a discretionary decision made by the contracting professional. Sometimes the contracting professional must blend more than one contract type into a solicitation, such as including both firm-fixed-price and time-and-material line items when appropriate. The choice of contract type and method is frequently a business decision, influenced by a variety of organizational and marketplace dynamics. The contracting professional should strive to ensure that the contract type and method chosen are consistent with the level of complexity and uncertainty inherent in the statement of work; reflects an acceptable level of risk sharing between the buyer and seller; conforms to applicable law, regulation, or corporate policy; and helps promote the successful accomplishment of the contracting function and overall goals of the organization.

4.1.3 Terms and Conditions

In addition to the statement of work, and contract type and method, terms and conditions are another component of the requirements package that help define the business relationship between the buyer and seller, and the rights and obligations of both parties to the contract. The primary function of terms and conditions is to eliminate or reduce the risk of contract ambiguity—often the source of disputes and misunderstandings. Most government and commercial contracting organizations include standard terms and conditions related to certain contract types in all solicitations and resulting contracts. In many cases, the selection of clauses that comprise the terms and conditions is an automated function that occurs within the buyer's contract writing software programs. In other cases, terms and conditions can be selected from a "shopping list" provided for the appropriate contract type. In still other cases, specific clauses must be crafted to meet an individual need, usually with the assistance of legal counsel and other professionals. Though frequently referred to as "boilerplate," and sometimes included in solicitations as little more than an afterthought, terms and conditions are another risk mitigating tool that can be used by the contracting professional to enhance the likelihood of success. A careful review of terms and conditions to be included in the solicitation can reveal gaps that could cause confusion, unnecessary terms, and conditions that could adversely affect price or performance, or terms and conditions that conflict with each other. Terms and conditions should be reviewed to ensure that each one included serves a legitimate purpose, is required or provides a direct benefit to the acquisition in question, promotes an acceptable level of risk-sharing between buyer and seller, and does not impose unreasonable burdens on prospective offerors.

4.1.4 Evaluation Procedures

The solicitation package should clearly indicate the general procedures that will be used to evaluate proposals and the decisions that will be used as the basis for an award. The method of acquisition normally determines the basis for the award. The use of an invitation for bids (IFBs) requires that the selection be based on price. The use of a request for proposal (RFP) indicates a negotiated procurement where various factors, with potentially different degrees of relative significance, will serve as the basis for award. The evaluation procedures can influence, either positively or negatively, the quality of proposals received from offerors. Great care must be taken in determining evaluation factors. Too few factors may result in the receipt of inadequate proposals that are impossible to evaluate. Too many factors may result in the receipt of exceedingly complex proposals—or none at all. Though price will normally be included as an evaluation factor, other factors such as cost realism, technical excellence, management capability, past performance, and other relevant factors can and should be included as appropriate. Each evaluation factor should be independent of the other factors to reduce the potential for confusion. It is also important to advise potential offerors of the relative significance of the evaluation factors to each other. Though it is usually neither required nor desirable to provide all the details of the evaluation plan in the solicitation, it is important for potential offerors to understand how proposals will be evaluated, the factors that will make up the evaluation, and the relative importance of each evaluation factor to each other and to the overall acquisition.

4.1.5 Instructions for Proposal Preparation and Submission

The final piece of the solicitation package is the instructions provided to potential offerors for preparing and submitting proposals. The purpose of the instructions is to help ensure that uniform (or nearly uniform) submissions are received from offerors to permit a fair and unbiased evaluation process. Contractors usually pay close attention to the instructions since failure to comply with them may result in a proposal not being considered. The instructions can be very specific or very general, depending on the needs of the buying organization. Instructions usually contain information regarding page format and page number limitations, the order of topic presentation, required content to be addressed, whether separate technical and price proposals are required, if the award will be made with or without discussions, if oral presentations will be required, the number of copies to submit, the media proposals may be submitted on, the place to submit proposals to, the due date and time, and similar types of information. The contracting professional has to balance the need for the information required to be provided in the proposal with the costs offerors will incur in proposal preparation. The instructions should be constructed so as to enable the offerors to submit the best possible proposals while also ensuring that the information received in the proposals will provide the necessary data for a thorough and appropriate evaluation and award decision.

4.1.6 Other Requirements Preparation Consideration

Once the solicitation package has been completed, there are a number of techniques that can be used to validate the completeness and accuracy of the package before it is formally issued. Some of these techniques include an independent technical review obtaining marketplace comments, and presolicitation notices and conferences.

Independent Technical Review

The solicitation package can be reviewed by technical experts, legal counsel, and other resources within the organization to ensure it is complete and accurate. Normally, this independent technical review team is composed of people who had no prior involvement with the solicitation package.

Marketplace Comments

A draft of the solicitation package can be issued requesting review and comments, or suggestions from contractors that might become offerors. This pre-release review sometimes yields useful suggestions for revision that might otherwise have been overlooked. However, the contracting professional needs to be aware of the possibility that potential offerors may use this opportunity for preliminary marketing purposes, and may try to influence content changes in the solicitation that enhance their ability to successfully compete for the contract.

Presolicitation Notices and Conferences

Presolicitation notices and conferences can be used to help identify potential interested sources and can provide a forum to explain technical or complicated aspects of the solicitation. These efforts can sometimes separate the interested potential sources from the merely curious ones.

4.2 Publicity

The issuance of solicitation packages and the degree to which competitive proposals are sought often depends on the organization performing the buying function. Government contracting professionals are subject to a law- and regulation-based preference for fully competitive procurements. Though there are a number of authorized exceptions permitting less than full and open competition and sole-source acquisition, the general rule in government contracting is to seek the maximum level of meaningful competition whenever possible. Commercial contracting professionals sometimes work in organizations that also have a preference for competitive acquisition. However, sometimes other commercial considerations, such as supply-chain agreements, approved source lists, and other business decisions, can have an influence on the degree to which competition is pursued. When competition is a goal, the buying organization normally uses publicizing as a technique to ensure adequate competition.

Government Agencies

Government contracting organizations are normally required to post solicitation packages exceeding certain dollar thresholds (i.e., the simplified acquisition threshold) for full and open competition on an official Web site. Though certain limitations can apply to these postings; including small business set-asides, restricting competition to firms that hold General Services Administration (GSA) Federal Supply Service (FSS) contracts, and other discriminators; the fundamental intent of these postings at a single location is to provide a uniform source of information to the business community in pursuit of a required or desired level of competition.

Solicitation packages that do not exceed certain dollar thresholds are normally competed by selecting an appropriate number of potential offerors and issuing the solicitation to them. Though the number of firms solicited usually varies depending on the dollar value and complexity of the acquisition, the intent is to seek a level of competition that will reasonably result in the receipt of multiple proposals that will produce a competitive award, and will not cause undue administrative burden to the agency.

Some government agencies also advertise open solicitations on their official Web site, usually under a title such as "Business Opportunities," "Current Business Opportunities," "Doing Business With...," or a similar title.

Commercial Organizations

Commercial contracting organizations may advertise their requirements in newspapers, trade journals, professional publications, and similar media. They may also provide the solicitation to capable firms in their supply chain, or as the result of other business agreements.

Commercial firms may also advertise business opportunities on their official Web site in much the same manner as government agencies.

Though the methods for publicizing active solicitation packages may vary, the basic purpose does not. When competition is required or desired, the solicitation should be advertised uniformly to ensure that the target market of potential offerors is aware of the opportunity. Additionally, some other concepts should be used to make the publicity effort more meaningful.

Solicitations should remain open or active for a period of time sufficient to permit potential offerors to carefully and completely review and analyze all aspects of the requirement, make an informed bid/no-bid decision, and prepare and submit their best proposal. Though the contracting professional often faces internal pressures to reduce the acquisition cycle time, the length of time a solicitation remains open can have a direct impact on the number and quality of proposals received, and the success or failure of the overall acquisition.

Contracting professionals should normally provide a period of time, within the solicitation period, for potential offerors to submit written questions and/or attend pre-proposal conferences. These activities are often very valuable in clarifying the buyer's intent, as well as technical or other complex aspects related to the acquisition. These conferences can sometimes include a "walk-through" when the contract will be performed at the buyer's location, or other pertinent information that could be of value to potential offerors.

The need for changes or amendments to a solicitation may become evident after responding to written questions or after a pre-proposal conference. When appropriate, the solicitation should be modified to reflect the necessary changes, and the due date for proposals should be extended to provide offerors the opportunity to respond to the changes. The degree to which solicitation packages are publicized usually has a direct impact on both the quality and quantity of competitive proposals received. The solicitation phase is often a target when trying to reduce acquisition cycle time, primarily because a reduction in the length of time a solicitation remains open has little or no immediate adverse impact on the buying organization. Contracting professionals need to remain aware, however, that an inadequate solicitation period often affects the overall quality of the acquisition.

4.3 Proposal Evaluation

Once the solicitation period has closed, the contracting professional will hopefully have a number of proposals to evaluate. In Chapter 3, the need for an evaluation plan, as part of the source selection planning process, was discussed. The evaluation methodology that was included in the source-selection plan should have been carefully crafted to evaluate elements of importance related to the acquisition objectives; should have been reviewed and approved by the multifunction acquisition planning team and other appropriate managers; may have been reviewed by legal counsel as appropriate; and should have been communicated clearly, though not necessarily in complete detail, to prospective offerors in the solicitation.

As is the case with acquisition plans and requirements packages, the evaluation plan may be simple or complex, with one or many factors and subfactors, depending on the dollar value and degree of complexity of the acquisition, and the contract type and method chosen. In any event, the evaluation plan must represent the key areas of consideration relative to source selection, and must provide for a meaningful comparison of and the ability to discriminate between various aspects of competing proposals. It is also essential that the proposals actually be evaluated according to the evaluation plan and source-selection plan, and that new or different criteria not be introduced into the process at this point.

4.3.1 Typical Evaluation Considerations

Generally speaking, like the solicitation, the evaluation process normally focuses on the price, technical capabilities, management capabilities, and past performance.

Price

Price (or cost) should always be an evaluation factor. In some cases, such as sealed bidding, price is the only factor. In other cases, such as with negotiated procurements, price is always included, but may be of secondary or even lesser significance compared to other evaluation criteria.

Technical Capabilities

Often required as a separate volume of the proposal, technical considerations relate to how well the offerors understand the requirement, and how effective their proposed solution is in achieving the objectives of the acquisition. The evaluation plan should mirror the statement of work and the instructions provided to offerors. It should contain evaluation factors that relate directly to issues that offerors were required to address.

Management Capabilities

How the offerors intend to manage the work required under contract is often an important evaluation factor. When such information is required by the solicitation, appropriate evaluation factors should assess the proposed organization structure, management capability, experience and controls, and other pertinent factors.

Past Performance

Relevant information concerning how well an offeror has performed similar work in the past is often used as a significant evaluation factor. Offerors are normally required to submit past performance data that references other contracts they have performed that are similar in nature to the current requirement. When required by the solicitation, the evaluation plan must address how past performance issues will be evaluated, including the effect (usually neutral) of an offeror having little or no pertinent past performance. Evaluation factors for past performance normally require the evaluators or the contracting professional to attempt to verify the accuracy of past performance information submitted by an offeror. This is usually accomplished by contacting the sources provided by the offeror and obtaining answers to an established set of past performance questions.

Relative Significance of Evaluation Factors

The evaluation plan should also address the relative significance of all evaluation factors to be used as a basis for selection, as well as the relative significance of price factors to nonprice factors. This factor-ranking process is particularly important in negotiated procurements, because the award is often made to some offeror other than the lowest price. As with all other evaluation factors, the relative significance of the factors should have also been addressed in the solicitation.

4.3.2 Typical Evaluation Techniques

The intent of the evaluation process is to uniformly rate the quality and content of all proposals received against a clear set of pertinent criteria in order to arrive at an award recommendation decision that provides the maximum benefit to the buying organization. Several methods are often used to help ensure that the evaluation process is logical, unbiased, and defendable.

Separate Evaluation of Technical Aspects

The solicitation package may have required the submission of separate technical and price proposals. However, even if separate proposal volumes were not required, the evaluation team should review technical considerations on their own merits. The proposals can be edited before review to eliminate any pricing information. Since there are defined evaluation criteria, and since price is always included as an evaluation factor, it is important not to allow the evaluation of one factor to be influenced by other evaluation factors at this stage.

Compliance Matrix

Organizations frequently use a prepared evaluation checklist or document to promote uniformity in the evaluation process. This checklist should contain a compliance matrix that usually consists of all evaluation factors and subfactors; the rating scale to be applied; weights to be applied to factors, if appropriate; and room for evaluator comments. The use of such a matrix can ensure that each proposal received a thorough and comprehensive review. Offerors often use a similar compliance matrix when preparing proposals to ensure they have addressed all pertinent requirements.

Independent Evaluation

Each member of the evaluation team should evaluate each proposal independently without any input from other team members. Each member of the team brings unique experiences, knowledge, insight, perspective, and expectations to the evaluation process. These personal differences should be viewed as assets that can be used to enhance the evaluation process. Though a consensus will eventually be required, the initial evaluation phase should normally be as uninhibited as possible. This preferred independence can be enhanced even further by removing the names of the offerors from the proposals, if this is possible.

Uniform Rating Scale

As noted earlier, the evaluation checklist or documentation will usually include the rating scale, which is used to assign value to the factors evaluated in the proposals. Rating scales often take one of several forms.

Numeric Scales

In numeric rating scales, a range of points (e.g., 0-10, 0-25, 0-100) is assigned to each evaluation factor, with the highest possible rating equaling the sum of the maximum points available for each factor. Numeric scales most easily accommodate weighted evaluation factors. For example, if a technical approach is twice as important as past performance, 20 total points can be allocated to technical approach and 10 points to past performance. Numeric scales are often preferred because they are most easily understood and yield a definitive "answer"—the score. Many contracting professionals do not favor the numeric scoring method because they understand that the definitive score it provides can often be much more subjective that it appears.

Color Scales

Many contracting professionals, most notably those from the government and military, use a color-based scale to evaluate proposals. Color scales are normally constructed with three, four, or five ranges. A three-range scale might consist of red for unsatisfactory, yellow for satisfactory, and green for excellent. For four- and five-range scales, more colors and related scoring ranges are added. The rationale for assigning a particular color rating is usually provided in the comments section. Color scales yield results that are easy to compare, but may be difficult to defend if the comments that support the rating are inadequate.

Adjectival Scales

Adjectival scales are very similar to color scales, but they eliminate the colors in favor of terms indicating the value assigned. As with color scales, adjectival scales usually have three, four, or five ranges and descriptions that often include unsatisfactory, marginal, satisfactory, highly satisfactory and exceptional; good, better, and exceptional; etc. The evaluators are required to provide comments to support the ratings in a manner similar to the color method scale. Adjectival scales are sometimes thought to produce results that are more consistent and defendable, primarily because they do not rely on visual or numeric devices to describe a score. However, the overall quality of the rating is still a dependent on the quality of the evaluators' comments. The following table is a sample of a typical adjectival evaluation rating system.

Adjectival Evaluation Rating System

Adjective	Explanation
Excellent (E)	Thorough and comprehensive ability to meet the criteria. Exceptional added value that will have a significant favorable effect on the government's ability to accomplish its mission, as reflected by the presence of numerous major strengths and no major weaknesses.
Very Good (VG)	Thorough and comprehensive ability to meet the criteria. Added value that will have a favorable effect on the government's ability to accomplish its mission, as reflected by the presence of major strengths and no major weaknesses.
Good (G)	Thorough ability to meet the criteria. Offers some value and will have a favorable effect on the government's ability to accomplish its mission.
Minimally Acceptable (MA)	Ability to meet all of the minimum requirements set forth in the criteria, but offers no added value.
Unacceptable (U)	Inability to meet all of the minimum requirements set forth in the criteria.

Compare Results and Reach Consensus

After each member of the evaluation team has completed his or her ratings, the team should come together and compare results. This process will often reveal significant differences in perceptions among team members concerning the relative quality of the proposals. These differences should be viewed as positive because they should require a spirited and collaborative deliberation process. Evaluation team members should avoid simply averaging individual scores, as this diminishes the benefits gained from the individual review process. Rather, each team member should both share and solicit information regarding how ratings were derived. The resulting consensus should be documented thoroughly, with the strengths and weaknesses of each proposal explained. Sometimes proposals are also ranked in order of preference by the evaluation team. It is also important to thoroughly document problems, issues requiring clarification, and other unresolved matters related to each proposal, since these often serve as the basis for negotiations with the offerors.

4.4 Source Selection

Selection of the "winning" proposal is often referred to as the source selection, although the term is sometimes used to represent all activities inherent in the evaluation process. The source selection is sometimes made by the contracting professional or the senior contracting professional in the organization, sometimes by a senior manager in the customer's organization, and sometimes by a neutral senior manager that has had no prior involvement in the acquisition process. Regardless of who makes the selection, the selection decision is normally intended to reflect the independent judgment of the selection official. A typical source selection structure is shown below:

In practice, the selection official will normally make the selection recommended if the evaluation team does a complete, thorough, and professional job; if the evaluation reports reflect compliance with the acquisition plan, the solicitation, and the evaluation plan; and if the resulting recommendation is logical, reasonable, and supportable.

Source-Selection Process

The chart on page 40 is a depiction of a typical source-selection process. Every procurement is unique, so the sequence or number of events may be slightly different.

Though the selection official will usually rely heavily on the analysis and recommendations provided by the evaluation team, there is usually no requirement that the selection official concur with the recommendations. The selection official is normally required to document the reasons for the selection made, and to explain additional considerations made in the source selection process.

CMBOK 2nd Edition section 2

RFP Release → Initial Proposals → Review for Completeness → Notification from Contract Official → Compliance Evaluation → Develop Requests for Clarifications → Initial Technical Evaluation/Report / Initial Business Evaluation/Report

Clarifications/Deficiencies → Determination of Disqualified Responses → Discussions + Negotiations Take Place → Request Best Offer → Best Offer Proposals Received → Technical Evaluation/Report / Business Evaluation/Report

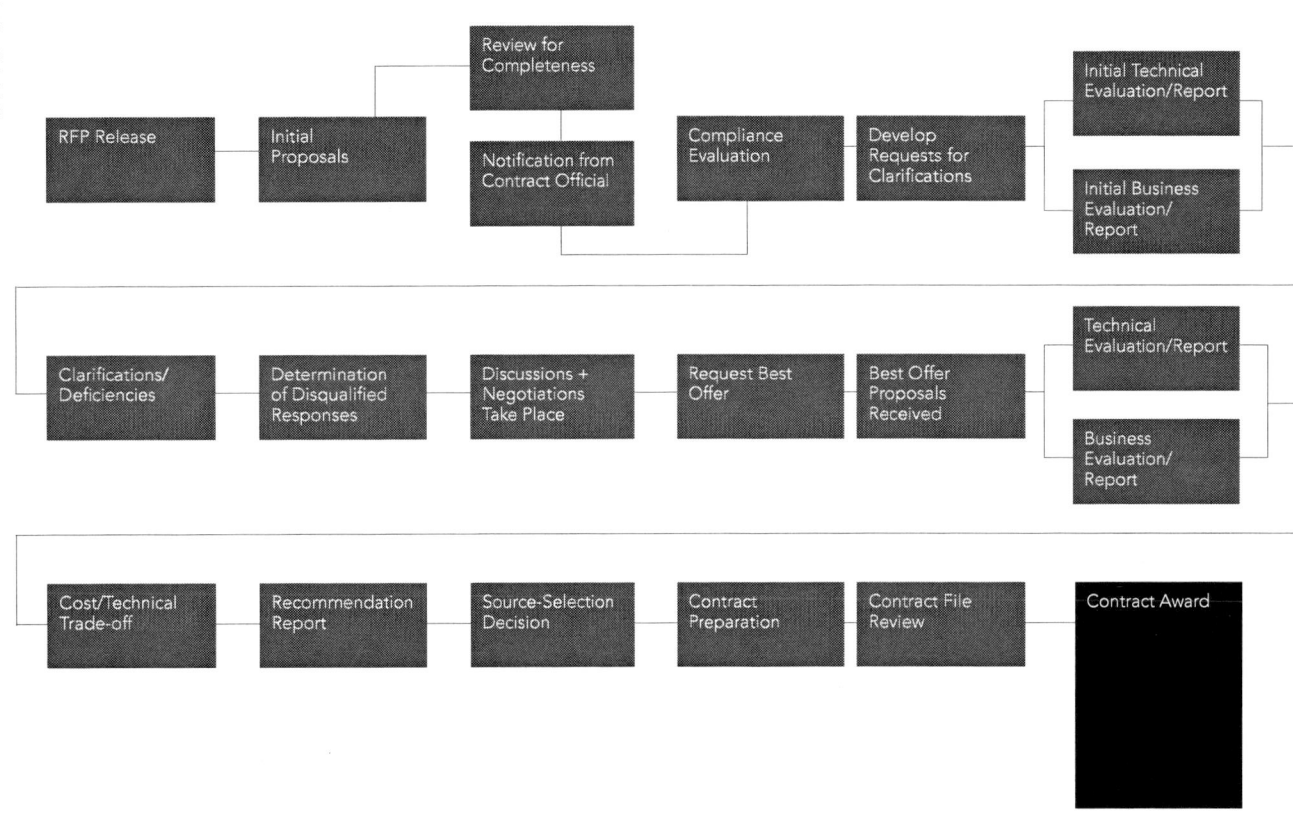

Cost/Technical Trade-off → Recommendation Report → Source-Selection Decision → Contract Preparation → Contract File Review → Contract Award

40

4.5 Negotiations

Negotiation is a communication process where two parties attempt to reach agreement. Negotiation does not need to be a process where one party wins at the other's expense. It is possible and preferable that both parties finish negotiations feeling that they have "won." Despite the fact that both parties have different interests, they have a common goal—to negotiate a fair and reasonable contract.

4.5.1 Preparation

Preparation is the most important step in the negotiation process. Buyers and sellers each have unique advantages going into negotiations. Buyers know how much money is available, and the amount and nature of competition. Sellers know the basis for cost estimates and where there is flexibility in their proposal. Nonetheless, both parties must plan for negotiations. Thorough preparations can lead to smooth negotiations, a good contract, fewer changes, and successful performance.

The first step in the preparation process is understanding the acquisition. The buyer must know what is being purchased, why it is needed, and whether it was purchased before. Although it is not always possible for every buyer to do an in-depth analysis of each acquisition, it is important to get to know as much as possible before entering negotiations. Sellers must also understand the acquisition. They should know the purpose of the acquisition, the buyer's objectives, whether the buyer is the end-user, and if not, who is the end-user, and the end-user's needs.

After the buyer receives the seller's proposal, they review and analyze it in response to the requirements stated in the solicitation. The buyer's first source of information is the offeror's proposal. Buyers compare the data in the proposal to previous contracts of a similar nature. The seller's source of information is previous experience and the assumptions used to price the proposal.

The buyer looks at the differences between the offer and previous contracts or the buyer's estimate. The buyer then gathers facts, analyzes the facts, establishes negotiation objectives, and plans the negotiation strategy. Gathering and analyzing facts is done throughout the acquisition cycle. It is important for both parties to document those facts for use in negotiation. Discrepancies are resolved by providing documentation to justify a position. Without adequate documentation, it may be difficult to reach a negotiation objective.

4.5.2 The Negotiation Team

Large and/or complex acquisitions usually require different people to participate in the negotiations, with each person contributing a special skill. Selection of team members depends on the nature of the acquisition and the experience that each member brings to the team. Team members on each side may include, but are not limited to, the contract professional, financial analyst, cost analyst, legal counsel, design engineer, production specialist, quality control specialist, and note taker. The negotiation teams for the buyer and sellers designate a lead negotiator for their team, which most often is the contract professional depending on the entity's practice and industry. In the case of federal contracting, the lead negotiator is always the contracting officer.

The team members usually have worked together on the acquisition since its early stages from solicitation to proposal submission. After proposal submission, they work together again to reach an agreement with the other party. It can be a long process that takes months or more, so it is important to put together a team that works well together. Each member of the team must understand and agree with the group's goal or the team will be ineffective. The group must function as a team, reporting to the lead negotiator. It is ineffective to have individuals who conduct side negotiations to protect their own interests—this will jeopardize the team's goals.

4.5.3 Negotiation Objectives

The facts are different for each negotiation even if the acquisition is for the same item that was previously purchased. The market may be different, the delivery schedule may be different, or the economy may be different. All of these factors influence pricing decisions and negotiation objectives.

Establishing the negotiation objectives entails more than cost analysis and comparison. Most aspects of a solicitation are negotiable, such as the statement of work, delivery schedule, warranties, payment terms, terms and conditions, and/or reporting requirements. These aspects may be negotiable depending on the circumstances surrounding the acquisition.

Both buyers and sellers need to establish specific and realistic negotiation objectives. An objective of "the best price we can get" is neither specific nor realistic, as there would be no way of knowing if the result was the best price. Establishing negotiation objectives is an ongoing process because the negotiation objectives will change as the situation changes.

Based on the review of proposed costs, a negotiation objective is prepared based on the best information available. Since the circumstances change, the objective needs to be flexible. A way to ensure flexibility is to develop three positions in preparing an objective—the minimum, objective, and maximum. By doing so, a range is established that permits movement one way or another depending on the situation. When the seller's objective overlaps with the buyer's objective, both parties are satisfied with the final agreement.

The tables below demonstrate examples of a negotiation objective for a firm-fixed-price contract and for a cost-plus-fixed-fee contract.

Negotiation Objective for a Firm-Fixed-Price Contract

	Minimum	Objective	Maximum
Unit Price	$	$	$

Negotiation Objective for a Cost-Plus-Fixed-Fee Contract

Cost Element	Minimum	Objective	Maximum
Direct	$	$	$
Indirect	$	$	$
Total Cost	$	$	$
Profit	$	$	$
Total Cost	$	$	$

For the seller, the minimum position is the lowest acceptable price. The seller's minimum position might be the lowest possible cost, plus a reasonable profit given a perfect situation. For the buyer, the lowest price is usually the first counter-proposal and may be based on a previous contract. If the contract is cost type, cost overruns are likely if the price agreement is too low. If the resulting contract is fixed price, an unreasonable low profit or even a potential loss may result. This may result in poor quality or nonperformance. For these reasons, a buyer's objective of the lowest price possible is not always a good idea.

The objective is the price at which final agreement can be reached. It is an amount between the minimum and the maximum. If the parties' objectives are far apart, a final agreement may be difficult to achieve.

The seller's maximum position is the initial proposal. The buyer's maximum position is usually the funding limit. In this instance, the buyer has an advantage because it knows the seller's maximum position (the initial proposal) and the buyer's own funding limit, whereas the seller only knows the initial proposal.

The amount for each position must be defensible. The negotiators must know the exact figures, the reasons for arriving at those numbers, and the means to justify the figures. Document how the amounts were reached, because as the facts surrounding your assumptions change, the positions will change.

The degree of competition, if any, also affects the relevance of negotiation objectives. If the acquisition is competitive, competition sets the price.

Another step in establishing negotiation objectives is to identify important issues to discuss. Each side must organize and gather facts to support the issues it believes are important. Issues might include requirements in the statement of work, terms and conditions, and cost proposal details. Identification of issues is based on experience with the required work and with the buyer or seller.

Upper management usually makes recommendations on positions by reviewing the documentation and justification prior to negotiations. Management review of the negotiation objectives is a vital step to entering negotiations. For private firms, it gives the negotiator the authority to agree to a certain price. In private firms, the negotiator may have a continuous delegation of authority to negotiate procurements up to a certain dollar level. For a negotiator to go beyond that prescribed authority requires further management review and approval. Consultation with management is an ongoing process in both commercial and federal contracting negotiations, especially when unanticipated problems arise.

Government contracting officers have authority to commit the government up to the amount specified in the contracting officer's warrant if limited by a specified dollar amount. If the contracting officer has an unlimited warrant, then he or she is constrained only by available funds, but management reviews are done nonetheless. A negotiator's authority is the first item discussed in the negotiation. Each negotiator must know the limits of his/her authority before entering into negotiations.

Discussion of negotiation objectives during the management review also sets the stage for establishing basic strategies. Pre-negotiation presentation of objectives and strategies helps the negotiators prepare for the negotiation by explaining the plan to upper management. Experience with products or services and with an individual buyer or seller prepares the negotiator, but each negotiation is different.

The strategy should consider negotiating terms and conditions as well, such as payment terms, delivery schedule, and contract type, as they too can affect the price.

4.5.4 Negotiation Guidelines

Although both parties enter negotiations intending to reach agreement, the fact remains that they approach it from different perspectives.

Lack of respect seriously reduces the possibility of reaching agreement. Respect for the individual and his or her authority is paramount to effective negotiations. Each side takes on certain risks when entering a contract, and it is important for the opposing side to not only recognize those risks, but to understand them as well. The first step in understanding is listening carefully to the other side's position and trying to understand it. The only way an agreement can be reached is for both parties to be flexible and compromise.

Caucus and concession are two techniques employed in negotiations. A caucus is used to break away from formal negotiations for the team to consider a point. When a counter-offer is made, a caucus can be used to confer with your negotiation team to consider all aspects of the counter-offer. A caucus is useful to discuss anything about the ongoing negotiation that you don't want the other team to hear. A caucus can be used when a team member wants to bring to the negotiator's attention an important fact, or if a fact needs to be checked with a team member, or if management approval is necessary to make a concession or counter-offer.

Concessions are also necessary to the negotiation process. Entering into negotiations without an intention to concede any point will not result in a mutual agreement. Sometimes it is necessary to concede an item if your objectives can be met at the same time.

4.5.5 Strategies and Tactics

In addition to these guidelines, certain strategies or techniques can be used to achieve negotiation objectives. The use and effectiveness of any strategy depends on a number of factors, including the nature of the acquisition and each parties' long- and short-term objectives. In addition to the long- and short-term objectives, the parties must evaluate the nature of their relationship. On the one hand, if a long-term, continuing relationship is important, then the strategies and tactics used are usually cooperative. On the other hand, if the relationship is only a one-time, short-term relationship, then a more competitive strategy may be effective.

Four basic tactics include the cooperative mode, competitive mode, time restrictions, and deadlock.

1. The cooperative mode presumes that reasonable people are needed to achieve reasonable outcomes. Planning before the negotiation includes developing justifications and explanations for a party's position. This allows for compromise and cooperation during negotiations because it allows the other party to understand and recognize the reasonableness and validity of the positions. Each party recognizes that the other party might have a position that meets the objectives of both parties, resulting in a mutually agreeable result. This tactic requires patience as the mutually agreeable result may not be presented immediately.

2. The competitive mode is used when each party views the other as an adversary, and concessions are gained at the expense of the other party. Lack of planning can lead to this approach, such as not having justifiable reasons for a position. The ability to convincingly apply pressure is helpful in this mode. However, one should be careful not to issue rash threats; the other party may accept the threat rather than concede a point.

3. Time restrictions are usually present at any negotiation—the contract must be awarded so deliveries can be met. Learning to work under this pressure is important because concessions made due to time limits may not meet negotiation objectives. Extreme deadlines make adequate preparation difficult and may lead unprepared negotiators to make decisions based solely on time constraints. Time restrictions can be worked around by negotiating delivery schedule, inspection requirement, compensated overtime, or a letter contract. Time tactics can range from "my flight's scheduled to leave in an hour" to "the funding will not be available unless the contract is awarded today."

4. Deadlock is the inability to continue negotiations because the parties cannot or will not be flexible in their position. If the negotiations break down and there is a deadlock, the party with time on its side usually benefits. Patience is also important when a deadlock occurs because new objectives must be established requiring additional management reviews. While objectives are re-established, both parties should consider how to allow the other party a "face-saving" way to concede: give the other party an opening allowing a concession. After a deadlock happens, one party usually welcomes the other party back into negotiations. If the buyer has begun negotiating with a second seller, the position of the seller is greatly reduced when they enter back into negotiations. A deadlock can sometimes be resolved by introducing new people into the negotiation process to allow another perspective.

4.5.6 The Negotiation

A common understanding and validation of the facts to be used in negotiations is done by asking questions of the other party. The process of validating assumptions is known as fact-finding, and is initiated by the buyer. Fact-finding can be done through telephone calls, correspondence, and meetings. It can take place before the formal negotiation session, or at the very beginning of the session depending on the circumstances. Fact-finding may affect both parties' objectives. If an assumption for the objective is invalid or even slightly different, the basis for objectives also changes. Thus, effectively conducted fact-finding is a vital element of successful negotiations.

The buyer is usually the host in negotiations and is responsible for ensuring that adequate facilities are available to ensure the negotiations run smoothly. The facilities should include a room large enough to comfortably accommodate everyone, a separate caucus room close to the negotiation room, a nearby private telephone, note paper and pencils for everyone, and visual aides, such as a viewgraph or white board.

The negotiation conference must be conducted without interruption, so full use of the room for as long as necessary should be scheduled in advance. The host should find out in advance how many people are going to attend and if there are any special audio/visual requirements.

The negotiation conference begins with a formal introduction of everyone present. The buyer's lead negotiator, as the host, begins the introductions. All the team members are introduced by announcing members' names and roles in the negotiation. The lead negotiators for both teams should indicate whether or not they have the authority to bind their organization. Some negotiators can verbally bind their organization, but do not have the signature authority for the contract, so they must return to the office to get the appropriate signature. In the case of federal contracting, contracting officers may bind the government up to a certain amount stipulated in their warrant.

Agendas are given to everyone present. The agenda establishes the major issues of the negotiation, and both sides may have different ideas of what the major issues are. In some cases, both parties arrive at negotiations with established agendas, and in other cases, negotiations begin by establishing the items to be discussed.

The basic format of negotiations is question and answer. The buyer might begin by asking the seller to justify a proposed price or term, and the seller responds by describing their justification. Or the seller may ask the buyer about an item in the statement of work, and the buyer responds by describing how that item fits into the program. Regardless of who is answering, it is vital that each party be allowed to answer completely. Interruptions not only distract the person from answering but also prevent listeners from obtaining important information.

It is helpful to secure easy agreements first. List all potential issues to be discussed, and cross off the items upon which there is no disagreement. This method narrows down the list of items quickly and makes the issues remaining appear manageable. Each agreement should be documented by writing it down on paper or on a white board so that everyone knows that discussion on that item is considered closed. Re-opening a closed item is considered unethical and should not be done unless additional facts come to light in the interim.

4.5.7 Agreement

As multiple concessions bring the parties closer to the negotiation range, final agreement also becomes more imminent. Convincing the other party of your counter-proposal's reasonableness takes logic and salesmanship. Not only does one have to present the basis for why it is reasonable, but one also has to convince the other party that it is in their best interest to accept it.

As an agreement is reached, both parties must document it. At the least, the documentation must explain the facts considered to reach agreement. The purpose of documentation is to establish that the final agreement has been accepted by both parties. A lot of paperwork is accumulated by the end of negotiations. The negotiation documentation summarizes the accumulated documentation, and takes the reader through each step—solicitation, proposal, negotiation objectives, concessions, and final agreement.

Although the narrative may have different formats or styles, some basic information should be included, such as

- A description of the supplies or services to be purchased, quantities, and delivery schedule;
- The solicitation/proposal number;
- The parties involved, including complete names, addresses, and phone numbers;
- The acquisition history, including information gathered;
- Negotiation objectives and their justifications; and
- Negotiation summary including
- Concessions made and their effect on negotiation objectives;
- Major items discussed and the parties' positions and outcomes;
- Use of and reliance upon data (including, but not limited to price and cost) submitted; and
- Copy of the agreed-to final position.

This documentation is kept in the contract file and provides an explanation of the final agreement and why it is reasonable. It will allow other personnel who were not involved in the negotiations to track how the final agreement was reached.

Chapter 5
Contract Award Competencies

In Chapter 4, a discussion was presented regarding the need for and uses of various types of pre-award competencies. This chapter presents a brief overview of competencies related to various award activities. Though some of the subjects more closely relate to government contracting operations, commercial contracting professionals can also use some of the information presented, consistent with their corporate goals, processes, and procedures.

5.1 Award

The notification of award to the successful offeror should normally occur immediately after the conclusion of all source selection activities. Though the notification is usually made by issuing the contract, in some cases, the award notification is made by separate correspondence, or by a telephone call or e-mail, followed by the written contract or official correspondence. In any event, there should be little or no delay in making the award once the source selection process has been completed.

5.1.1 Preparation of Contract Document

The contract document is prepared to document the terms of the agreement and the expectations of each party. The enforceability of the contract and the nature of the parties' obligations can be greatly affected by the format in which the contract is written, and the language used to express the agreement. Agreements made during preliminary negotiations may not be evident in the written contract and therefore, may be unenforceable. The terms and conditions within the contract will dictate its legal effect. Ambiguities in a written contract may cause differences in interpretation of the contract requirements. Internal conflict in the terms and conditions of a contract may lead to disagreement between the parties on which term should prevail.

It is important to prepare a contract document that accurately and concisely reflects the agreement between the two parties.

The contract document is prepared using the appropriate format and terms and conditions for the type of contract being awarded and the type of organization awarding the document. The contract document may contain standard contract language that has been formulated for the specific type of purchase or it may be necessary to write new contract language to fit the unique requirements of the contract. A large number of commercial contracts are form contracts. Commercial contracts for products, as a common practice in the every day transactions under the *UCC*, include the quantity of goods to be purchased, the time for performance, terms related to payment, delivery, passage of title, risk of loss terms, interest in goods, warranty, and returns of goods.

In the case of more complex requirements, a contract may include a statement of work, specifications, management plan, quality control plan, list of contract deliverables, licensing agreements, subcontracting plans, program and financial reporting requirements, and so on.

In the case of the federal government, a standard uniform contract format is used for many procurements, excluding contracts for commercial items, basic agreements, and construction or architect–engineering contracts. The sections in this format are as follows:

Section A	Solicitation/Contract Form
Section B	Supplies or Services and Prices/Cost Schedule
Section C	Statement of Work or Other Description of Item Purchased
Section D	Packaging and Marking
Section E	Inspection and Acceptance
Section F	Deliveries or Performance
Section G	Contract Administration Data
Section H	Special Contract Requirements
Section I	Contract Clauses
Section J	List of Attachments
Section K	Representations, Certifications, and Other Statements of Offerors
Section L	Instructions, Conditions, and Notices to Offerors
Section M	Evaluation Factors for Award

A successful contract reflects the agreed-upon business transaction, and addresses areas where there may be ambiguities regarding the expected performance of each party. If a contract does not adequately address these areas, the parties may end up in legal proceedings asking for the court's interpretation of the terms of the contracts. The goal of the contract professional is to prepare a document that minimizes the risk to their organization, reflects the agreed-to understanding between the parties, and successfully closes the business deal.

After the contract is signed and performance begins, the parties may realize that their agreement is not as clear as first thought. Thus, contract interpretation becomes necessary. Contract interpretation refers to determining the meaning of a contract or a term in the contract based on the original intent of the parties. Contract interpretation may begin by attempting to give all parts of the contract some meaning, (as opposed to some sections being rendered meaningless through certain interpretations,) and by the assertion of the specific over the general.

Most organizations have an instituted process for review of the contract document or items within by various stakeholders in the process. It is usually the responsibility of the contract professional to coordinate this review and obtain any necessary approvals within the organization before the document is signed. Often in organizations, the level of approval and review necessary is dependent upon the dollar value of the contract.

5.1.2 Contract File

It is important that all contracts, regardless of dollar value, be properly documented so a complete record of pre-solicitation activities; the solicitation, evaluation, and award process; and the administration of the contract through closeout is provided.

Often a contract file has a table of contents organized in chronological order. For example, it could have six separate sections for pre-solicitation documents, solicitation documents, evaluation documents, award documents, administration documents, and contract closeout documents. Depending on the size of the contract, a separate contract file can be maintained for modifications or delivery orders.

In addition to the contract document itself, pertinent items often assembled in the file might include solicitation documentation, such as sole-source or sole-make justification or consultant justifications, purchase requests, initial statement of work, specifications, drawings, independent cost estimate detail, make-buy documentation, request for information, acquisition planning, market survey, source selection evaluation plan, solicitation revisions, other miscellaneous correspondence, pre-proposal conference minutes and agenda, and proposals received. It might include the contract award documentation, such as an abstract of purchase, technical evaluation, cost/price analysis report, pre-award audit report, subcontracting plan with approval, prenegotiation plan, record of negotiations, financial approval, regret letters, legal approval, other supporting documentation (i.e., undefined terms or revision documentation), audits, procurement action summaries, winning proposal, revisions and proposals, non-winning proposals, and supplier's correspondence. It might also include contract administration information, such as invoice actions, shipments, cost forecasting/status reports, general correspondence, contract closeout documentation, and fee documentation.

The contract professional should review each proposed contractual document and its supporting file for completeness and accuracy. Each contract file should contain all pertinent information applicable to the proposed action. Each contract file should be in sufficient detail to permit reconstruction of all significant events by any subsequent reviewer without referral to the individual responsible for the contractual action.

5.1.3 Post-award Conference

A post-award conference, meeting, or some other form of post-award contact between the contracting professional and the successful offeror is sometimes held, particularly if the contract is complex, represents a significant undertaking, or has a high-dollar value. The intent of the post-award conference should be to help promote a good working relationship between the buyer and seller, to ensure that both parties to the contract have a clear and complete understanding of all contract requirements, and to identify and resolve questions, issues, and potential problems that may exist. However, the post-award conference is not intended to be a forum to "fix" problems that should more appropriately have been resolved in the pre-award phase. The contracting professional representing the buyer needs to exercise caution to ensure that the contract professional representing the seller does not use the post-award conference as a means to reopen negotiations. The decision to have a post-award conference, as well as all arrangements and agenda items related to the conference normally remain under the control of the buyer's contracting professional. Post-award conferences are usually attended by representatives of the buyer's and seller's contracting function, the buyer's customer, and the seller's staff that will be performing the work. In lieu of an actual meeting, the exchange of correspondence or teleconference is sometimes used to convey post-award communication.

5.2 Notification

In addition to the prompt notification of the successful offeror, all unsuccessful offerors should be notified of their status immediately or very soon after award. In some cases, notification is provided to offerors who have been eliminated from competition prior to the award decision.

Chapter 6
Post–award Competencies

The acquisition strategy, pre-award, and award competencies discussed in previous chapters are arguably the most glamorous aspects of contract management. In many organizations, the bulk of the professional contracting resources are devoted to "getting the contract issued," or "winning the award." However, once a contract has been awarded, there are many significant and important activities required that often determine how successful the contractual relationship will be. This chapter discusses the competencies required in the post-award environment.

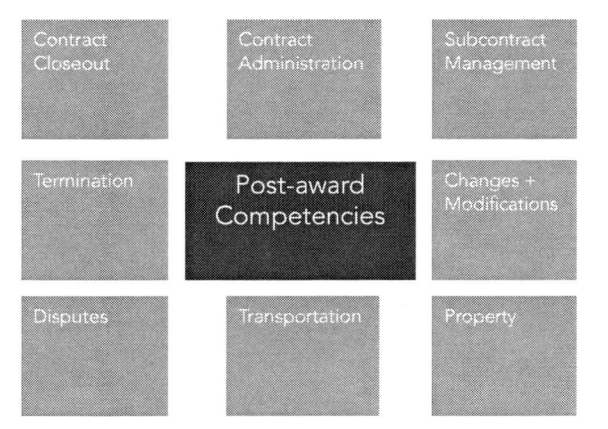

Contract Closeout	Contract Administration	Subcontract Management
Termination	**Post-award Competencies**	Changes + Modifications
Disputes	Transportation	Property

6.1 Contract Administration

Once a contract award has been made, and assuming that no significant issues presented themselves during the immediate post-award phase (i.e. the protest period), the tasks associated with ensuring appropriate contract performance begin, and are usually referred to using the generic term "contract administration." The range and extent of contract administration activities required will vary greatly, depending primarily on the complexity, dollar value, and organizational significance of the contract. It is also important to note that effective contract administration is a shared responsibility of both the buyer and seller. The contract specifies the duties, obligations, and benefits that both parties are responsible for and entitled to. The contract administration function provides <u>the oversight required to ensure that contractual promises are kept</u>. Contract administration can be straightforward, particularly when the contracting parties are individuals or small organizations. The complexities often associated with effective contract administration tend to be more prevalent and important as the size and complexity of the buyer's and seller's organizations increase. Contracting professionals in large, complex organizations frequently find themselves simultaneously responsible for administration activities on multiple contracts, and usually require some technical assistance and ongoing input from their internal customers, internal professional resources, management, and other stakeholders. The increasing level of complexity and the dependence upon resources external to the contracting function frequently present significant contract challenges for the contracting professionals for both the buyer and seller.

6.1.1 Effective Communication

An essential element of effective contract administration is establishing and maintaining effective communications. Maintaining a productive, two-way professional dialogue between buyer and seller during the period of contract performance is perhaps the most difficult, but potentially the most beneficial, aspect of contract administration. All too often, other business priorities and demands seem to force the contracting professional to relegate many administration activities to the "back burner." When this occurs, it is usually the customers in both the buyer's and seller's organizations who "pick up the slack" and run with the contract. Since these individuals often have little or no contacting experience, the results of inadequate oversight can be problematic.

6.1.2 Post-award Meeting

A post-award meeting can help mitigate the potential for issues and problems during contract performance. A discussion of the benefits of conducting a post-award conference was presented in Chapter 5. In addition to that conference, a more comprehensive post-award, pre-performance meeting can set the foundation for good communication between the buyer and seller. When conducted, this meeting should be chaired by contracting professionals from the buyer and seller, and include appropriate managers and staff personnel from the buyer's organization (i.e., the customer who will interface with and receive the benefits from the contractor's work), and appropriate managers and staff personnel from the seller's organization (i.e., the contractor's resources that will interface with and perform work for the customer).

A post-award meeting should include a detailed review of the contract, including all work to be performed and related terms and conditions. The intent of this review is to achieve a clear, mutual understanding of what needs to be done and who will do the work. It could include the development of a procedure for continuing written and verbal communication. This procedure should clearly specify, for both the buyer and seller, who is authorized to communicate, subject matter appropriate for communication, subject matter inappropriate for communication, the level of negotiation authority of the communicator (if any), and the form and format such communication should take. Since many of the players on both sides will not be contracting professionals, this agreement can be of significant value in reducing or eliminating issues related to constructive changes, apparent authority, etc. At the post-award meeting, there is usually discussion and agreement on progress reporting requirements, including the frequency, format and content of required reports, procedures for reporting unusual or urgent issues, and similar subjects. There is also discussion and agreement on methods and processes to be used to resolve minor disagreements or questions about contract interpretation, with provisions for escalation when appropriate. The subjects discussed and agreements reached during these meetings should be thoroughly documented, approved by both the buyer and seller, and distributed throughout both organizations.

6.1.3 Periodic Status Review Meetings

Updated information on status, issues, and concerns should be shared between the buyer and seller during periodic face-to-face meetings. The frequency, content, and required attendees for these meetings should be mutually agreed upon, and each should have a written agenda. These meetings should be used to augment any written reports required and help serve as a means to continue an open and honest dialogue for issues related to contract performance.

6.1.4 Written Status Reports

When appropriate and useful, the contractor should provide written status reports to keep the buyer's contacting professionals and customers aware of progress and issues. These reports can be narrative, statistical—or a combination of the two—and consistent with the need for the information. These types of reporting requirements, as well as the pre-performance meeting and periodic status meetings discussed earlier, are normally included in the contract language as required deliverables. All reporting requirements should directly relate to some aspect of required performance, create the smallest administrative burden possible, and only be required when the information they contain will actually be used for some legitimate contract management purpose.

6.1.5 Observation

In addition to the information provided by a contractor in various meetings and reports, observation is a tool often used by the buyer's contract professionals and management staff to validate information received from other sources. Indirect observation is usually obtained through the receipt of various types of reports from the contractor, from reviews or audits performed by either the buyer's management staff or by internal or external auditors, from various forms of pre- and post-production testing and sampling, and a variety of other methods. Indirect observation can provide valuable information regarding issues such as cost, schedule, and quality that might not otherwise be available. If the work effort is primarily physical in nature, indirect observation is often augmented by direct observation. Direct observation is the actual physical presence of the contracting professional or other appropriate manager on site to visually check on progress or compare actual work completed to planned work completed.

6.1.6 Documentation

A continuous stream of pertinent documentation should be generated and maintained throughout the life of the contract. The documentation can take many forms—formal correspondence, memoranda for the record, telephone logs, e-mails, personal notes, journal entries, etc. The documentation serves as a written record of all meetings, discussions, issues, problems, solutions, and agreements. The record can be used as a ready reference source to reflect the intent of the parties over time, as a means to guide future actions based on agreements reached in the past, or as evidence in the event of litigation.

The communications, reporting, and observation aspects of contract administration form the basis for many of the other administration functions to be discussed later in this chapter.

6.2 Subcontract Administration

Although the contractual relationship between the buyer and the seller (i.e., the prime contract) is normally the most important aspect of contract administration, the buying contract professional also needs to pay attention to the relationship between the seller and its subcontractors. In many cases, the ability of a prime contractor to successfully meet contractual obligations is at least partially, and sometimes significantly, dependent on the ability of subcontractors to meet contractual obligations to the seller. In some cases, the subcontractor is simply a supplier of goods or raw materials to the seller for use in production or fabrication. In other cases, the subcontractor may perform specialized, intellectual, or highly technical work for a seller in direct support of the seller's contract with the buyer. Though in both cases, the seller's ability to successfully perform is dependent on the action of their subcontractors, the buyer's contracting professionals should normally be more attuned to and concerned with subcontractor performance when that performance plays a direct and significant role in the overall contract performance.

In some cases, particularly in certain types of government contracting, the buying government organization may require that it consent to subcontracts anticipated by the prime contractor. In other cases, the government may require that the seller's purchasing system be periodically reviewed by government personnel. In both these cases, the primary intent of the oversight is to ensure that government funds provided to the prime contractor are used appropriately.

In other cases, it may be a matter of prudent management, whether in the public or private sector, for a buyer to be cognizant of the relationships between sellers and their subcontractors. When the performance of subcontractors is anticipated to have a significant impact on the ability of the prime contractor to perform, the buying organization may consider including subcontractors in some or all of the communications-related activities mentioned in paragraph 6.1, particularly the face-to-face meetings. Including the subcontractor in meetings can

- Enhance the level of open communications,
- Provide both the buyer and seller with a more complete understanding of all actions required for performance,

- Alert both the buyer and seller to issues and potential subcontractor problems that may be referred to their level,
- Encourage the seller to maintain an effective relationship with their subcontractors,
- Provide the subcontractor with valuable insight regarding the nature of the relationship between the prime contractor and the buyer, and
- Can assist the subcontractor in understanding how their performance affects the seller and the overall achievement of the contractual relationship between the buyer and seller.

When subcontractors are included, the buying organization needs to exercise a degree of caution. The buyer has no privity of contract with the seller's subcontractors, and should therefore be careful regarding communications with and the role played in meetings by subcontractors. The prime contractor should always be the conduit through which information is relayed from the buyer and the subcontractor to the other party. The buyer should not allow a subcontractor to bring issues or problems with the seller to the buyer for resolution. The buyer should normally not meet with the subcontractor without representatives of the seller present. The buyer should, by word and deed, clearly communicate to the subcontractor that the buyer's contractual relationship with the seller forms the framework for the relationship. The buyer should also be careful not to give the appearance of undercutting the authority of the seller over its subcontractors.

6.3 Changes and Modifications

In a perfect world, the buyer and seller negotiate and agree on all aspects of a contractual action, the contract is issued, the contractor performs flawlessly, all required work is completed on or ahead of schedule and at or below expected cost, all goods and services are received, the contractor is paid accurately and promptly, and both sides happily move on to the next matter of business. Though the perfect contract is a goal both buyers and sellers should pursue, the reality is that we live in an imperfect world, and the parties need to deal with inevitable changes that may occur during the contract. Generally, there are three types of changes—directed changes, constructive changes, and cardinal changes.

Most contracts contain a changes clause that gives the buyer the right to direct changes during contract performance. The clause describes what type of changes the buyer can direct, the procedure for ordering the change, and a provision for "equitable adjustment" to the contract amount or period of performance if there is a resultant change in cost or schedule. A directed change usually must be within the original scope of the contract.

A constructive change is a change resulting from buyer actions or directives that impact the cost or schedule for performance. A constructive change generally occurs when the buyer impliedly or expressly orders the seller to perform work that is not in the contract. In government contracting, equitable adjustment is granted for constructive changes only if the change caused injury or liability to the seller.

Cardinal changes are changes that are beyond the scope of the contract and materially alter the nature of the contract that the parties entered into. A cardinal change could be considered a breach of contract.

Accordingly, both parties to a contract should adhere to an agreed upon change management process that seeks to fairly and equitably deal with the impact of change on the contract.

6.3.1 Prompt Notification of Apparent Noncompliance

Both parties should require their respective staffs to promptly report, preferably in writing, any perceived action or lack of action that appears to be in conflict with contractual requirements. Both parties should notify the other promptly, in writing, of the issues and request an explanation. These issues often are the precursor of the need for changes, and if left unattended, can cause relatively insignificant issues to become major roadblocks to performance.

6.3.2 Early Identification of Potential Changes

The honest and open exchange of pertinent information, in meetings, reports, and through other appropriate forums, can often result in the early identification of issues that may result in contract changes. Though both parties may be initially reluctant to share potentially "bad" information, or may be tempted to put a "spin" on potentially negative information, the long-term effects of hiding important facts are often more damaging to the contract and the relationship. For the buyer, such data as the potential for funding reductions, project cancellation or downsizing, and related issues should be shared with the seller to the maximum extent permitted by government regulation or corporate policy. For the seller, information related to the loss of key personnel, problems with subcontractors, new contracts that strain available resources, corporate mergers, changes in the economic environment, and other related matters should be shared with the buyer as openly as possible. However, both the buyer and seller should be sensitive to the possibility that such information, once shared, could be used in a manner they had not intended. Trust and honesty are essential elements that will dictate the extent to which important information is shared.

6.3.3 Agreement of Authority to Affect Change

It is critical that both the buyer and seller clearly identify the individuals in their respective organizations that have the requisite authority to make changes. Many times, individuals from both organizations who lack the authority to legally bind their organization contractually will nonetheless make verbal agreements and other arrangements that inappropriately alter the fundamental structure of the contract. If the buyer and seller agree in advance to honor only those changes made by authorized personnel, and to promptly notify the other if unauthorized personnel attempt to make changes, many problems can be avoided.

6.3.4 Agreement on Estimating Processes

If the buyer and seller can agree on a process to estimate the financial, quality, schedule, and other potential consequences of a possible change, the likelihood of protracted, difficult negotiations on the impact of the change, and who will pay for it, can be minimized. This cooperation can be carried a step further if the parties agree to perform this analysis jointly rather than separately. The buyer and seller should be more likely to agree with the results of an analysis, even though the results are less than pleasurable, if the results were determined together.

6.3.5 Written Concurrence

Both parties should provide written agreement on the nature, scope, cost, and effect of any change before the change is implemented. This written documentation reduces or eliminates the possibility of confusion later regarding just what was agreed upon.

Changes that are agreed upon should be formally issued as contract modifications, with bilateral signatures indicating mutual agreement on the change. It is imperative that the contract provides an accurate, current written record of the totality of the agreement at any point in time. Both the buyer and seller should maintain current copies of the contract and distribute it internally to appropriate personnel who have a continuing need for access to it. The completeness of distributed copies should be periodically verified. The original signed copy of the contract and all modifications should always be retained by the buyer's contracting professional.

6.4 Property

Generally speaking, most contracts require total performance from the contractor. That is, under the requirements and terms and conditions contained in the contract, the contractor is usually required to provide all the resources required for successful performance. In some cases, however, various forms of property can be provided to a contractor or subcontractor by the buyer. The fundamental reason for the buyer to provide property to the seller is cost savings. It may be less expensive for a buyer to provide property to a contractor for use during performance than it would be for the contractor to purchase the property, particularly when the property can be re-used for future contracts. The post-award administration of property is a highly specialized aspect of contract administration, normally handled by a trained subspecialist within the buyer's contracting organization. However, there are some general concepts related to property that are important, including ownership, accountability, competitive advantage, and property administration.

6.4.1 Ownership

Usually, the buyer retains ownership of and all rights to buyer-provided property. The question of ownership of property acquired by the seller to perform the contract is sometimes more complex, and may be dependent on the type of contract the seller is performing under.

6.4.2 Accountability

The buying organization usually retains internal organizational accountability for all property the buyer provides to a seller.

6.4.3 Competitive Advantage

Particularly as it relates to government contracting, the possession of buyer-furnished property can provide an incumbent contractor with a competitive advantage when competing with other sellers for future contracts. Contracting professionals often "level the playing field" in such cases by taking the value of the property into account when evaluating competing offers.

6.4.4 Property Administration

When buyer-furnished property is provided to a contractor, several property administration issues are normally part of the acquisition. The availability of buyer-furnished property is usually included in the solicitation, and potential offerors normally are provided an opportunity to review and inspect the property to verify its existence and condition.

The buyer is most often responsible for the delivery of buyer-furnished property to the contractor. Care should be taken to ensure that delivery delays do not occur, since that may adversely affect contractor performance.

The contractor is usually required to have a system in place to ensure that all property provided by the buyer is accounted for, maintained as appropriate, and used as specified in the contract. Both the buyer and seller should periodically review or audit these control systems to ensure they are operating properly.

Upon completion or termination of a contract, the contractor is usually held responsible for requesting property disposition instructions from the buyer for disposing of the property as directed.

6.5 Transportation

When contracting for goods, the costs associated with transportation are sometimes little more than a minor afterthought for many contracting professionals. However, transportation issues can sometimes represent a significant expense, particularly when a large quantity of goods are purchased, or when the goods are extremely heavy, cumbersome, fragile, subject to spoilage, or otherwise difficult to transport. Transportation is another technical subspecialty, and many organizations have some expertise in their transportation, logistics, or shipping and receiving functions that the contracting professional can consult with and use to evaluate the cost considerations of various transportation options.

Some of the more common transportation considerations include required receipt dates, mode of transportation, transportation-related services, and responsibility for transportation charges.

6.5.1 Required Receipt Dates

The date that goods are due to be received at the place designated by the buyer is sometimes a determinant of transportation costs. The contracting professional should be aware of the potential for increased transportation costs that may be a result of a specific receipt date, particularly when the delivery schedule is aggressive, or when the delivery schedule is accelerated by modification due to a change in plans or to overcome some issue or problem in production.

6.5.2 Mode of Transportation

The mode of transportation (i.e., rail, motor freight, air, etc.) is sometimes dictated by the nature of the goods being purchased, and is always a factor in determining appropriate transportation methods. Consistent with other contract requirements and industry standards, the mode of transportation selected should reflect a thoughtful balance among speed, reliability, need, and cost.

6.5.3 Transportation-Related Services

Additional transportation considerations sometimes result from the need for transportation-related services, which may include storage, packing, marking, loading, and unloading, etc.

6.5.4 Responsibility for Transportation Charges

Costs associated with the transportation of goods can be the responsibility of either the buyer or the seller. The responsibility is defined by the applicable clause in the contract.

If the contract stipulates free-on-board (FOB) destination, the seller is responsible for payment of transportation costs associated with delivering the goods from their facility to the place or places specified by the buyer in the contract. Such costs are normally included in the seller's price. An advantage to the buyer is that the title to the goods does not pass from the seller to the buyer until the goods have been received, thereby insulating the buyer from in-transit loss or damage issues.

If the contract stipulates FOB origin, the buyer is responsible for payment of transportation costs associated with delivering the goods from the seller's facility to the place or places specified by the buyer in the contract. This option may be advantageous to the buyer when the buyer can obtain the transportation at lower costs than the seller could, or when the buyer has its own transportation capability. Title to the goods transfers from the seller to the buyer when the goods leave the seller's facility.

6.6 Disputes

Notwithstanding the advantages that can result from the buyer and seller adopting a collaborative and cooperative approach toward all aspects of contract management, sometimes issues arise in the performance of contract requirements that are difficult to resolve. As a general rule, contracting professionals should always seek to resolve differences in the least formal and most collaborative manner possible. Though formal legal action is always a possibility, both buyers and sellers should be hesitant to pursue resolution through legal proceedings for many excellent reasons, including time, expense, uncertainty of outcome, and the effect on the business relationship.

Formal legal proceedings often require many months or years to achieve a resolution. Preparing for and participating in legal proceedings can require the expenditure of substantial amounts of funds, which can sometimes have a negative impact on other aspects of the organization's business.

Few, if any, organizations will pursue legal action if they do not believe they will prevail. However, in most actions there are winners and losers, and parties to litigation often find themselves the recipient of unpleasant surprises. Since legal proceedings are, by nature, adversarial, they can have a permanently negative effect on the relationship between the litigants. This negative effect can prevent the parties from engaging in mutually beneficial business relationships in the future.
In recent years, both government and commercial contracting organizations have made progress toward pursuing a variety of informal, less formal, and formal dispute resolution methods in lieu of formal legal proceedings, including informal collaboration, negotiation, and alternate dispute resolution.

6.6.1 Informal Collaboration

The collaborative sharing of information, issues, and potential problems discussed in paragraph 6.1 can often be used to quickly resolve differences informally.

6.6.2 Negotiation

Negotiation is another method preferred by both buyers and sellers for resolving disputes. Negotiation is often preferred because most parties are familiar with and experienced in the process, and because it is much more efficient and less expensive than other dispute resolution processes. Agreements resulting from negotiations can be easily implemented as contract modifications.

6.6.3 Alternative Dispute Resolution (ADR)

When the less formal methods of collaboration and negotiation between parties does not produce a satisfactory result, ADR procedures can often be used to arrive at a mutually agreeable solution. ADR encompasses practices for managing and quickly resolving disputes at modes cost and with minimal adverse effect on the relationship between the contracting parties.

These processes significantly broaden dispute resolution options beyond litigation or traditional unassisted negotiation. Some ADR procedures, such as binding arbitration and private judging, are similar to expedited litigation in that they involve a third-party decision-maker with authority to impose a resolution if the parties so desire. Other procedures, such as mediation and the mini-trial, are collaborative, with a neutral third party helping a group of individuals or entities with divergent views to reach a goal or complete a task to their mutual satisfaction.

Some examples of ADR techniques include interest-based negotiation, mediation, mini-trials, nonbinding arbitration, and binding arbitration.
Traditional negotiation involves each side beginning with a proposed solution, followed by a series of counterproposals, offers and counteroffers, argument, persuasion, and concessions until an acceptable compromise is reached. Interest-based negotiation is a more collaborative process that involves the parties becoming educated about the needs, concerns, and interests of the other, followed by joint problem-solving to identify the most acceptable way to meet all or most of the interests of both parties.

Mediation is a private, informal process in which the parties are assisted by one or more neutral third parties in efforts to achieve settlement. Mediators do not judge or arbitrate, rather they advise and consult impartially with the parties in an attempt to bring about a mutually agreeable resolution.

A mini-trial is a structured process where the attorney for each party presents an abbreviated version of that side's case. This information exchange allows each party to hear the strengths and weaknesses of the other party's case as well as their own. Following the presentation, the attorneys meet to see if they can negotiate a settlement. A neutral party can oversee the process if desired, and provide an opinion on what the potential court outcome might be.

Nonbinding arbitration involves an evidentiary hearing before a third party, composed of one or more arbitrators, that draws conclusions regarding the issues in dispute. These hearings typically include broad fact-finding activities, which assist in educating the third party about the matters in dispute. Upon completion of presentations by each party, the third party renders its decision. The parties are not bound by the arbitrator's decision, and either or both sides may reject it. The intent of nonbinding arbitration is to predict the likely adjudicated outcome of the case as an aid to settlement.

Parties that submit to binding arbitration submit their disputes to a neutral third person or panel for a decision that both parties must accept. Binding arbitration is commonly used in private sector contracting, but is rarely used in government contracting due to the absolute nature of the binding decision.

6.6.4 Resolution Through Available Legal Means

When the parties cannot resolve or accommodate disagreements about the meaning of terms of an agreement, a court may be required to decide what the contract requires. Both commercial and government contracting allows resolution using available legal means.

Government contracting allows the filing of claims and appeal to the boards and courts when less formal methods do not produce satisfactory results. A contractor may submit a claim with the government contracting officer who issued the contract. There are a number of procedural and time-sensitive requirements imposed on both the contractor and the government contracting officer when a claim is submitted. The government contracting officer is required to formally accept or reject the claim, in writing, within a specified period of time. When a government contracting officer denies a claim, the contractor may appeal that decision to the appropriate agency Board of Contract Appeals (BCA) or to the U.S. Court of Federal Claims.

Depending on the type of agreement and facts of the case, there are a variety of remedies available to a party who prevails in a lawsuit for breach of contract. These include money damages and equitable remedies.

Money damages include compensatory damages for the purpose of putting the nonbreaching party in the position that it would have been in if the contract had not been breached. Consequential damages are those damages not directly associated with the seller's breach, but traceable to it nonetheless because the seller had reason to know of the buyer's general or particular needs at the time of contracting. Consequential damages also include injury to person or property proximately resulting from any breach of warranty. Incidental damages include damages resulting from seller's breach, (e.g., expenses reasonably incurred in inspection; receipt, transportation, and care and custody of goods rightfully rejected; any commercially reasonable charges, expenses, or commissions in connection with effecting cover; and any other reasonable expense incident to the delay or other breach.) In the case of fraud or malice, punitive damages may be awarded to the non-breaching party to punish the party that breached, which is meant to discourage him from committing the same offense again. Liquidated damages are those money damages the parties agreed to in their contract should breach of contract occur.

Equitable remedies include an order of specific performance, restitution, and recession. In the case of goods or real property, an order of specific performance can require the breaching party to perform in accordance with the contract. Restitution, as an equitable remedy, seeks to restore the nonbreaching party to the position the party was in before the formation of the contract. Rescission, as an equitable remedy, allows the cancellation of the contract, usually when mutually agreed to between the parties. In some cases, the contract or statutes allow unilateral rescission for a specified period of time, such in the case of mortgages and real estate purchases.

In the case of commercial contracts, questions involving the legality or interpretation of a contract are generally governed by the law of the state where the contract was made. Questions related to contract performance are generally governed by the law of the state where such performance occurs.

Regardless of whether the contracting professional is operating in the government or commercial arena, the prompt and efficient resolution of all disputes, at the lowest organizational level possible, should always be the goal.

6.7 Termination

In some cases, it becomes necessary to end performance on a contract before the contractual period of performance ends. This premature ending of a contract is referred to as a termination, and usually takes one of the following forms.

6.7.1 Termination for Default

Termination for default, also referred to as termination for cause, is normally a right of law as well as a right vested as the result of the inclusion of appropriate terms and conditions in the contract. Termination for default can result from one party's failure to perform one or more actions required by the contract. Typical reasons to terminate for default include:

- **Failure to Perform.** Failure on the part of the seller to provide the goods or services contracted for is a valid reason to terminate for default.
- **Failure to Adhere to Schedule.** If a seller fails to completely perform during the specified period of performance, that failure may be justification for a termination for default. The buyer should exercise good business judgment in this situation to determine if the failure is significant enough to justify the termination.
- **Failure to Comply with Other Terms and Conditions.** The failure of a seller to comply with other significant terms and conditions contained in the contract can serve as justification for termination for default. This is another area in which the buyer should exercise sound business judgment and good faith in determining if the seller's failures are damaging enough to warrant termination.
- **Repudiation.** A contract may be terminated for default if either the buyer or seller clearly indicates to the other party, by word or deed, that it cannot or will not perform.

6.7.2 Termination for Convenience

In government contracting, the government buyer always has the unilateral right to terminate a contract for the convenience of the government when the contract no longer serves the best interests of the government. Terminations for convenience often result from a change in government priorities, program termination, or downsizing, or other significant events that were not anticipated at the time of contract formation. When the government pursues a termination for convenience, a termination settlement is negotiated with the seller.

6.7.3 Termination by Mutual Consent

Commonly used in the commercial contracting environment, termination by mutual consent is a bilateral agreement indicating that the parties no longer wish to be bound by the contract, and terminates both parties' respective rights and obligations. Termination by mutual consent clauses are sometimes included in the basic contract, though they can also be negotiated and executed during the period of performance.

6.7.4 No-Cost Cancellation

A no-cost cancellation is a type of quasi-termination that usually occurs shortly after contract execution, often because the seller realizes that they will be unable to perform. If both parties agree, no debts or obligations are due, and if the buyer can obtain performance from other sources, a no-cost cancellation can be a quick and efficient way to sever a contractual relationship.

6.8 Contract Closeout

Contracting activities are responsible for initiating each contract closeout. This administrative process should begin as soon as possible after the contract is physically completed, which means that the seller has delivered the required supplies and the buyer has inspected and accepted them, or the seller has performed and the buyer has accepted all services required by the contract, and the base period and any option periods exercised have expired.

Contract closeout consists of completing a number of procedural and administrative tasks to change the status of a contract from active to complete. These required tasks normally include:

- Verification that all required goods or services have been received and accepted;
- Verification that all contractor invoices have been received and paid;
- The return or appropriate disposition of any buyer-furnished property;
- Subcontracts have been appropriately settled by the seller;
- Both parties agree that no claims, issues, or unresolved matters exist;
- A formal notice of contract completion has been signed and issued; and
- Excess funds remaining on the contract are de-obligated from the contract (in federal contracting) by the buyer.

Upon completion of all required closeout actions, completed contract files should be retained for the appropriate period of time required by law, regulation, or corporate policy.

Chapter 7
Specialized Knowledge Competencies

Certain types of contracting actions require highly specialized experience and knowledge to perform effectively. This chapter presents a brief overview of various contracting specialty areas. It also describes some of the areas that relate exclusively to government contracting, commercial contracting, and some that have a degree of application to both the government and commercial sectors.

7.1 Research and Development (R&D)

When research and development services are procured it is difficult to define the requirement other than to describe the problem. This creates a departure from the general guideline used when contracting for other types of products or services. The contract specialist cannot define clearly the requirement, define specific acceptance criteria, and negotiate a low price based on the market. R&D contracting necessitates a different philosophy than is necessary for other types of procurement.

7.1.1 Commercial Research and Development

In the commercial world, the phrase "research and development" has a special commercial significance apart from its conventional meaning of "research and technological development." In the context of commerce, R&D normally refers to future-oriented, longer-term activities in science and technology. Profits are not realized until after successful discovery, development, and application of a new technology, which only occurs after diligent and systematic research.

During a company's lengthy product development phase, it takes large amounts of capital to fund research and development activities. Most companies prefer to perform research and development internally so they own the resultant technology. To share the burden, a company may purchase a noncontrolling equity stake in another company as part of a strategic alliance with the other company to conduct research and develop products jointly. They may also choose to use public funds for research in their areas of interest, and provide research and development services to the government.

If a corporation contracts for R&D services from another corporation, the most important issue becomes acceptable clauses in the areas of intellectual data, data rights, ownership of inventions, license-to-use, and patents. These clauses are also important when a commercial company enters a contract to provide these services to the government. The vast majority of research and development contracts are between commercial firms contracting with the federal, state, or local governments. We provide a discussion of the process the government uses to contract with commercial firms for research and development services.

7.1.2 Government Research and Development

When used by the government, the primary purpose of research and development contracts and programs is to advance scientific and technical knowledge and apply that knowledge to achieve organizational and national goals. Unlike most other type of contracts, R&D contracts are intended to achieve objectives for which the work or methods cannot be precisely defined in advance. It is also frequently difficult to estimate the effort required for various R&D technical approaches, particularly when some of the approaches may offer little or no early indications or assurances that they will be successful. Due to this level of uncertainty, contracting professionals should use R&D contracting in a manner that will encourage the best scientific and industrial sources to participate. The contracts should be structured so that they provide an environment in which the work can be pursued with reasonable flexibility and minimum administrative burden.

Publicizing Requirements

As is the case for any competitive requirement, R&D requirements should be publicized as widely as possible. Chapter 4 presented strategies for publicizing requirements. Additionally, since a primary issue in R&D contracting is obtaining the best scientific and industrial sources, contracting professionals handling R&D requirements should continually search for and develop information on potential additional sources capable of competent performance, and encourage the early, appropriate information exchange between and involvement of potential sources with internal technical experts.

Statement of Work

A clear and complete SOW, detailing the area of exploration for basic research or the end objectives for development and applied research, is essential. The SOW should provide contractors with the freedom required to exercise innovation and creativity, while adhering to the overall objectives of the R&D effort. R&D SOWs often include some or all of the following:

- A statement of the area of exploration, tasks to be performed, and objectives of the R&D effort;
- Appropriate background information to help achieve clear understanding of the requirement;
- Information on factors that might constrain the results of the effort, including personnel, environment, or interface issues;
- Reporting requirements and/or other items that the contractor will be required to furnish as the work progresses;
- The type of contract anticipated, and an estimate of the professional and technical effort required for level-of-effort requirements; and
- Any other considerations that relate to the work to be performed.

Contract Method and Type

The fundamental nature of R&D contracting usually precludes the use of the sealed bid method, and often makes fixed-price contracts inappropriate. Because of the typical absence of precise specifications and the associated difficulties in estimating costs, R&D contracts are often cost-reimbursement contracts, sometimes with appropriate incentives. Contracting professionals should consult extensively with internal technical experts regarding the contract type to be selected.

Solicitations

R&D solicitations generally should be distributed only to sources that have been identified; as a result of publicizing requirements, consultation with internal technical personnel and other means; or as technically qualified to perform the required work. Such evaluations of technical competence usually include factors such as present and past performance of similar work, professional stature and reputation, relative position in a particular field of endeavor, ability to acquire and retain the technical capability required to perform the work, and other relevant factors. If it is not practical to initially solicit all apparently qualified sources, a reasonable number should be solicited to obtain meaningful competition.

Solicitations normally should require offerors to describe their technical and management approach, identify technical uncertainties, and make specific proposals to resolve the uncertainties. The solicitation should also require the offeror to disclose any planned subcontracting of scientific or technical work, and may require the submission of separate technical and cost proposals.

The evaluation factors in R&D solicitations used to determine the most technically competent usually include:

- The offerors understanding of the scope of the work;
- The approach proposed to accomplish the scientific and technical objectives of the contract or the merit of the ideas and concepts proposed;
- The availability and competence of experienced technical personnel;
- The offerors experience;
- Pertinent novel ideas in the specific branch of science and technology involved; and
- The availability, from any source, of necessary research, test, laboratory, or shop facilities.

Evaluation

Generally speaking, R&D contracts most often are awarded to the offeror that proposes the best ideas or concepts, and has the highest competence in the specific field involved. However, the contracting professional should use caution and not obtain technical capabilities that clearly exceed those required by the solicitation or those required for successful performance of the requirement. It is also customary to evaluate the offerors proposed cost or price, as a means to verify that the offeror has a clear understanding of the scope of the project, perception of risks involved, and the ability to organize and perform the work.

7.2 Architect, Engineering, and Construction Services

Contracts for architect, engineering, and construction services are highly technical in nature, and often are awarded by specialized contracting professionals with extensive experience in and knowledge of the skills and abilities required for successful performance. Some of the terminology associated with this type of contracting includes:

- **Design**—Defining a construction requirement, including the functional relationships and technical systems to be used; producing the technical specifications and drawings; and preparing the construction cost estimate.
- **Design-bid-build**—The traditional construction delivery method where design and construction are sequential and contracted for separately with two contracts and two contractors.
- **Design-build**—Combining the design and construction requirements in a single contract with one contractor.
- **Two-phase design-build**—A selection procedure that selects a number of offerors based on qualifications in the first phase to submit detailed proposals for evaluation and award in the second phase.

7.2.1 Architect and Engineering Services

When acquiring architect and engineering services, the government normally publicizes all requirements for such services, and negotiates contracts based on the demonstrated competence and qualifications of prospective contractors to perform the services at fair and reasonable prices. Architect–engineering services are generally defined to include:

- Professional services of an architectural or engineering nature, as defined by applicable state law, which the state law requires to be performed by a registered architect or engineer;
- Professional architectural or engineering services associated with the design or construction of real property;
- Other professional architectural or engineering services related to studies, investigations,

surveying, mapping, soils engineering, construction phase conceptual design, and similar tasks that require performance by a registered architect, engineer, or their employees; and

- Professional surveying and mapping services, when the mapping services are associated with the construction or alteration of real property.

Selection Criteria

Normal evaluation and selection criteria for architect and engineering services usually include:

- Professional qualifications necessary for satisfactory performance of the required services;
- Specialized experience and technical competence in the type of work required;
- The capacity to accomplish the work in the required time;
- Past performance in both the government and commercial sectors in terms of cost control, quality of work, and compliance with performance schedules; and
- Proximity to the general geographical area of the project and knowledge of the local conditions.

The selection process usually results in the preparation of a selection report that ranks competent contractors in order of preference. The contracting professional then begins specific negotiations with the contractor(s) to agree upon and award a contract.

7.2.2 Construction Services

In commercial construction contracting, there are both formal and informal policies and procedures used in acquiring construction services. Construction contracts are subject to many outside restraints that have an impact on the successful contract performance, such as inspections, permits, and licenses. Careful planning is necessary to ensure adequate coordination of the acquisition.

In government contracting, sealed bid procedures are often used for construction contracts. The following processes are also normally part of a construction contracting effort.

- **Presolicitation Notice.** A presolicitation notice contains sufficient detail to identify the nature, volume, location, and schedule for the requirement. These notices are usually issued well in advance of the invitation to bid in order to stimulate the interest of the greatest number of prospective bidders.
- **Invitation for bids.** The invitation for bids should allow sufficient time for bidders to perform the many tasks and issues associated with the bid process, including site inspection, collection of required subcontracting bids, examination of plans and specifications, and preparation of the required estimates.
- **Prebid Conferences.** Prebid conferences often are held to ensure that all prospective bidders have a clear and complete understanding of all aspects of the requirement.
- **Notice of Award.**
- **Preconstruction Orientation.** A preconstruction conference often is held with the successful offeror, before the construction effort begins, to again ensure that there is complete understanding of all issues related to the effort.

7.3 Information Technology

Information technology requirements often present a unique set of challenges for the contracting professional. The rapid pace of technological advancements often makes it difficult to acquire state-of-the-art information technology items without exposing the buying organization to a significant amount of inherent risk.

Common risk elements include schedule risk, risk of technical obsolescence, cost risk, technical feasibility, dependencies between new projects and existing projects or systems, the number of simultaneous high-risk projects to be monitored, funding availability, and program management risk.

Typical techniques to manage and mitigate risks associated with information technology acquisitions include prudent project management, thorough acquisition planning related to budget planning, continuous collection and evaluation of risk-based assessment data, preparation of prototype systems prior to implementation, post-implementation reviews to determine actual costs and benefits, use of quantifiable measures to assess risks and returns, and the use of modular contracting.

7.3.1 Modular Contracting

Modular contracting is intended to reduce program risk and incentivize contractor performance, while providing for the timely access to rapidly changing technology. Modular contracting consists of dividing the acquisition of a system of information technology into smaller acquisition increments. There are numerous benefits of modular contracting.

- Smaller increments are easier to manage than would be possible in one comprehensive acquisition.
- Complex information technology objectives are addressed incrementally, enhancing the likelihood of achieving workable solutions for each of the objectives.
- Each increment can be tested and implemented, resulting in a functional system or solution that is not dependent on any subsequent increment in order to perform its principal functions.
- Subsequent increments can take advantage of evolutionary enhancements in technology or changes in needs that occur during the implementation and use of preceding increments.
- Potential adverse consequences can be isolated, mitigated, or resolved without potentially affecting the entire project.

7.4 Service Contracts

Many organizations have increased the number and scope of service contacts in recent years. Organizations, with increasing frequency, are contracting for a variety of services rather than performing the related functions with internal resources, especially when the functions are not part of the core mission or purpose of the organization. The increase in the use of service contracts, particularly in government contracting, brings with it the need for additional skills and knowledge.

Service Contract

A contract that directly engages the time and effort of a contractor to perform an identifiable task, rather than to furnish an end item or good. Service contracts can be nonpersonal or personal, professional or nonprofessional.

Nonpersonal Service Contract

A contract under which the personnel providing the services are not subject, either by the contract's terms or the manner in which it is administered, to the supervision and control usually prevailing in relationships between employers and employees.

Personal Services Contracts

A contract under which the personnel providing the services are subject, either by the contract's terms or the manner in which it is administered, to the supervision and control usually prevailing in relationships between employers and employees.

7.4.1 Performance-Based Contacting

Commercial contracting has included performance-based contracting as a standard practice. However, these methods are relatively new for government contracting. Performance-based contracting is intended to ensure that required outcome quality levels are achieved and that total payment is related to the degree that achieved outcomes meet contract standards. Performance-based contracts should:

- Describe the requirements in terms of results required rather than the methods of performing the work,
- Use measurable performance standards and quality assurance plans,
- Specify procedures for reductions of fees or for reductions to the price of fixed-price contracts when services are not performed or do not meet certain specified requirements, and
- Include performance incentives where appropriate.

7.5 Contracting with State and Local Governments

When viewed as a single entity, the purchasing power of state and local governments represents a huge, and often untapped, source of business for commercial contracting professionals. However, the unfortunate reality is that state and local government is not a homogenous market segment, but rather a somewhat artificial category that, in fact, is comprised of literally thousands of buying entities, often with their own unique processes, procedures, and challenges.

Nonetheless, there are definite advantages to both the seller and the government entity in pursuing business in the state and local government sector.

- State and local governments tend to be more commercially oriented than their federal counterparts. Many potentially new customers already exist for firms that deal in commercial goods and services.
- The local government can benefit from the close proximity of a company that can provide high-quality goods and services at competitive prices, and that can be available for consultation and advice.
- The success of local businesses generates additional tax revenue for the state and local governments, which can be used to help provide additional government services, and also to reinvest in the local business community and infrastructure to create more businesses and economic growth.
- Dealing locally tends to help both the buyer and the seller by developing personal, long-term relationships based on mutual need and mutual benefit.

There are also some disadvantages inherent in dealing with the state and local government segment.

- There is often a lack of standardized processes, procedures, and regulatory guidance. Many state and local government entities have unique requirements, forms, and local ordinances that may increase the cost to the seller of doing business with multiple entities simultaneously.
- Many local governments seek out the best value, which may make some local businesses, particularly smaller ones, less competitive.
- Local and regional politics often influence purchasing decisions. Vendors should be aware that sometimes buying decisions are made based on facts or perceptions that have little or nothing to do with price, quality, or service.

Organizations seeking to do business with state and local governments can enhance their chances for success by following several simple rules.

- Learn the rules and procedures for each government entity you wish to do business with and follow them. Trying to get a local government purchasing official to change their procedures to accommodate your standard corporate policies is probably a waste of time.
- Whenever possible, standardize and be consistent with the interpretation of terms, conditions, clauses, and similar issues.
- Understand the standard business practices of each government entity you wish to do business with. It is not uncommon to discover that one entity's processes are slightly different than another's, particularly in billing and payment functions.
- Take the time to develop personal relationships with the buyer's purchasing personnel. Particularly at the local government level, purchasing decisions are frequently made based on a level of trust and confidence that must be developed and nurtured over time.

7.6 Supply-Chain Management

The concept of supply-chain management as a natural, evolutionary managerial advancement over the traditional purchasing function has become more prevalent and commonly accepted in recent years. Traditional supply-chain management theory holds that an organization can reduce procurement costs, reduce procurement cycle time, and add value to the procurement process by taking the following actions.

- Reducing the number of suppliers used. Many organizations have found that maintaining large numbers of suppliers for the same or similar products or services, and attempting to manage that supplier base was more expensive than the savings potentially realized from extensive competition among the suppliers for orders. Having many suppliers also introduced quality and consistent performance issues that were more difficult to manage.
- Negotiating long-term contracts with the few preferred suppliers. Cost savings can be realized by making significant commitments to a few suppliers as opposed to making only short-term commitments to many suppliers.
- Conducting more rigorous and detailed timeliness and quality tracking of the preferred supplier base. The significant purchase commitments made to a few suppliers are coupled with increased requirements for quality and performance.
- Analyzing and seeking to improve every action and link in the supply chain, from the end customer to the lowest level supplier, with involvement, input and cooperation from all stakeholders.

Supply-chain management concepts recognize that the acquisition function does not operate in a reactive vacuum, but rather is a component in a larger management system that provides value and profitability by merging customer needs and supplier capabilities with the value-added processes of the organization. Supply-chain management also recognizes the inter-dependencies and inter-relationships between and among all members of the supply chain, and seeks to maximize the power and competitiveness of the entire supply chain through collaboration, cooperation, continuous improvement, and the maintenance of long-term relationships that benefit all members of the chain.

7.7   International Contracting

Contracting domestically is sometimes a difficult process, as evidenced by the misunderstandings, lack of compliance with terms and conditions, late delivery, and payment issues that can develop. When contracting internationally, the potential for problems can expand almost exponentially. Whether functioning as a buyer or seller, contracting professionals who operate in the international market require an enhanced set of skills and knowledge to be effective. International contracting can sometimes result in lower costs and improved quality for buyers, and increased sales and profitability for sellers. However, there are many significant differences between operating in the domestic market and the international market. Some of those differences include the following:

Language

There are obvious potential issues when multiple languages are introduced into the contracting process. Some international firms have personnel who are multi-lingual. In other cases, the use of third-party interpreters may be appropriate. Regardless, the contracting professional needs to ensure that the sometimes subtle context and nuances inherent in one language are accurately reflected in translation to a different language.

Location

Dealing with organizations located abroad can present a number of challenges related to time differences and distance. Buyers and sellers may need to adjust their work hours to be able to converse directly with international firms, or they may have to accept the fact that most communication will be indirect.

Different Meanings of Common Business Terms

Common business terms, such as "bi-monthly" or "relationship," often have different meanings in different countries and can be the source of unintended issues.

Currency Differences

Currency differences, and constantly changing exchange rates, can impact the business relationship and feasibility of doing business in certain countries.

More Third-Party Involvement

Buying and selling internationally often requires the use of various third-party entities, such as trading companies, local representatives, foreign banks, freight forwarders, customs brokers, etc. Some foreign countries require an in-country firm on the company team.

Social Customs

Business, cultural, and social customs and norms, to the degree that they are different from one's experience and expectations, can present significant obstacles to the successful completion of business agreements.

Different Processes

Some companies in less developed countries may be less sophisticated and knowledgeable in various production, quality control, or management processes, and may be unable or reluctant to modify their systems and procedures to conform to one's expectations.

Legal Processes

Legal terms and processes may differ significantly in various countries, and can inject additional risk in the contracting process. Local laws vary widely from country to country in the areas of employment, labor, and severance. In the cases where contract performance will be done in-country, this can impose substantial financial burden on a company.

Tax Implications

The tax-cost implications of doing business in foreign countries can be tremendous; for example, the foreign country may have a right to assess its own income or value-added tax on the company's global earnings that have a connection to that country.

There may be personal tax implications for company employees who are temporarily transferred to the country for contract performance.

Export Issues

Export is defined as the transfer of commodities, technical data, articles, or services from the United States to a foreign person, corporation, or other entity. The company may be required to obtain export permission from the Bureau of Export Administration within the Department of Commerce or the Office of Defense Trade Controls within the U.S. Department of State.

Political Climate

The political and social climate in many countries is sometimes subject to abrupt and significant change. Contracting professionals must have a thorough understanding of past, present, and future trends that may influence the degree to which business in a foreign country may be affected by changes in the political and social climate.

International contracting presents many positive opportunities, but also presents many challenges that are not present in the domestic sector. Contracting professionals should ensure they have a complete understanding of this more dynamic environment, and use appropriate caution to avoid mistakes.

Chapter 8
Unique Commercial Contracting Competencies

Commercial contracting refers to contractual agreements between two commercial (nongovernment) parties. This chapter addresses further competencies that are normally unique to the commercial contracting sector.

8.1 Commercial Contract Law Basics

The states, not the federal government, are the primary source of law on commercial transactions in the United States. This includes state statutory, common (judge-made) law, and private law. Private law principally includes the terms of the agreement between the parties who have exchanged promises for consideration. These terms may override rules established by state law. Statutory law may require some contracts be put in writing and executed using specific procedures.

8.1.1 Agency

The law of agency is important in commercial contracting. It recognizes that most corporations operate exclusively through agents. Agency law is concerned with any "principal–agent" relationship—a relationship in which one person has legal authority to act for another. This relationship can result from explicit appointment where the principal authorizes the agent to represent his or her interests and perform acts that bind the principal; or this relationship can result by implication where it is implied by the conduct of the parties.

An agent acts on behalf of another person and is subject to that person's control. The one for whom action is taken is the principal; the one who acts on behalf of the principal is the agent.

A universal agent provides broad authority for an agent to act on behalf of the principal.

A general agent is authorized to conduct a limited series of transactions involving continuity of service, and may be empowered to enter into contracts which are binding on the principal.

A special agent's power and authority is limited to accomplishing a specific and limited assignment, and does not have the power or authority to enter into contracts on behalf of the principal.

8.1.2 Authority

To bind the principal, the agent must act within the authority granted by the principal. This authority may be actual, expressed, implied, or apparent.

Actual authority is an agent's specific authority that the principal intentionally confers on the agent. It confers a power to the agent to affect legal relations of the principals with third persons.

Expressed authority is authority plainly granted, either verbally or in writing, to an agent by a principal. It is direction provided to the agent by the principal to do specific actions.

Implied authority is authority given by a principal to an agent that is not actually expressed or otherwise communicated. This allows the agent to perform all the usual and necessary tasks to exercise the agent's expressed authority. The direction to do something is not provided expressly from the principal's words, but implied from what is understood as customary in the industry.

Apparent authority is the appearance of being a principal's agent with the power to act for the principal. Corporations are liable for an employee's acts and promises to a third party if it appears to the third party that the employee has been granted authority by his or her corporate employer (principal) to do those acts which bind the corporation.

8.1.3 *Uniform Commercial Code*

Many aspects of commercial transactions in the United States are governed by the *Uniform Commercial Code* (*UCC*), which is a set of uniform provisions dealing with varied areas of law ranging from the sale of goods and bulk sale transactions to negotiable instruments, secured transactions, and leases of personal property.

The underlying purposes of the *UCC*, as stated in Section 1-102 of the code, are to

(a) Simplify, clarify, and modernize the law governing commercial transactions;

(b) Permit the continued expansion of commercial practices through custom, usage and agreement of the parties; and

(c) Make uniform the law among the various jurisdictions.

The *UCC*, or portions of it, has been adopted by all states (except Louisiana) in an effort to create a standardized legal environment for commercial activities throughout the U.S. Some states have not adopted all of the *UCC*'s articles or have enacted modified versions of the *UCC*. Therefore, when the *UCC* applies to a transaction, the requirements of each state need to be separately considered as applicable.

The overriding philosophy of the *Uniform Commercial Code* is to allow people to make the contracts they want, but to fill in any missing provisions or gaps where the agreements they make are silent. Current law governing contracts for the sale of any kind of "goods" between two U.S. corporations is Article 2 of the Uniform Commercial Code. The *UCC* applies to goods, but not services. Services contracts can become voluminous because there are no "missing provision" or "gap filler" provisions as under the *UCC* to protect buyers and sellers, so buyers and sellers create provisions that are suitable for their own needs. Article 2 is intended to be the sole source of law governing sales of goods supplemented by state law only if not addressed by a provision within the code (UCC § 1-103). The table below lists the parts within Article 2.

Uniform Commercial Code—Article 2 (Sales)	
Part 1	Short title, general construction, and subject matter
Part 2	Form, formation, and readjustment of contract
Part 3	General obligation and construction of contract
Part 4	Title, creditors, and good faith purchasers
Part 5	Performance
Part 6	Breach, repudiation, and excuse
Part 7	Remedies

The complete text of the standard *UCC* may be found at **www.law.cornell.edu/wex/index.php/commercial_law**.

Article 2 addresses such issues as contract formation, nonperformance, performance of contractual obligations, repudiation of contract, contract termination, remedies for non performance, cure rights of a party who fails to perform, implicit and explicit warranties, waiver or disclaimer of such warranties, and risk of loss. We provide a limited discussion of some of these items in the following paragraphs.

Underlying Concepts in UCC

In regards to contracts, the UCC has several underlying concepts—(1) merchants are professionals in their field and should be held to higher standards than a casual buyer, (2) every contract imposes an obligation of good faith in its performance or enforcement, and (3) a reasonable amount of time for taking any action depends on the nature, purpose, and circumstances of such action.

Formation of a Sales Contract

Article 2 states that to contract for the sale of goods with a price of $500 or more to be enforceable, it must be in writing sufficient to indicate that a contract for sale has been made between the parties, and signed by the party against whom enforcement is sought or by his authorized agent or broker. Article 2 contains three requirements of the written contract.

1. It must provide evidence there was a contract for the sale of goods,
2. It must be signed by the party to be charged, and
3. It must specify a quantity.

This implies that the price, time, and place of payment or delivery, the general quality of the goods, or any particular warranties may be omitted, and if the above three requirements are included, the contract is enforceable. Thus, contracts can be written on a cocktail napkin for sufficient evidence of a real transaction.

If not in writing, a contract can also be validated if there is "partial performance" as evidenced that goods have been accepted and payment has been made and accepted. This provides evidence that the contract actually exists. The party receiving the contract must give written notice of objection within 10 days after it is received, or the contract could be enforceable.

A signed offer to buy or sell goods remains irrevocable for a reasonable period not to exceed three months, or for the period stated in the offer. Acceptance of the offer may be made by any reasonable manner, including either shipment or a prompt promise to ship, or the beginning of performance by an offeree.

Often in commercial transactions, the offeree has a standard boilerplate of terms on which the offer is printed. When the offeror accepts the offer, the offeror states additional terms or different terms from those offered. The UCC allows for those additional terms to be construed as proposals for additional terms to the contract. Such terms are incorporated into the contract unless the offer stated that the offer expressly limits the terms of the offer, the acceptance was expressly made conditional on agreement on different terms, the additional terms materially alter the offer, or an objection of the additional terms is sent within a reasonable time. Article § 2–207 states "In such case the terms of the particular contract consist of those terms on which the writings of the parties agree, together with any supplementary terms incorporated under any other provisions of the UCC."

In addition to the express terms of the contract, there are other factors that can be relevant when interpretation of the contract is required. These include course of performance, course of dealing, and usage of trade.

- Course of performance refers to any acts in the performance of the contract by either party that are not objected to. These acts can be interpreted as consistent with the express terms.

- Course of dealing is a series of previous conduct between the parties to a particular transaction that can be regarded as establishing a common basis of understanding for terminology and conduct.

- A usage of trade is practices or methods of dealing that are regularly observed and justifies an expectation that they will apply to the transaction in question.

Contract Modification

An existing contract, under UCC rules, can be modified without consideration, but the modification must satisfy the "statute of frauds" provision. A contract can be modified or rescinded only if done in writing on a form provided by the merchant and signed by the other party. Contract modifications must meet the test of good faith and cannot be used to escape performance obligations under the contract. A modification that does not meet the above requirements can be considered a waiver.

Performance

The general obligation of the seller under the contract is to transfer and deliver, and that of the buyer is to accept and pay in accordance with the contract. The contract "imposes an obligation by the seller to use best efforts to supply the goods, and an obligation by the buyer to use best efforts to promote their sale (*UCC*)."

After the seller has manufactured the product, he may be unwilling to forward the product to the buyer until he receives payment. Likewise, the buyer may be unwilling to pay until he receives and inspects the product. The concept of tender entitles the seller, upon shipment, to the acceptance of goods and to payment according to the terms of the contract, and entitles the buyer, upon payment, to the receipt of conforming goods. The seller's goods must conform in all respects to the terms of the contract or the buyer may reject the goods and not perform further. This is in addition to other rights the buyer may have. The concept of tender allows each party to be confident that the other party will perform so the seller and buyer can ship the product and make payment respectively.

The *UCC* states that acceptance of goods occurs when the buyer, "…after a reasonable opportunity to inspect the goods, signifies to the seller that the goods are conforming or that he will take or retain them in spite of their nonconformity." Acceptance can also occur when the buyer fails to reject them or commits actions that are inconsistent with rejection.

The buyer has the right to reject the goods if they "fail in any respect to conform to the contract." The seller has a right to cure defects if the time for performance has not run out, and seller can cure within that time, or the seller has reason to believe the buyer would accept nonconforming goods (in which case the seller can take a reasonable amount of extra time, beyond the time for original performance, in curing the defects).

In certain situations a buyer may revoke a prior acceptance of nonconforming goods (as long as he notifies the seller of revocation in a reasonable time after he discovered or should have discovered the nonconformity) when the defect has substantially impaired their value. A prior acceptance can be revoked if acceptance was made on the reasonable assumption that the defects would be cured in a reasonable time, but they haven't been, or acceptance was predicated on the seller's assurances of conformity, or the defect was difficult to discover before acceptance. The goods must be in the same condition as when they were delivered to the buyer except for changes caused by the defects themselves in order for the revocation to be effective. A revocation puts the buyer in the same position as if he had rejected the goods initially.

Implied Warranties

Under the *UCC*, every sale of goods gives rise to certain implied warranties, including implied warranty of merchantability, and implied warranty of fitness for a particular purpose.

Implied Warranty of Merchantability. A warranty a merchant makes that guarantees that goods are reasonably fit for the general purpose for which they are sold.

Implied Warranty of Fitness for a Particular Purpose. A seller knows or has reason to know of a particular purpose for which some item is being purchased by the buyer, the seller is guaranteeing that the item is fit for that particular purpose and if the buyer is relying on the seller's expertise to select suitable goods.

An implied warranty can be expressly disclaimed but has strict requirements in how it is disclaimed. In a contract to purchase by the inclusion of the words, "as is" or "with all faults" must appear distinctly in the contract in a different kind of print or font that makes it stand out. A disclaimer of the implied warranty of merchantability must use the word "merchantability." Contractual language can also limit the remedies available for breach of an implied warranty—for example, capping recoverable damages or limiting the remedy to a replacement of a defective item

Repudiation

Repudiation is the refusal, especially by public authorities, to acknowledge a contract or debt. In the case of repudiation, a party can wait a commercially reasonable time for the repudiating party to perform or resort to any remedy for breach, even if he's notified the repudiating party that he's waiting for performance and urges him to retract the repudiation.

The repudiating party can retract his repudiation, until his next performance is due unless since the repudiation, the aggrieved party has cancelled or materially changed his position or the aggrieved party has indicated he considers the repudiation final. A retraction must be accompanied by "adequate assurances" within a reasonable time of the retraction.

Adequate assurances may be demanded in writing by any party when he has reasonable grounds for insecurity with respect to the performance of the other party. Until he receives such assurances, he may suspend his own performance. These adequate assurances would need to make a reasonable merchant believe the promised performance will be forthcoming.

When anticipatory repudiation substantially impairs the value of the contract, the innocent party may resort to any remedy, including suing immediately for breach, even if he is still negotiating with the repudiating party for performance or retraction. The innocent party can, if he chooses, wait for a commercially reasonable time for the repudiating party to perform. Either way, taking some action now or waiting, the innocent party can suspend his performance.

The Sarbanes-Oxley Act (SOX)

The Sarbanes-Oxley Act or SOX was signed into law on July 30, 2002. The substance of the law is to create requirements to prevent companies from accounting for profits not realized in an effort to portray value where none exists. SOX has had a significant impact on the accounting practices of nearly all companies doing business in the United States. Indirectly, SOX has had a significant impact on the contract management functions as well. A sales contract is typically the primary record underlying a revenue transaction. Prior to SOX many, even very large, companies, did not have standard practices for contract creation or management. Under SOX firms could no longer be laissez faire in how they created, recorded, and managed contracts. Since SOX was passed into law, a mini-industry for creation and implementation of contract management software systems has boomed. And many firms have devoted more attention to the contract management function than ever before in order to ensure SOX compliance.

SOX has had a disproportionate impact on commercial companies, versus those that do business principally with the U.S. federal government. This is because companies who did substantial business with the federal government were already required to maintain a higher standard of contract management and cost accounting systems in order to comply with the *Federal Acquisition Regulation* and associated laws and regulations.

Additional information about the Sarbanes-Oxley Act can be found at **www.soxinstitute.org**.

Chapter 9
Unique Federal Contracting Competencies

This chapter addresses competencies that are normally unique to the federal contracting sector.

9.1 Government Contract Law Basics

The government contracting process involves all three branches of the U.S. government—legislative, executive, and judicial. Congress, as the legislative branch, enacts laws that impact the contracting process and provide funding. The agencies, as part of the executive branch, draft regulations implementing the laws, solicit offers, and award and administer contracts. The federal courts, representing the judicial branch, interpret legislation and sometimes resolve disputes. These three branches thus work together to preserve the system of checks and balances necessary for the U.S. government. Each has an integral function to serve in the procurement process.

Some may argue, that as the sovereign, the U.S. government receives special consideration in the contracting process. Although certain conflicts exist between the government as lawmaker and the government as contracting party, the laws have been designed to ensure that there is no special treatment conferred to the government. The government must be treated as other contracting parties to maintain a fair and equitable business relationship and to protect those with whom the government deals. Nonetheless, as the sovereign, the government can and does specify exactly how it will conduct its business. This includes how it will use contracting to implement social policy; how it will allow a contract to be canceled (e.g., termination process); and how, when, and in which courts it can be sued. All of these are significant differences between government contracts and commercial contracts.

The origin of the government's authority to enter into contract comes from the U.S. Constitution and is subject to various statutes and regulations. Although the U.S. Constitution does not specifically refer to government contracts, the government has the implied power to use contracts to fulfill its responsibilities. For example, Article 1, § 8, Clause 18, gives Congress the power to

Make all laws which shall be necessary and proper for carrying into execution the foregoing powers and all other powers vested by this Constitution of the government of the United States, or in any department or officer thereof.

The clause is called the "necessary and proper" clause and provides, by implication, the power for the government to enter into contracts to fulfill its obligations by providing and paying for the common defense and general welfare of the United States. Additionally, Article I, § 8, Clause 12, gives Congress the power to "raise and support armies." Congress also has the authority to appropriate funds to federal agencies to fulfill their obligations. Article I, § 9, of the Constitution provides, "No money shall be drawn from the Treasury, but in consequence of appropriations made by law…." This section is the basis of Congress' power of the purse. It means that no debt may be paid out of public funds unless Congress has made an appropriation for that purpose.

9.1.1 Statutes and Regulations

In addition, many statutory provisions implement the Constitution's requirement for Congressional appropriations, as well as limit a federal agency's powers. For example, the Anti-Deficiency Act states

> No officer or employee of the United States shall make or authorize expenditure from or create or authorize an obligation under any appropriation or fund in excess of the amount available therein; nor shall any such officer or employee involve the government in any contract or other obligation, for payment of money for any purpose, in advance of appropriations made for such purpose, unless such contract or obligation is authorized by law. (31 U.S.C. § 665(a))

Congress has extremely broad power to pass laws affecting the procurement process. Many of the laws are substantive, i.e., they describe how the process must be conducted. Examples of these laws would include the Armed Services Procurement Act, the Federal Property and Administrative Services Act, the Competition in Contracting Act, and the Streamlining Acquisition Regulations Act. These acts are a primary means by which Congress grants contracting powers to an agency, as well as places limitations on the way an agency exercises those powers. Congress also places limitations through Authorization and Appropriation Acts.

Other laws Congress passes each year deal principally with fiscal matters. Each "pot of money" from Congress must pass two key gates. The first is an Authorization Act. This law authorizes the various congressional committees to propose appropriations within a defined ceiling. The second gate is the Appropriation Act, which makes the specified funds available to the agencies. Both acts must be followed by agencies. If a particular program is authorized but not funded (i.e., no appropriation made), the program cannot survive. Conversely, if funds are appropriated, but the program is not authorized, it likewise cannot survive.

There are certain steps in the budgeting process. The first step is for the agencies to compile a budget from their various commands, installations, or field sites. This is presented to the Office of Management and Budget (OMB), which negotiates with the agencies, in concert with the president's desires, to compile a proposed federal budget. This federal budget is sent to Congress, which holds hearings and debates to finally settle on proper "authorized" and "appropriated" budgets for the various agencies. Once the acts become law by the president's signature, this budget is returned to OMB, which then allocates it to the agencies, which then makes allotments and sub-allotments, as appropriate, to their various segments.

The funds appropriated by Congress are commonly restricted in two principal ways—by intended use and time of availability. The executive branch has limited ability to reprogram funds to alter their intended use, and no authority to obligate funds beyond their period of availability (usually one year). However, obligating funds should not be confused with actually paying those funds to a contractor. An obligation occurs when the funds are specifically designated to a particular contract or grant by the actual "award" of the contract or grant. Congress requires that all obligations be recorded by some clear documentary evidence (31 U.S.C § 1501). Once obligated, however, it may be some time (sometimes years) before the work is completed and the contractor paid with those funds. Thus, expenditure occurs after the obligation.

If contracting officers are not clear whether a particular use of funds is proper, they can seek the guidance of the General Accounting Office (GAO), a part of the legislative branch which will issue an opinion that is binding, since GAO has the authority to "settle all accounts" of the government (31 U.S.C. § 3526).

If the appropriation does not conclude by the beginning of the next fiscal year, October 1, the Congress may pass a "continuing resolution" to provide authority for agencies to continue to operate until the regular appropriation is enacted.

9.1.2 The Role of the FAR

Regulations, which implement statutes, are detailed procedures for use in awarding government contracts. An example of such a regulation is the *Federal Acquisition Regulation* (*FAR*).

The *FAR* has been in place since April 1, 1984. The *FAR* system was developed in accordance with the Office of Federal Procurement Policy Act (P.L. 93-400) of 1974, as amended by P.L. 96-83 and Office of Federal Procurement Policy (OFPP) policy letter 85-1, dated August 19, 1985. The *FAR* system consists of the *FAR* and various agency acquisition regulations that supplement the *FAR*. The *FAR* is prepared, issued, and maintained jointly by the Secretary of Defense and the administrators of the General Services Administration (GSA) and the National Aeronautics and Space Administration (NASA). The *FAR* establishes uniform policies and procedures for federal agency acquisitions and governs all military and civilian agencies.

Although the *FAR* was intended to be the single comprehensive source of procurement regulations, many agencies have extensive *FAR* supplements (e.g., the *Defense Federal Acquisition Regulations*, *DFARS*) and sub-supplements (e.g., the *Army Federal Acquisition Regulation Supplement*, *AFARS*). In addition, there are OMB circulars, Office of Federal Procurement Policy (OFPP) policy letters, agency directives and instructions, and agency handbooks and manuals.

None of these regulations, however, define the word "contract." Nor do the statutes previously discussed provide an exclusive guidepost for contract management. All of the applicable statutes, regulations, and contract law basics must be used together to effectively manage federal government contracts. Relying solely on the *FAR* may not answer every contract manager's questions about contract law. Generally contract principles come from case law and court decisions, which are summarized in the "Restatement of the Law, Second," Contracts. The "Restatement" is a presentation of contract law by the American Law Institute. It is regarded as an authoritative reference and is relied upon in judicial opinions.

In addition to the Restatement, the *Uniform Commercial Code* (*UCC*) is the current legal guideline for commercial transactions. The *UCC* is a law drafted by the National Conference of Commissioners on Uniform State Laws Governing Commercial Transactions, and is applicable in nearly every state. While the "Restatement" and the *UCC* are not binding on federal government contracting, they provide useful examples to determine the rights and obligations of contracting parties, and serve as a significant source of legal principles applicable to government contracts.

9.1.3 Ratification

Ratification is the act of approving an unauthorized commitment by an official who has the authority to do so (FAR 1.602-3). "Unauthorized commitment" is a nonbinding agreement made by a government representative who lacks the authority to enter into the agreement on behalf of the government (FAR 1.602.3). The government is not bound by unauthorized acts of its agents. The agent's unauthorized action may become binding, however, if the principal chooses to ratify the agent's act. A principal may ratify an unauthorized act of his or her agent only if the principal could have authorized the agent to act when the agent performed the unauthorized act.

Commitments that cannot be ratified may be subject to extraordinary contractual relief as authorized by Public Law (P.L.) 85-804. Or, commitments that cannot be ratified may be subject to resolution by the General Accounting Office under its account settlement authority.

9.2 Operational Practices Unique to Federal Contracting

In this section we will expand on some of the operational practices that are unique to federal contracting, and for the most part do not apply to commercial contracting. This list is not all inclusive but will be expanded on in a future edition of this guide.

In the operational world of federal contracting, the act of obligating the government to a contract is considered an inherently governmental activity. It is considered an inherently governmental activity because this act is so intimately related to the public interest that it mandates performance by federal employees. Although contractors can be used to provide contract specialist support to the contracting officer, only a contracting officer can sign a contractual document.

9.2.1 Pre-award Practices Unique to Federal Contracting

As it relates to contracting for general services, the government's policy includes the following precepts:

- Performance-based contracting is the preferred method for obtaining services.
- Government agencies shall generally rely on the private sector for commercial services.
- Agencies shall not award a contract for the performance of inherently governmental functions.
- Program officials are responsible for accurately describing the service contracting requirement in a manner that ensures full understanding and performance by contractors.
- Services should be obtained in the most cost-effective manner, without barriers to full and open competition, and free of any potential conflicts of interest.

Personal Services Contracts

Personal services contracts in government contracting are of particular concern to contracting professionals. A personal services contract is characterized by the employer–employee relationship it creates between the government agency and the contractor's personnel. The government is normally required to obtain its employees under direct hire under competitive appointment or other procedures required by civil service law. Obtaining personal services by contract, rather than by direct hire can circumvent those laws. Accordingly,

- Agencies are prohibited from awarding personal service contracts, except when specifically authorized by statute to do so.
- A nonpersonal service contract can, in effect, become a personal services contract, based on the manner in which the contract is administered after award. This can occur when contractor personnel are subject to the relatively continuous supervision and control of a government manager or employee.
- Certain aspects of the contract and its administration can be used as a guide in assessing whether a proposed contract is personal in nature, including:
  - Performance on site;
  - Principal tools and equipment furnished by the government;

- Services are applied directly to the integral effort of the agency in furtherance of assigned mission or functions;
- Comparable services, meeting comparable needs, are performed in the same or similar agency using government personnel;
- The need for the service is expected to last for more than one year; and
- The nature of the service, or the manner in which it is provided, requires the direct or indirect government direction or supervision of contractor employees.

Service Contract Act

The Service Contract Act of 1965 provides for minimum wages and fringe benefits as well as other conditions of work under certain types of service contracts. Contracting professionals need to be aware of the potential impact of this law on potential service contracts.

Government Use of Private Sector Temporaries

Government contracting professionals may enter into contracts with temporary help service firms for brief or intermittent periods without having these contracts regarded or treated as personal services contracts. Temporary help service contracts may not be used in lieu of regular recruitment under civil service laws or to replace a federal employee. Detailed information regarding the authority, criteria and conditions for the use of private sector temporaries is contained in 5 CFR Part 300.

Advisory and Assistance Services

The acquisition of advisory and assistance services is sometimes used to help government managers achieve maximum effectiveness or economy in their operations. Advisory and assistance service contracts can be used to

- Obtain outside points of view to avoid limited judgment on critical issues;
- Obtain advice regarding developments in industry, university, or foundation research;
- Obtain the opinions, special knowledge or skills of noted experts;
- Enhance the understanding of, and develop alternative solutions to, complex issues;
- Support and improve the operation of organizations; and
- Ensure the more efficient or effective operation of managerial or hardware systems.

Advisory and assistance service contracts may not be used to

- Perform work of a policy, decision-making or managerial nature, which is the direct responsibility of agency officials;
- Bypass or undermine personnel ceilings, pay limitations, or competitive employment procedures;
- Contract for, on a preferential basis, former federal employees;
- Specifically aid in influencing or enacting legislation; and
- Obtain professional or other technical advice, which is readily available within the agency or another federal agency.

Major Systems

The Office of Management and Budget Circular A-109 outlines policies and procedures for the acquisition of government major systems. Major systems are defined as:

> Those programs that, as determined by the agency head, are directed at and critical to fulfilling an agency mission need should entail allocating relatively large resources for the particular agency and warrant special management attention, including specific agency-head decisions.

Major systems acquisition policies are designed to ensure that agencies acquire major systems in the most effective, economical, and timely manner. The policies require agencies to

> Promote innovation and full and open competition in the development of major system concepts by expressing agency needs and program objectives in terms of the agency's mission and not in terms of specified systems to satisfy needs, focusing agency resources and special management attention on activities conducted in the initial stage of major programs, and to sustain effective competition between alternative system concepts and sources for as long as it is beneficial.

As it relates to major systems acquisition, effective competition is defined as a market condition that exists when two or more contractors, acting independently, actively contend for the government's business in a manner that ensures that the government will be offered the lowest cost or price alternative or best technical design meeting its minimum needs.

Major systems acquisition requires the direct involvement of senior agency management, including the agency head, in the planning, execution and continuing evaluation of the status of the program.

Certificate of Current Cost or Pricing Data

If no exceptions apply, contractors are required to submit a certificate of current cost and pricing data to the contracting officer. Cost or pricing data are all facts at the time of price agreement that prudent buyers and sellers would reasonably expect to affect price negotiations significantly. These data are factual, not judgmental, and therefore are verifiable. The Truth in Negotiations Act requires cost and pricing data to be accurate, current, and complete as of the date of price agreement, or some other date agreed to by the parties. Since the assembly and evaluation of cost or pricing data is costly and time consuming for both parties, data submissions are not required in every procurement.

The time of price agreement is the date of the final price agreement or the "shake hands" date. All facts reasonably available as of that date must be disclosed, but facts that become available after that date do not need to be disclosed. A potential problem for contractors is the lag time between the last data submission and the shake hands date, and the lag time between creation of data within the company and communication to the negotiator. The requirement for current data on the certification does not permit any substantial lag time. Contractors must review all supplier information regarding price and validity periods. Any changes in direct and/or indirect rate structures also needs to be disclosed.

9.2.2 Award Practices Unique to Federal Contracting

Pre-award Notification

When an offeror has been eliminated from competition before an award decision has been made, the contracting professional should promptly notify the offeror in writing of their exclusion and the underlying reason for the decision. Pre-award notifications are normally made when elimination from further competition was made based on the offerors exclusion from a pre-determined competitive range or for other appropriate reason.

Post-award Notification

Each unsuccessful offeror usually receives written correspondence from the contracting professional that notifies the offeror of their nonselection and provides additional information concerning:

- The number of offerors solicited, if known;
- The number of proposals received;
- The name and address of the successful offeror;
- A list of items, quantities and unit prices in the award, or the total dollar value of the award if listing items is not practical; and
- The general reason or reasons that the offerors proposal was not selected for award, unless the price paid provides the obvious reason.

The contracting professional should take care not to reveal proprietary information, trade secrets, detailed financial breakdowns, or any other confidential or sensitive data related to the successful offerors proposal, or related to any other unsuccessful offerors proposal, when providing this notice to unsuccessful offerors. The contracting professional should also be aware that this notice often serves as the prelude to a request for a formal debriefing.

Debriefing

Once notified, an unsuccessful offeror may request a formal debriefing. Normally such a request should be received by the contracting officer within three days of the initial notification of nonselection or pre-award elimination. The types of information appropriate for sharing depends on whether the debriefing occurs pre-award or post-award.

Pre-award Debriefing

An unsuccessful offeror may request a debriefing prior to contract award when the offeror has been notified of their elimination from the competitive range, or has otherwise been eliminated from further competition. The offeror may also elect to defer the debriefing until an award has been made. Under certain circumstances, the contracting officer may deny a request for a pre-award briefing in favor of a post-award debriefing. When conducted, pre-award debriefings are somewhat more restrictive than post-award debriefings. The debriefing may be conducted in person, by written correspondence, or by any other manner deemed appropriate by the contracting professional. Pre-award debriefings usually include information concerning the result of the evaluation of significant elements contained in the offerors proposal. It usually includes a summary of the reasons that the offerors proposal was eliminated from the competition. Reasonable responses to pertinent questions are also usually given concerning the degree to which source selection procedures defined in the solicitation were actually followed.

It is important to note that information in the pre-award debriefing is restricted to conversations related only to the offerors proposal and how it was evaluated.

Post-award Debriefing

Post-award debriefings are requested by unsuccessful offerors in much the same manner as pre-award debriefings. However, the permissible content of post-award debriefings is somewhat more extensive. The debriefing may be conducted in person, by written correspondence, or by any other manner deemed appropriate by the contracting professional.

Post-award debriefings usually include information concerning the evaluation of significant weaknesses or deficiencies in the offeror's proposal, the price, and technical ratings of the successful offeror, as well as that of the unsuccessful offeror and the overall ranking of all offerors, if a ranking process was used. The debriefing also usually includes a summary of the rationale used to select the successful offeror and reasonable responses to pertinent questions concerning the degree to which source selection procedures defined in the solicitation were actually followed.

It is important to emphasize that the purpose of a debriefing is to provide useful information to an unsuccessful offeror so that they are aware of how they might improve their chances for selection in future acquisitions. Debriefings are not intended to provide an unsuccessful offeror with the opportunity to perform a complete and detailed analysis of the relative strengths and weaknesses of all aspects of their proposal as compared to the successful offeror or to other unsuccessful offerors. The contracting professional should also be aware of the need to protect proprietary information, trade secrets, financial data, and other sensitive information of all offerors in the same manner as done in the notification process.

Mistakes and Protests

The period immediately following contract award is the time frame when contracting professionals are most likely to be presented with potentially time-consuming and damaging issues, sometimes generated by both the successful offeror as well as unsuccessful offerors. These issues usually are presented by offerors as either mistakes or protests. Though they can also surface in the pre-award phase, charges of mistakes or protests usually are reserved for the immediate post-award period. This section will not deal with the detailed and rigorous processes and venues used to resolve mistakes and protests, but rather, will briefly discuss some of the more common reasons for mistakes and protests. An awareness of the more common types of mistake and protest related issues can be used by the contracting professional when crafting solicitation packages to hopefully avoid ambiguities and prevent or reduce the frequency of such issues arising in the post-award environment.

If a contractor alleges a mistake, it is incumbent on the contractor to present clear and convincing evidence to support the allegation that a mistake was made. Depending on the extent and quality of the evidence provided by the contractor, the contracting professional normally resolves the issue in one of the following manners:

- The mistake can be corrected by issuing a contract modification, provided that the modification would be favorable to the buyer and does not materially alter the essential requirements of the contract.

- If the mistake was mutual or, if unilateral by the contractor and so apparent that the contracting officer should have realized the likelihood of a mistake, then the contract can be rescinded or reformed to eliminate the mistake. Reformed contracts may result in a price increase, but that increase may not exceed the price of the next most acceptable proposal.

- The contract can remain unchanged if the evidence presented by the contractor is insufficient to substantiate the mistake.

Protests are formal challenges to some aspect or aspects of the acquisition process. Like mistakes, protests can be lodged in either the pre-award or post-award phase. Though the specific grounds for a protest can vary widely and will depend on the particular circumstances of an acquisition and the contractors' perceptions, protests generally relate to some of the following issues.

Typical pre-award protest issues include:

- **Restrictive Requirements.** The protestor may claim that the requirements or specifications are unnecessarily restrictive and thereby prohibit or limit meaningful competition.
- **Inappropriate Sole-Source Requirement.** A protestor may claim that a requirement advertised as a sole-source procurement is not, in fact, a valid use of sole-source authority and that the possibility for competition exists.
- **Ambiguous or Erroneous Evaluation Criteria.** A protestor may claim that the criteria to be used to evaluate proposals is flawed or inaccurate or ambiguous in some material way so as to negatively impact the protestor's ability to fairly compete.
- **Ambiguous or Incomplete Requirements.** The protestor may claim that the statement of work is so incomplete or ambiguous so as to preclude a clear understanding of the full nature and scope of the requirement to be performed.
- **Exclusion from the Competitive Range.** A protestor may claim that their exclusion from the competitive range, when such a range was pre-established, was inappropriate or that the establishment of a competitive range was not revealed or sufficiently clear in the solicitation.

Typical post-award protest issues include:

- **Unfair Evaluation Criteria.** The protestor may assert that one or more of the criteria used to evaluate proposals were unreasonable, unfair, or otherwise inappropriate.
- **Failure to Evaluate as Advertised.** The protestor may claim that the method used to actually evaluate proposals was significantly different than the evaluation criteria specified in the solicitation.
- **Unreasonable Best-Value Analysis.** A protestor may indicate that, in a best-value procurement, the cost or tradeoff analysis used to justify an award to other than the highest rated or lowest price proposal was flawed, inaccurate or otherwise unreasonable in some material way.
- **Unequal Treatment.** A protestor may claim that other offerors received some form of special treatment or that all offerors were not treated equally, thereby adversely impacting the protestor's ability to compete effectively.
- **Failure to Conduct Meaningful Discussions.** A protestor may claim that they were not the recipient of meaningful discussions during pre-award negotiations, which unfairly prevented them from having the opportunity to submit a more competitive, revised proposal.

Regardless of the specific nature of a pre-award or post-award protest, the underlying issue usually relates to some real or perceived flaw or error or shortcoming in some facet of the pre-award process. As was discussed in Chapters 3 and 4, a thorough and comprehensive acquisition planning effort, and the logical implementation of the acquisition plan in the solicitation phase can result in a better procurement and fewer post-award issues to resolve. Once a protest is received, the contracting professional should take all reasonable and appropriate steps necessary to resolve the issue at the lowest possible level.

Small Business Programs

It is the policy of the government to provide the maximum practicable opportunities in its acquisitions to small business, veteran-owned small business, service-disabled veteran-owned small business, HUBZone small business, small disadvantaged business, and women-owned small business concerns. Such concerns must also have the maximum practicable opportunity to participate as subcontractors in the contracts awarded by any executive agency, consistent with efficient contract performance. The Small Business Administration (SBA) counsels and assists small business concerns and assists government contracting personnel to ensure that a fair proportion of contracts for goods and services is placed with small business.

Government contracting professionals are responsible for effectively implementing the small business programs within their activities, including achieving program goals. Government contracting offices are required to establish an Office of Small and Disadvantaged Business Utilization.

Small Business Policies

Small business concerns shall be afforded an equitable opportunity to compete for all contracts that they can perform to the extent consistent with the government's interest.

Contracting professionals shall, when appropriate,

- Divide proposed acquisitions, except construction, into reasonable small lots to permit offers on less than the total requirement;
- Plan acquisitions such that more than one small business concern may perform the work, if the work exceeds the amount for which a surety may be guaranteed by the SBA against loss;
- Ensure that delivery schedules are established on a realistic basis that will encourage small business participation;
- Encourage prime contractors to subcontract with small business concerns; and
- Provide copies of proposed acquisition packages to the SBA, under certain circumstances.

Contracting professionals should make every reasonable effort to find additional small business concerns, unless existing lists are excessively long.

Small Business Set-Asides

A small business set-aside is the reserving of an acquisition exclusively for participation by small business concerns. A small business set-aside may be open to all small businesses. A small business set-aside may relate to a single acquisition or a class of acquisitions and may be total or partial. Normally, all acquisitions exceeding $2,500 but not more than $100,000 are automatically set-aside for small business. Small business set-asides may be withdrawn by the contracting professional if award would be detrimental to the public interest (e.g., payment of more than a fair market price).

Types of Small Businesses

Small Business—A concern, including its affiliates, that is independently owned and operated, not dominant in the field of operation in which it is bidding on government contracts, and qualified as a small business under the criteria and size standards contained in 13 CFR Part 121.

Small Business 8(a)—A small business operating in conjunction with the SBA's Business Development (BD) Program, authorized by Section 8(a) of the Small Business Act. Fundamentally, the SBA acts as a prime contractor for other government agencies and issues subcontracts to 8(a) firms. The SBA sometimes delegates contract execution authority to the requiring agency. 8(a) contracts may be awarded competitively or noncompetitively.

Veteran-Owned Small Business—A small business not less than 51 percent of which is owned by one or more veterans or; in the case of publicly owned businesses, not less than 51 percent of the stock of which is owned by one or more veterans; and the management and daily business operations of which are controlled by one or more veterans.

Service-Disabled Veteran-Owned Small Business—A veteran-owned small business in which the 51 percent veteran criteria refers to veterans with a disability that is service-connected.

Small Disadvantaged Business—A small business that has received certification as a small disadvantaged business consistent with 13 CFR Part 124.

HUBZone Small Business—A small business that operates in a historically underutilized business zone that is in an area located within one or more qualified census tracts, qualified non-metropolitan counties, or lands within the external boundaries of an Indian reservation. The business must also appear on the List of Qualified HUBZone Small Business concerns maintained by the SBA.

Woman-Owned Small Business—A small business that is at least 51 percent owned by one or more women; or in the case of publicly owned business, at least 51 percent of the stock of which is owned by one or more women; and whose management and daily business operations are controlled by one or more women.

Other Socioeconomic Programs

Federal contracting professionals need to be aware of and comply with federal laws and policies that have some form of socioeconomic implication. Commercial contracting professionals whose organizations perform under federal contracts are also often bound by these laws and policies, which are normally included as terms and conditions in government contracts. Some of the significant socioeconomic programs include:

Indian Incentive Program—Government policy states that Indian organizations and Indian-owned economic enterprises shall have the maximum practicable opportunity to participate in performing contracts awarded by federal agencies. The policy also provides for incentive payments to Indian-owned economic enterprises that perform as subcontractors.

Disaster or Emergency Assistance Activities—When contracting for disaster or emergency assistance services following a major disaster or emergency, the government provides a preference to organizations, firms or individuals residing or doing business in the area affected by the disaster or emergency. Such services can include debris clearance, distribution of supplies or reconstruction.

Historically Black Colleges and Universities and Minority Institutions—The government promotes the participation of historically black colleges and universities and minority institutions in federal procurement, in compliance with Executive Order 12928, particularly for the types of services normally acquired from higher educational institutions.

Application of Labor Laws to Government Acquisitions

Labor laws frequently are a matter of concern for contracting professionals, particularly as they relate to service contracts. As a matter of policy, the government seeks to maintain sound relations with both industry and labor and usually remains impartial concerning disputes between labor and contractor management. Some of the significant issues and policies related to the application of labor laws include:

- Restrictions on the use of convict labor;
- The requirement to pay at least the prevailing wage rate for construction contracts subject to the Davis-Bacon Act;
- The Anti-Kickback provisions of the Copeland Act, which make it illegal to require, induce, intimidate or otherwise force employees on construction contracts to give up any part of their compensation;
- The requirement to pay overtime for work in excess of 40 hours per week as governed by the contract work hours and Safety Standards Act;
- The provisions of the Walsh-Healy Public Contracts Act, which require various stipulations regarding minimum wages, maximum hours, child labor, convict labor, and safe and sanitary working conditions for certain types of supply contracts;
- The provisions of the Service Contract Act of 1965 regarding minimum wages and fringe benefits, safe and sanitary working conditions, and notification to employees of the minimum allowable compensation for contracts covered by the act; and
- Various laws, executive orders, and policies that deal with equal employment opportunity, age discrimination, veterans preference, providing employment opportunities for the disabled, and other related matters.

Environmental and Workplace Considerations

The government seeks to implement, in part, various workplace and environmental policies, through the acquisition process. Some of these considerations include:

Drug-Free Workplace—Contractors are sometimes required to agree to take specified steps, including the establishment of an ongoing drug awareness program; providing published statements to its employees prohibiting the manufacture, distribution, dispensing, possession or use of controlled substances; and taking appropriate action against employees who violate the policies.

Energy Conservation—Some contracts contain clauses that help implement government policies to acquire goods and services that promote energy and water efficiency, advance the use of renewable energy products, and help foster markets for emerging technology.

Hazardous Materials—Sometimes contractors are required to provide information to the government regarding hazardous materials that may be introduced into the workplace as a result of performance on a government contract.

Recovered Materials—The government seeks to acquire products that meet performance requirements and are composed of the highest percentage of recovered materials practicable.

Ozone Depleting Substances—Government policy strives to minimize the procurement of materials and substances that contribute to the depletion of stratospheric ozone, and gives preference to the procurement of alternative products that reduce overall risks to human health and the environment.

Privacy and Freedom of Information

The Privacy Act of 1974 and the Freedom of Information Act have implications that sometimes affect government contracts. When a contract requires a contractor to design, develop or operate a system of records on individuals, the contracting agency is required to apply the requirements of the Privacy Act to the contractor and its employees. The Freedom of Information Act generally provides that information contained in government records be made available to the public. There are some exceptions to the general rule that apply to acquisitions. For example, proposals submitted in response to a competitive solicitation may not be released under the Freedom of Information Act. Also, there are exceptions that relate to classified information, trade secrets confidential commercial or financial information, and other matters.

9.2.3 Post-award Practices Unique to Federal Contracting

Property

When the U.S. government contracts for supplies and services, the contractor is generally required to provide all necessary resources to successfully meet the terms and conditions of such a contract. These "resources" also include all property necessary to perform the work required under government contracts. Re-utilization of government property promotes cost savings and efficiency for the government. The federal government also has a responsibility to protect the public trust, and serves as the guardian of the property purchased with public funds.

Government property means all property, owned by, leased to, or acquired by the government under the terms of a contract. It includes property delivered or otherwise made available to the contractor (for example, government-furnished property), and property provided by the contractor (property purchased by the contractor for use in performance of the contract), title in the latter case depends on the type of contract used and the specific provisions of the contract.

Government-furnished property (GFP) refers to any property in the possession of or directly acquired by the government and subsequently made available to a contractor. The *FAR* distinguishes between government-furnished property and contractor-acquired property under contracts. A simple definition of GFP is any property the government makes available or provides to a contractor for use in performance of a contract.

Contractor-acquired property (CAP) is defined as property that is acquired or otherwise provided by the contractor for performing a contract and to which the government has title. Under the terms of a contract, a contractor may be required to buy certain materials, equipment, or other property to perform the contract. The rights to title for such property purchased for use in performing a contract are generally placed (vested) in the government.

Ownership means the collection of rights to use and enjoy property, including the right to transmit or convey these rights to others. Title defines the right to control and dispose of property.

FAR Part 45 classifies property into five categories—(1) facilities, (2) material, (3) special tooling, (4) special test equipment, and (5) agency-peculiar property.

The term "facilities" refers to property used in production, maintenance, research, development, or testing. It includes plant equipment (such as machine tools, test equipment, and furniture) and real property (i.e., land, buildings, and other structures). It does not include any of the other categories of property mentioned earlier.

The term "material" means property that may be incorporated into or attached to a deliverable end item (i.e., steel used to make bolts) or that may be consumed or expended in performing a contract (i.e., solvents, cleansers, or paint). It also includes assemblies, components, parts, raw and processed materials, and small tools and supplies that may be consumed while performing a contract.

"Special tooling" means jigs (a device guiding a tool or for holding a machine work in place); dies (a device used for cutting out, forming, or stamping material); fixtures; molds; patterns; taps (a tool for cutting internal screw threads); gauges; other equipment and manufacturing aides; all components of these items; and replacement of these items; all of which are of such a specialized nature that without substantial modification or alteration, their use is limited to the development or production of particular supplies or parts thereof or to the performance of particular services. In other words, special tooling must be used only for the manufacture of specialty items.

"Special test equipment" refers to either single or multipurpose integrated test units engineered, designed, fabricated, or modified to accomplish special purpose testing in performing a contract. It consists of items or assemblies of equipment, including standard or general purpose items, or components that are interconnected and interdependent so as to become a new factional entity for special testing purposes. In other words, although special test equipment may consist of components that are used for normal testing purposes, it must be used only for special testing purposes as required in performing a contract.

Finally, "agency-peculiar property" means government-owned property that is peculiar to the mission of one agency (i.e., military hardware, such as an aircraft carrier, or space equipment, such as a space shuttle).

If the government plans to award a contract requiring the use of such property, there are formal procedures for the incorporation of such property based on some fundamental considerations. There are four major phases and key activities associated with property—(1) solicitation, (2) delivery of property, (3) control, accountability and use, and (4) disposition. During the solicitation phase, property is identified and made available for inspection or used "as is." Existing GFP is also identified, and a determination is made whether to include it in the procurement. If such property is included, it is made available for inspection and is offered either "as is" or with a guarantee of suitability for use in the procurement. Contractors are allowed to inspect property to verify the suitability or the "as is" condition of such for use in performance of the contract.

The government is responsible for providing the property in accordance with the contract schedule, or in such time to allow the contractor to reasonably meet delivery requirements. The contractor may receive an equitable adjustment due to the late delivery or other circumstances that may jeopardize performance in accordance with the agree-upon terms of the contract.

The contractor is generally responsible for having a property control system as required by the contract and FAR Part 45. The contractor is generally required to maintain property in good condition, less normal wear and tear, while also keeping custodial records that include information regarding the location, cost, allocability to contracts, condition and disposition of government property.

Upon completion or termination of a contract, the contractor is generally responsible for requesting disposition instructions and disposing of any property as directed by the government.

Contract Financing

According to the FAR Part 32, when a contractor requests financing, the government contracting officer is to consider the following order of preference for methods of contract financing.

Private financing without government guarantee includes loans from financial institutions, sale of bonds or stocks, and loans from family members or other private sources. However, it is not intended that the contractor be required to obtain private financing at unreasonable terms or from other agencies. In addition, under assignment of claims provisions, a financing institution can receive payments directly from the government in consideration for making a private loan to a contractor.

Progress payments based on incurred costs at customary progress payment rates can be made on the basis of costs incurred by the contractor as work progresses under a fixed-price contract.

If a contractor applies for a conventional loan to finance a government contract, the private financial institution involved may submit an application for a loan guarantee to the Federal Reserve Bank in its district. The Federal Reserve Bank acts as a fiscal agent and transmits the application to the guaranteeing agency. The president has designated seven agencies as guaranteeing agencies—(1) Department of Defense, (2) Department of Energy, (3) Department of Commerce, (4) Department of the Interior, (5) Department of Agriculture, (6) General Services Administration, and (7) National Aeronautics and Space Administration. The guaranteeing agency makes a determination of eligibility in accordance with the applicable *FAR* provisions. If the loan guarantee is approved, the private financial institution makes the loan and collects interest from the contractor, the guaranteeing agency guarantees the loan, and the Federal Reserve Bank acts as the "intermediary", or fiscal agent that processes the paperwork between the private financial institution and the contractor.

FAR Subpart 32 provides guidance for customary progress payments, i.e., the customary progress payment rate, the cost base, frequency of payment, and liquidation rates. Any progress payments that do not comply with this guidance for "customary" progress payments are considered "unusual." As such, unusual progress payments require advance agency approve.

Advance payments are advances of money by the government to a contractor. They are not measured by performance; they are made in anticipation of performance. Advance payments are the least preferred method of contract financing and generally should not be authorized if other types of financing are reasonably available to the contractor in adequate amounts. Loans and credit at excessive interest rates or other exorbitant charges, or loans from other government agencies, are not considered reasonably available financing. Contractors may apply for advance payments before or after the award of a contract. If advance payments are approved, a special bank account may be required. Interest is usually charged on the advance payments, and any interest earned is refundable to the government.

Contract Management Body of Knowledge

NCMA Certifications Examinations **Chapter 10**

section three

Chapter 10
NCMA Certification Examinations

In conjunction with the CMBOK updates, NCMA is developing certification examinations. The current examination format consists of multiple-choice questions. Former CACM candidates will recognize the type of examination. Former CPCM candidates who are familiar with an essay-style exam will need to become familiar with this new format.

Many people assume multiple-choice questions are easy to answer because they have had experience with tests that are not psychometrically sound. This means that every test question has undergone the full rigor of educational and statistical testing necessary to ensure that it elicits the exact response desired, that it is unambiguous, and that it has only one correct answer. However, three other plausible possible answers will separate those who know and understand the material from those who don't. Furthermore, multiple-choice testing can test more than simple recall of facts and recognition of words. It can test for understanding of content and for responses that indicate application of principles to a situation.

The benefits of multiple-choice examination lie in the objective assessment of question answers. There is no scope for alternative interpretation of results. That is not to say that every question is perfect. Rather, the multiple-choice format has the flexibility that allows NCMA, working in conjunction with psychometricians, or test developers, to change the examination and make every question a fair, valid, and reliable one.

Using a computer-based, multiple-choice examination allows NCMA to provide candidates with their results before they leave the testing site. Although this will not happen during the beta phase of the program, it does improve immeasurably on the four-month wait for results that CPCM candidates currently must endure.

An additional benefit is that candidates may schedule an exam anonymously. They may simply tell their office colleagues they will be out on that day and take the exam without peer pressure. When the candidates pass, they can share the news with their colleagues, but they no longer need to admit failure in an open forum.

Multiple-choice questions allow for a wider sampling of the body of knowledge. On the one hand, this means that candidates are bound to find areas with which they are familiar. On the other hand, it means that candidates may be unsure exactly where to concentrate their study. However, candidates should feel confident that the examination will ask only those questions that determine whether a contract manager has the knowledge to be a good practitioner. NCMA will not be testing on extraneous or trivial matter.

The computer has hastened the acceptance of multiple-choice examinations. Familiarity with this style of testing begins as early as elementary school. Because the future contract management community is in the hands of the demographic strata of the population that has either grown up with or grown familiar with computers, this style of testing will gain even wider acceptance. Furthermore, because multiple-choice examinations lend themselves to computer delivery, test developers can readily discern trends and make judgments about the examination or the underlying practice. In either case, the examination can be changed to correct or reflect the practice.

An examination delivered through computer can be delivered to many more people than can an examination that is graded by hand and by volunteer experts. In the latter case, the population can avail itself of an examination opportunity that is constrained by limited resources. With computers, examinations can be delivered and scored continuously, with the limiting factor being the number of computers to which the exam is delivered. The new program, while unable to offer worldwide 24-7 testing opportunities, will vastly increase the capacity of the program. This will allow NCMA to bring the certification program to those outside the membership community who may not previously have been aware of the program. This expansion will increase the influence of NCMA, increase the testing pool, and improve thee chance that changes to the practice will be readily noticed. And, thus, it will change the examinations to reflect the practice, which will increase the validity, reliability, and influence of the program.

Using the results of the testing program, NCMA will be better positioned to provide its membership, and the entire contract management community, with the education and information they need, almost as soon as they need it. NCMA is working toward an examination that will cause candidates to say, "That was a tough exam; it really made me think about what I do."

10.1 The Anatomy of a Multiple-Choice Question

A multiple-choice question has its own terminology. The question itself is called the "stem." The stem should contain all the information needed to provide the correct answer. The stem should be phrased in clear, unambiguous language that will leave no doubt what is being asked. A knowledgeable candidate should be able to discern the correct answer upon reading only the stem.

The answers also have specific terminology. The correct answer is the key, and the other possible answers are the distracters. The key is the only correct answer; no other answer should be able to be construed as correct. The distracters are plausible answers only to those who don't know the correct answer.

10.2 How to Study

Given that the examinations will now sample a wider slice of the body of knowledge, how should a candidate prepare? First of all, candidates should relax. Examinations will not include "everything but the kitchen sink." Rather, the examinations will reflect the sum of the eligibility requirements and current contract management practice.

Self-assessment is the first step to a study program. Does the candidate work well in a group or alone? Given the CMBOK, are there areas about which the candidate has little or no knowledge? Are there areas that the candidate is confident enough to teach others? In a review program, the areas where the candidate is confident would be areas of less intense concentration.

Even working alone, it is good to have a study plan. For example, candidates might plan to study one hour on a weekend for the next eight weeks, or three hours per week during the day for the next six weeks. Even as little as half an hour of study can help candidates gain knowledge and increase comprehension.

An alternative study method would be to join a group—for example, a group of office colleagues or a study group at the chapter level. NCMA chapters have provided study groups to hundreds of examination candidates. Study groups successfully allow for multiple points of view, as well as for sharing information and resources. Furthermore, chapter study group sessions are often lead by experts in the field. In terms of time spent, expert information beats informed research almost any day. Candidates may contact their local chapters for stuffy group information. Chapters may be accessed through the NCMA Web site by clicking on the "Membership" drop-down menu and selecting "Chapter Information" from the menu list.

10.3 Test Specifications for Certification Examination

Certification candidates must take and pass examinations consisting of multiple-choice questions. The distribution of certification examination questions is explained below. The CMCAB developed this distribution with the aid of a team of psychometricians and from the results of the body of knowledge revision. This includes research, the input of subject matter experts, and the results of surveys.

The answers to the questions in the examination are based on common terms and concepts found in publications, including this guide, readily available and normally found in public libraries, Web sites, or through NCMA.

10.4 How to Approach the Certification Examinations

It is easiest to first talk about the physical side of testing. Candidates should leave for the testing center early enough to allow for traffic delays and unfamiliar locations. They should arrive at the exam site well rested and energetic. To take the exam, candidates must present a photo identification card (ID). Note that the candidate must provide the photo ID with the same name as that under which he or she registered for the exam. For example, if Mary Smith applied and was accepted under her marital name of Mary Smith-Jones but presents an ID for Mary Smith or Mary Jones, she may be denied entrance to the examination.

Candidates may schedule two exam modules in one day. NCMA does not, however, advise that anyone attempt to schedule and take three exam modules in one day. Candidates may schedule either module or take both, and may take them in whatever order they choose.

During the beta phase of NCMA's certification program, results were not instantly provided. The passing score was not set until a sufficient number of persons had taken the exam to provide data for the scoring process. Candidates who passed the beta test are considered to have earned the certification and will be issued certificates. However, candidates who take the certification examinations now will receive results almost instantly. Within seconds or minutes of hitting the "Submit" button, the results of the examination will be displayed. Those who pass will be advised of that fact but will not be given the exact score. Those who were unsuccessful will be given a diagnostic report, which can be used to aid further study.

For the harder, mental side of examinations, here are a few good test-taking techniques:

1. Relax. The examination is based on your profession.
2. Read the questions carefully, answering those you can easily and quickly answer. It is usually a good idea to go with your first impression when answering a question; second-guessing can cause you to change a correct answer to an incorrect one.
3. Skip over or flag questions that appear too difficult and return to them later.
4. Don't stop. Keep going. Keep reading questions until you find one you can answer. The questions you've read will be in the back of your mind; when you return to them, you'll have a fresh perspective.
5. Avoid overanalyzing and second-guessing the question. Chose the correct answer for the question as it is written. Do not make assumptions about what the question means. Don't regard questions as being "trick questions" or concentrate on the exceptions to normal practice.
6. Keep an eye on the clock. Judge the time you have, so you don't spend a lot of time puzzling over one question to the detriment of being able to answer several others. Flag questions you are having trouble with and move on (see numbers 3 and 4).
7. Don't try to "game" the system by choosing answers to ensure that an equal number of As, Bs, Cs, and so on are selected. In the long run (over a lifetime), this may be a good technique, but in the short run (for one examination) the statistical underpinning for this myth has not been proven.
8. Try to answer the question in your mind before you read the choices. Good test questions are constructed to allow the knowledgeable examination candidate to do this.
9. If you can't readily identify the correct answer, make an educated guess. Eliminate the choices you know to be false and select from those remaining.
10. Look over your answers, if time permits. However, avoid trying to second-guess your answers (see number 5).
11. Don't worry about the examination. You may feel wrung out and exhausted at the end of the exam, but that is not an indication of hoe well or how poorly you may have performed (see number 1).

The CMBOK Lexicon

Federal Contracting

Commercial Contracting

section four

The CMBOK Lexicon for Federal Contracting

The CMBOK lexicon contains an explanation of the terms that are used directly or indirectly in Section 2. Multiple sources were consulted. However, where applicable, the terms were taken from the operational definitions published in NCMA's *Desktop Guide to Basic Contracting Terms, Sixth Edition (2006)*. These definitions reflect the collective opinion of the contract management community. In some instances, the definitions are excerpts with examples added for clarification. The purpose is to clearly convey the intended content of each CMBOK element. Definitions have been taken from the *Federal Acquisition Regulation (FAR)*, the *Uniform Commercial Code (UCC)* dictionaries, Web sites, official documents (Office of Management and Budget [OMB] circulars and legal casework, for example), textbooks, and accepted contract management practice.

A&E Selection Process —The unique process used to select Architect–Engineer firms pursuant to the Brooks Act.

Acceptance—That act of an authorized buyer representative by which the buyer assents to ownership of existing and identified supplies, or approves specific services rendered, as partial or complete performance of a contract.

Accounting —The principles and practices of systematically recording, presenting, and interpreting financial data.

Acquisition Methodology—A means of requesting or inviting offerors to submit offers, generally by issuance of a solicitation.

Acquisition Plan—A plan for an acquisition that serves as the basis for initiating the individual contracting actions necessary to acquire a system or support a program.

Acquisition Planning—The process by which efforts of all personnel responsible for an acquisition are coordinated and integrated through a comprehensive plan for fulfilling the organizations' need in a timely manner at a reasonable cost. It includes developing the overall strategy for managing the acquisition.

Acquisition Strategy—The conceptual framework for conducting an acquisition. It encompasses the broad concepts and objectives that direct and control the overall acquisition process.

Administrative Changes—Unilateral contract changes, in writing, that do not affect the substantive rights of the parties, such as a change in the paying office.

Administrative Closeout—Process of ensuring that all documentation, including releases, audits, reports, and final invoices has been completed and that contract files have been properly stored or disposed of.

Advisory and Assistance Services—Services acquired to support or improve agency policy development, decision-making, management, and administration, or to support or improve the operation of management systems.

Agency—A relationship whereby the principal authorizes another (the agent) to act for and on behalf of the principal and to bind the principal in contract.

Agreements and Restrictions—Agreements exist between the United States and its trading partners regarding international procurement. These include the General Agreement on Tariffs and Trade (GATT), the GATT Government Procurement Code, the North American Free Trade Agreement (NAFTA), as well as bilateral agreements that have been negotiated between the United States and other countries (such as the U.S.-Canada Free Trade Agreement). Congress has routinely included in appropriation acts restrictions on the procurement of certain foreign items, usually to protect domestic industries.

Alternate Disputes Resolution—Any procedure that is used, in lieu of litigation, to resolve issues in controversy, including but not limited to, settlement negotiations, conciliation, facilitation, mediation, fact-finding, mini-trials, and arbitration.

Apparent Authority—The right by an agent for a principal to exercise power where the principal knowing permits the agent to exercise authority, though not actually granted.

Arbitration—The use of an impartial third party to whom the parties to an agreement refer their disputes for resolution. Some contracts contain provisions that provide for binding arbitration of unsettled grievances.

Architect–Engineer (A&E) Services and Construction—A&E includes professional services of an architectural or engineering nature, which are required to be performed or approved by a person licensed, registered or certified to provide such services or are associated with research, planning, development, design, construction, alteration, or repair of real property, or other related professional services, such as studies and surveys. Construction means alteration or repair including dredging; excavating; and painting of buildings, structures, or other real property.

Audits—The systematic examination of records and documents and/or the securing of other evidence by confirmation, physical inspection, or otherwise, for one or more of the following purposes—determining the propriety or legality of proposed or completed transactions; ascertaining whether all transactions have been recorded and are reflected accurately in accounts; determining the existence of recorded assets and inclusiveness of recorded liabilities; determining the accuracy of financial or statistical statements or reports and the fairness of the facts they represent; determining the degree of compliance with established policies and procedures in terms of financial transactions and business management; and appraising an account system and making recommendations concerning it.

Authority—The sources from which entities or people receive their empowerment to engage in procurement activities, and which set forth the framework, parameters and extend to their empowerment. Such authority includes state statutes, state and local regulations charters, local ordinances, and administrative resolutions, policies, or edicts.

Basic Agreement—A written instrument of understanding, negotiated between an agency or contracting activity and a contractor that contains contract clauses applying to future contracts between the parties during its term and contemplates separate future contracts that will incorporate, by reference or attachment, the required and applicable clauses agreed on in the basic agreement. A basic agreement is not a contract.

Basic Ordering Agreement—A written instrument of understanding, negotiated between an agency, contracting activity, or contracting office and a contractor, that contains terms and clauses applying to future contracts (orders) between the parties during its term; a description, as specific as practicable, of supplies or services to be provided; and methods for pricing, issuing, and delivering future orders under the basic ordering agreement. A basic ordering agreement is not a contract.

Bid or No-Bid Decision—Determination made by seller's management whether or not to submit an offer usually in response to a customer request.

Bilateral and Unilateral—A bilateral contract is formed by the exchange of promises to perform reciprocal obligations for the other party. A unilateral contract is formed by the exchange of a promise of one party for an action by the other party.
Break Even Analysis—A means of determining the number of goods or services that must be sold at a given price to generate sufficient revenue to cover costs.

Budgeting—The planning, scheduling, and budgeting of organizational expenses for the fiscal period.

Capital Budgeting—The process of planning for the best selection and financing of long-term investment proposals, taking into account the time value of money.

Cash Budgeting—A schedule of expected cash receipts and disbursements for a designated period. The primary reason for a cash budget is to forecast a company's future financing needs. A cash budget is also used to avoid either unnecessary idle cash or possible cash shortages. In case of cash shortage, it indicates whether the shortage is temporary or permanent (i.e., whether short-term or long-term borrowing is needed).

Change Orders—Written orders signed by the contracting officer or buyer, which are authorized by contract clause, to modify contractual requirements within the scope of the contract.

Conflict of Interest—Term used in connection with public officials and fiduciaries and their relationship to matters of private interest or gain to them. Ethical problems connected therewith are covered by statutes in most jurisdictions and by federal statutes on the federal level. A conflict of interest arises when an employee's personal or financial interest conflicts or appears to conflict with his or her official responsibility.

Consent to Subcontracts—Situations in which the government must consent to a prime contractor's subcontract. Consent is required when subcontract work is complex, the dollar value is substantial, or the government's interest is not adequately protected by competition and the type of prime or subcontract.

Construction Contracts—The traditional method of construction contracting that uses the phases of design, bid, and build for construction projects.

Constructive Changes—Verbal or written acts or omissions by an authorized government official that are of such a nature that they have the same effect as written change orders.

Contract Administration—Management of issues that arise during the performance of a contract.

Contract Changes or Modifications—Any written alteration in the specification, delivery point, rate of delivery, contract period, price, quantity, or other provision of an existing contract, accomplished in accordance with a contract clause; may be unilateral or bilateral.

Contract Closeout—The process of declaring that the obligations under a contract have been satisfied and that a procurement file is both physically and administratively complete. A closeout can occur when (1) the contractor's supplies or services have been accepted and paid for, and (2) all documentation on the procurement is finalized and properly assembled.

Contract Financing—Obtaining the funds necessary for performing the contract including payment methods, loan guarantees, advanced payments, progress payments, and contract funding.

Contract Formation—The elements of offer, acceptance, mutuality of consideration, competent parties, legal subject matter, and mutuality of agreement.

Contract Performance or Quality Assurance—A planned and systematic pattern of actions necessary to provide adequate confidence that material, data, supplies, and services conform to established technical requirements, and to achieve satisfactory performance.

Contract Structures—Specific pricing arrangements employed for the performance of work under contract.

Contract Termination—Action taken pursuant to a contract clause in which the contracting officer unilaterally ends all or part of the work.

Contracting Methods—The process employed for soliciting offers, evaluating offers, and awarding a contract.

Contractor's Purchasing Systems Review—An evaluation of the efficiency and effectiveness with which the prime contractor spends government funds and complies with government policy when subcontracting.

Convenience Termination—Right reserved to the government, under the standard Termination for Convenience clause, to bring an end to contracts that are made obsolete by technological and other developments or that are otherwise no longer advantageous to the government.

Copyrights—Royalty-free, nonexclusive, and irrevocable license to reproduce, translate, publish, use, and dispose of written or recorded material and to authorize others to do so.

Cost—Concerned with the accounting system design for recording, accumulating, and reporting costs for specific products and services.

Cost Accounting Standards (CAS)—Federal standards designed to provide consistency and coherency in defense and other government contract accounting.

Cost Contract—Cost-reimbursement contract in which the contractor receives no fee.

Cost Incentives—Most incentive contracts include only cost incentives, which take the form of a profit or fee adjustment formula and are intended to motivate the contractor to effectively manage costs. No incentive contract may provide for other incentives without also providing a cost incentive (or constraint). Except for award fee contracts (see 16.404 and 16.405-2), incentive contracts include a target cost, a target profit or fee, and a profit or fee adjustment formula. These targets and the formula provide that (within the constraints of a price ceiling or minimum and maximum fee) (1) the actual cost that meets the target will result in the target profit fee; (2) the actual cost that exceeds the target will result in downward adjustment of target profit or fee; and (3) the actual cost that is below the target will result upward adjustment of target profit or fee.

Cost-Plus-Incentive-Fee Contract—A cost-reimbursement contract that provides for the initially negotiated fee to be adjusted later by a formula based on the relationship of total allowable costs to total target costs.

Cost/Price Analysis—A review to determine and evaluate the cost elements in an offeror's or contractor's proposal to determine how well the proposed costs represent what the cost of the contract should be, assuming reasonable economy and efficiency.

Cost Principles—The regulations that establish rules and policies relating to the general treatment of costs in government contracting, particularly the allowability of costs.

Cost Proposal—The instrument required of an offeror for the submission or identification of cost or pricing data by which an offeror submits to the buyer a summary of estimated (or incurred) costs, suitable for detailed review and analysis.

Cost Reimbursement—A form of pricing arrangement that provides for payment of allowable, allocable, and reasonable costs incurred in the performance of a contract to the extent that such costs are prescribed or permitted by the contract. This family of contracts includes cost-plus-award-fee (CPAF), cost-plus-fixed-fee (CPFF), cost-plus-incentive-fee, and cost-sharing contracts.

Cost-Sharing Contract—Cost-reimbursement contract in which the contractor receives no fee and is reimbursed only for an agreed-on portion of its allowable costs.

CPAF Contract—Cost-reimbursement contract that provides for a fee consisting of (1) a base amount (which may be zero) fixed at inception of the contract and (2) an award amount, based on a judgmental evaluation by the government, sufficient to provide motivation for excellence in contract performance.

CPFF Contract—Cost-reimbursement contract that provides for payment to the contractor of a negotiated fee that is fixed at the inception of the contract. The fixed fee does not vary with actual cost but may be adjusted as a result of changes in the work to be performed under the contract. This contract type permits contracting for efforts that might otherwise present too great a risk to contractors, but it provides the contractor only a minimum incentive to control costs.

Data—Recorded information, regardless of form or the media on which it may be recorded. Rights to use technical data developed by the contractor vary depending on the source of funds used to develop the item, component, process, software, or software documentation.

Data Rights—Rights of ownership of data under any contract. In any contract that may involve the production of scientific or technical data, the rights to those data must be clearly ascribed. Generally, a rights in data clause will protect the government's right to use and distribute— without limitation, free from payment of royalties, and with immunity against lawsuits for copyright infringement or misuse of data—any data produced under a contract funded by the government.

Database Management—Includes data modeling, query languages database design, and transaction processing.

Debriefings—An explanation given by government personnel to an offer or detailing the reasons its proposal was unsuccessful.

Default Termination—An action that the government may impose under the standard default clause for a contractor's failure to perform.

Defense Priorities and Allocations System (DPAS)—A Department of Commerce system controlling the use of critical material and facilities. Goals are to ensure the timely availability of industrial resources to meet current defense requirements and provide a framework for rapid industrial expansion in case of a national emergency.

Defense Production Act—An act passed in 1950 (50 U.S.C. app 2061 and the following ones) that authorizes the president to require the priority performance of contracts and orders necessary or appropriate to promote the national defense over other contracts or orders; to allocate materials, services, and facilities as necessary or appropriate to promote the national defense; and to require the allocation of, or the priority performance under contracts or orders relating to, supplies of materials, equipment, and services to ensure domestic energy supplies for national defense needs.

Definite Quantity Contract—Provides for delivery of a definite quantity of specific supplies or services for a fixed period, with deliveries or performance to be scheduled at designated locations upon order.

Delays—Contractual provisions designed to protect the contractor from sanctions for late performance. To the extent that it has been excusably delayed, the contractor is protected from default termination, liquidated damages, or excess costs of procurement or completion. Excusable delays (e.g., acts of God or the public enemy, acts of the government in either its sovereign or contractual capacity, fire, flood, quarantines, strikes, epidemics, unusually severe weather, or freight embargoes): also may lead to recovery of additional compensation if the government constructively accelerates performance.

Delegation of Authority—The conferring of authority, from one organization or representative to another, to accomplish specified tasks, such as contract administrative tasks. Such authority may be shared or recalled.

Delivery Incentives—Should be considered when improvement from a required delivery schedule is a significant government objective. It is important to determine the government's primary objectives in a given contract.

Delivery Order Contract—Contract for supplies that does not procure or specify a firm quantity of supplies (other than a minimum or maximum quantity) and that provides for the issuance of orders for the delivery of supplies during the period of the contract.

Design or Build—A method of construction contracting that combines the architectural, engineering, and construction services required for a project into a single agreement.

Discussions—Any verbal or written communication between the government and an offeror, other than communications conducted for the purpose of minor clarification, whether or not initiated by the government that (1) involves information essential for determining the acceptability of the proposals, or (2) provides the offeror an opportunity to revise or modify its proposal.

Disputes—Disagreements between the parties regarding their rights under a contract that will originate when a claim is denied by the party against which it is made.

Diversity—Programs designed to encourage a diverse workforce or education and training group; such as programs that prohibit employment or workplace discrimination based on race, color, religion, sex, or national origin, age, or disability.

Earned Value—A management technique that relates resource planning to schedules and to technical cost and schedule requirements. All work is planned, budgeted, and scheduled in time-phased "planned value" increments constituting a cost and schedule measurement baseline. There are two major objectives of an earned-value system: (1) to encourage contractors to use effective internal cost and schedule management control systems, and (2) to enable the customer to rely on timely data produced by those systems for determining product-oriented contract status.

Economics—The study of the problems arising when goods and services are scarce relative to human desires for those goods and services.

Electronic Commerce—A paperless process, including electronic mail, electronic bulletin boards, electronic funds transfer, electronic data interchange, and similar techniques for accomplishing business transactions.

Enterprise Resource Planning (ERP) System—A set of integrated business applications, or modules, to carry out most common business functions, including inventory control, general ledger accounting, accounts payable, accounts receivable, material requirements planning (MRP), order management, purchasing, and human resources. ERP modules are integrated, primarily through a common set of definitions and a common database, and the modules have been designed to reflect a particular way of doing business (i.e., a particular set of business processes).

Environmental Issues—Policies and procedures supporting the Government's program for ensuring a drug-free workplace and of protecting and improving the quality of the environment through pollution control, energy conservation, identification of hazardous material, and use of recovered materials.

Ethics—Of or relating to moral action, conduct, motive or character, as ethical emotion; professionally right or benefiting; conforming to professional standards of conduct.

Evaluation Factors—Factors that are tailored to each acquisition and the consideration of each proposal and that establish a baseline for proposal evaluation for recommendations regarding the source selection decision. Price, or cost to the government, and quality are addressed in every source selection. Other relevant factors may also be included.

Evaluation Procedures—The process used to evaluate offers against established selection criteria in accordance with the source selection plan.

Export Controls—The comprehensive set of controls that have been established to protect national security interests and to foster foreign policy initiatives. The Department of State monitors and controls the expert and re-export of goods and services in accordance with the *International Traffic in Arms Regulations (ITAR)*, and the Department of Commerce *Export Administration Regulation (EAR)* enforces the Export Administration Act.

Export Financing—Financing of international transactions in the exporting or importing of products and services. Addresses factors such as transit times, customs regulations, banking rules and regulations, buyer and seller credit, exchange rates, and political risk.

Extraordinary Contractual Relief—Form of relief for contractors under federal law giving the president the power to authorize federal agencies to enter into contracts, or amendments or modifications of contracts, without regard to other revisions of law relating to the making, performance, amendment, or modification of contracts, when the president believes the action will facilitate national defense.

Facilities Contract—A contract under which government facilities are provided to a contractor or subcontractor by the government for use in connection with performing one or more related contracts for supplies or services. It is used occasionally to provide special tooling or special test equipment. Facilities contracts are cost contracts; contractors receive no fee.

Fact-Finding—The process of identifying and obtaining information necessary to complete the evaluation of proposals.

Federal Regulations—Applicable directives and instructions issued by the several departments and agencies that establish and implement acquisition policies. Examples include the *Federal Acquisition Regulation (FAR)*, agency *FAR* supplements, and Office of Management and Budget circulars (OMB).

Federal Statutes—Applicable laws enacted by the legislative branch and signed by the president that affects acquisition. Examples include the Armed Services Procurement Act of (1947), the Federal Property and Administrative Services Act of (1949), the Competition in Contracting Act of (1984), and the Federal Acquisition Streamlining Act of (1994).

Federal Supply Schedules—A program directed and managed by the General Services Administration that provides federal agencies with a simplified process for obtaining commonly used supplies and services at prices associated with volume buying.

Federally Funded Research and Development Corporation (FFRDC)—Activity sponsored under a broad charter by a government agency (or agencies) for the purpose of performing, analyzing, integrating, supporting, and/or managing basic or applied research and/or development, and which receive 70 percent or more of its financial support from the government. If FFRDCs, a long-term relationship is contemplated; most or all of the facilities are owned or funded by the government; and the FFRDC has access to government and supplier data, employees, and facilities beyond that which is common in a normal contractual relationship. The operation, management, and administration of an FFRDC is performed by a university, consortium of universities, nonprofit organization, or industrial firm as an identifiable and separate operating unit of a parent organization. The Nation Science Foundation maintains the master list of FFRDCs.

Finance—Managing the money matters of the organization.

Financial Analysis—Includes international financial analysis, return on assets, return on investment, asset turnover, and variance analysis.

Financial Reporting—Includes financial statements, sales forecasting, planning and control.

Firm-Fixed-Price Contract—Provides for a price that is not subject to any adjustment on the basis of the contractor's cost experience in performing the contract. This contract type places on the contractor maximum risk and full responsibility for all costs and resulting profit or loss. It provides maximum incentives for the contractor to control costs and perform effectively and imposes a minimum administrative burden on the contracting parties.

Firm-Fixed-Price, Level-of-Effort Term Contract—Requires the contractor to provide a specified level of effort, over a stated period of time, on work that can be stated only in general terms; and requires the government to pay the contractor a fixed dollar amount.

Fixed Price—A type (family) of contracts providing for a firm pricing arrangement established by the parties at the time of contracting. This family of contracts includes firm-fixed-price, fixed-price with economic price adjustment, fixed-price incentive, fixed-price re-determination (prospective and retroactive), and firm-fixed-price level-of-effort.

Fixed-Price Contract with Award Fees—Used when the government wishes to motivate a contractor and other incentives cannot be used because contractor performance cannot be measured objectively. Such contracts shall establish a fixed price (including normal profit) for the effort that will be paid for satisfactory contract performance. Such contracts shall establish that the award fee earned (if any) will be paid in addition to that fixed price and provide for periodic evaluation of the contractor's performance against an award fee plan.

Fixed-Price Contract with Economic Price Adjustment—Provides for upward and downward revision of the stated contract price on the occurrence of specified contingencies. There are three general types of economics price adjustments: (1) Adjustments based on established prices where price adjustments are based on increases or decreases from an agreed-on level in published or otherwise established prices of specific items or the contract end items, (2) Adjustments based on actual costs of labor or material where price adjustments are based on increases or decreases in specified costs of labor or material that the contractor actually experiences during contract performance, and (3) Adjustments based on cost indexes of labor or material where price adjustments are based on increases or decreases in labor or material cost standards or indexes that are specifically identified in the contract.

Fixed-Price Contract with Prospective Price Redetermination—Provides for (1) a firm-fixed price for an initial period of contract deliveries or performance and (2) prospective re-determination, at a stated time or times during performance of the price for subsequent periods of performance.

Fixed-Price Contract with Retroactive Price Redetermination—Provides for (1) a fixed ceiling price and (2) retroactive price re-determination within the ceiling after completion of the contract.

Fixed-Price Incentive Contract—Provides for adjusting profit and establishing the final contract price by application a formula based on the relationship of total final negotiated cost to total target cost. The final price is subject to a price ceiling, negotiated at the outset. The two forms of fixed-price incentive contracts—firm target and successive target contracts—are discussed below.

Fixed-Price Incentive (Firm Target) Contract—Specifies a target cost, a target profit, a price ceiling (but not a profit ceiling or floor), and a profit adjustment formula. These elements are all negotiated at the outset.

Fixed-Price Incentive (Successive Targets) Contract—Specifies the following elements, all of which are negotiated at the outset: an initial target cost, an initial target profit, and an initial profit adjustment formula. These targets and formula are used to establish (1) the firm target profit, including a ceiling and floor for the firm target profit; (2) the production point at which the firm target cost and firm target profit will be negotiated (usually before delivery or shop completion of the first item); and (3) a ceiling price that is the maximum that may be paid to the contractor, except for any adjustment under other contract clauses providing for equitable adjustment or other revision of the contract price under stated circumstances.

Forecasting—An estimate of financial position, results of operations, and changes in cash flows for one or more future periods based on a set of assumptions representing the most probable outcomes. If the assumptions are not necessarily the most likely outcomes, the estimate is called a "projection."

Foreign Military Sales (FMS)—That portion of the US security assistance authorized by the Foreign Assistance Act of (1961), as amended, and the Arms Export Control Act, as amended, where the recipient provides reimbursement for defense articles and services transferred. FMS includes Department of Defense (DOD) cast sales from stocks; DOD guarantees covering financing by private or Federal Financing Bank sources for credit sales of defense articles and defense services; sales financed by appropriated direct credits; and sales funded by grants under the Military Assistance Program.

Forums—The administrative and judicial bodies that adjudicate protests.

Fraud—Acts or attempts to defraud the government or its agents; acts violating the False Claims Act or the Anti-Kickback Act.

Free on Board (FOB)—A term used in conjunction with a physical point to determine the responsibility and basis for payment of freight charges and, unless otherwise agreed, the point at which title for goods passes to the buyer or consignee.

General and Administrative (G&A)—A subcategory of overhead; includes costs necessary for overall management and operations but not directly associated with a specific cost objective or business segment. Typical G&A costs include sales staff salaries, insurance, executive compensation, and central office expenses.

General Business—Portions of other disciplines relevant to contract management.

Generally Accepted Accounting Principles (GAAP)—A term encompassing conventions, rules, and procedures of accounting that are "generally accepted" and have "substantial authoritative support." The GAAP have been developed by agreement on the basis of experience, reason, custom, usage, and to a certain extent, practical necessity, rather than being derived from a formal set of theories.

HUBZone—A historically underutilized business zone or area that is located within one or more qualified census tracts, qualified non-metropolitan counties, or lands within the boundaries of an Indian reservation. "Indian" means any person who is a member of any Indian tribe, band, group, pueblo, or community that is recognized by the federal government as eligible for services from the Bureau of Indian Affairs (BIA) in accordance with 25 U.S.C. 1452© and any "Native" as defined in the Alaska Native Claims Settlement Act (43 U.S.C. 1601).
Human Relations—Individual behavior, interpersonal relationships, group behavior and human problems in the work environment.

Improper Practices—A broad range of activities forbidden or limited by the FAR with regard to the award and performance of government contracts.
Incentive Contracts—Incentive contracts are appropriate when a firm fixed price contract not appropriate and the required supplies or services can be acquired at lower costs and, in certain instances, with improved delivery or technical performance, by relating the amount of profit or fee payable under the contract to the contractor's performance. Incentive contracts are designed to obtain specific acquisition objectives by (1) establishing reasonable and attainable targets that are clearly communicated to the contractor and (2) including appropriate incentive arrangements designed to motivate contractor efforts that might not otherwise be emphasized and discourage contractor inefficiency and waste.

Indefinite Delivery/Indefinite Quantity Contract (IDIQ)—IDIQ contracts provide for an indefinite quantity within stated limits of supplies or services to be furnished within a fixed period with deliveries or performance to be scheduled by placing orders with the contractor. Examples of these contracts are delivery order, task order, definite quantity, requirements, and indefinite quantity.

Governmentwide Agency Contract (GWAC)—Governmentwide acquisition contracts available to multiple buyers.

Indefinite Quantity Contract—Provides for an indefinite quantity, within stated limits, of supplies or services during a fixed period. The government places orders for individual requirements. Quantity limits may be stated as number of units or as dollar values.

Indemnification—Protections provided by the parties to each other; also to restore a loss, either in whole or in part, by payment, repair, or replacement.

Independent Research and Development (IR&D)—Contractor effort that is neither sponsored by a grant nor required in performing a contract and that falls within any of the following four areas: (a) basic research, (b) applied research, (c) development, and (d) systems and other concept formulation studies.

Information Management—The applications of information science to the practical aspects of specifying, designing, implementing and managing information systems.

Information Science—The technical, managerial, policy issues associated with computer based information systems in modern organizations.

Information Technology (IT)—The collection of technologies that deal specifically with processing, storing, and communicating information; includes all types of computer and communication systems. It involves those special policies and procedures applicable to the acquisition and use of computers, telecommunications, and related resources.

Inherently Governmental—An activity that is so intimately related to the public interest that it mandates performance by federal employees. Activities that meet these criteria are not in competition with commercial sources, are not generally available from commercial sources, and, therefore, are not subject to OMB Circular A-76 or its supplement.

Innovative Contracting Methods—Contracting methods focusing on an alternative aspect of cost-effective contract management that ensure total fulfillment of the contract goals. Examples of such innovative contracting methods are warranty flexibility, multi-parameter, and best-value contracting. Warranty contracting includes an extended warranty that places responsibility for product performance on the contractor, generating a longer lasting product and lower overall maintenance costs. In multi-parameter contracting, agencies determine contract winners based on the lowest combination of cost, time, and other parameters. Best-value contracting focuses on such factors as technical excellence, management capability, past performance, and personnel qualifications and makes trade-offs for lowest price.

Inspection—The examination (including testing) of supplies and services (including, when appropriate, raw materials, components, and intermediate assemblies) to determine whether the supplies and services conform to the contract requirements.

Integrated Project/Product Team (IPT)—Team composed of representatives from appropriate functional disciplines working together to build successful programs, identify and resolve issues, and make sound and timely recommendations to facilitate decision making. There are three types of IPTs: overarching IPTs (OIPTs), which focus on strategic guidance, program assessment, and issue resolution; working-level IPTs (WIPTs), which identify and resolve program issues, determine program status, and seek opportunities for acquisition reform; and program-level IPTs (PIPTs), which focus on program execution and may include representatives from both government and, after contract award, industry.

Intellectual Property—The kind of property that results from the fruits of mental labor. Intellectual property rights include any or all of the following: patent, trademark, copyright, trade secret, trade name, service mark, and the like.

Intergovernmental Relations—A range of cooperative activities between governments, including various forms of intergovernmental cooperative purchasing, joint or shared use of facilities and supplies, and procurements made by one government from another.

International Contracting—The policies and procedures that govern the acquisition and sale of goods and services with foreign nationals and governments.

International Organization for Standardization (ISO) Standards—The ISO Standards are families of standards consisting of standards and guidelines that relate to management systems and related supporting standards on terminology and specific tools, such as auditing (the process of checking that the management system conforms to the standard).

Invitation for Bids (IFBs)—Solicitation used in the sealed-bid method of procurement.

Labor Laws—Policies and procedures for implementing labor laws such as the Davis-Bacon Act, Contract Work Hours and Safety Standards Act, and the Service contract Act.

Labor Surplus Area—A geographical area identified by the Department of Labor as an area of concentrated unemployment or underemployment or an area of labor surplus.

Labor-Hour Contract—Variation of the time-and-materials contract, differing only in that materials are not supplied by the contractor.

Laws and Regulations—Refers to the statutes and regulations that provide the legal and regulatory framework for the acquisition of goods and services.

Leases—Rental agreements in which the lessor conveys to the lessee the right to use the lessor's personal or real property, usually in exchange for a payment of money.

Letter Contract—A written preliminary contractual instrument that authorizes the contractor to begin immediately manufacturing supplies or performing services.

Licensing—The sale of a license permitting the use of patents, trademarks, or other technology to another firm. A license covering a patent, technical or proprietary data, technical assistance, know-how, or any combination of these—granted by a U.S. firm to a foreign firm or government—to produce, co-produce, or sell a defense article or service within a given sales territory. An exclusive license grants this right without competition from any other licensees or from the licensor. For a nonexclusive license, competition may be permitted with other licensees and/or the licensor. Licensing involves the many procedures administrative agencies perform in conjunction with issuance of various types of licenses.

Logistics—Inventory management, transportation and traffic, and distribution supporting the product/service mission of the organization.

Major Systems—A combination of elements that will function together to produce the capabilities required to fulfill a mission need, including hardware, equipment, software, or any combination of these, but excluding construction.

Make-or-Buy-Program—That part of a contractor's written plan for the development or production of an end item outlining the subsystems, major components, assemblies, subassemblies, and parts intended to be manufactured, test-treated, or assembled by the seller (make); and those the seller intends to procure from another source (buy).

Management—The art and science of the processes of planning, organizing, directing and controlling the affairs of the organization.

Market Research—The process used for collecting and analyzing information about the entire market available to satisfy an agency's needs for the minimum information required to establish the most suitable approach to acquiring, distributing, and supporting supplies and services.

Marketing—Activities that direct the flow of goods and services from the producer to the consumers.

Modes of Transportation—Means of moving freight traffic utilizing transportation methods such as bills of lading, parcel post, bus service, air cargo, rail freight, carload and less than carload, motor freight, freight forwarder, and pipeline.

Modular Contracts—Use of one or more contracts to acquire information technology (IT) systems in successive, interoperable increments.

Multiple-Incentive Contracts—Such contracts should motivate the contractor to strive for outstanding results in all incentive areas and compel trade-off decisions among the incentive areas consistent with the government's overall objectives for the acquisition.

NCMA CMBOK—Definitive description of the elements making up the body of professional knowledge that applies to contract management.

Negotiation—The process of entering into or modifying a contract to the mutual agreement of the parties to the contract.

Negotiations—A method of contracting that uses either competitive or other-than-competitive proposals and (usually) discussions. It is a flexible process that includes the receipt of proposals from offerors, permits bargaining, and usually affords offerors an opportunity to revise their offers before award of a contract.

Negotiation Objectives—Determining the issues to be negotiated and the minimum and maximum positions for each issue.

Network Systems—Computer equipment or interconnected systems or subsystems of equipment used in the automatic acquisition, storage, manipulation, management, movement, control, display, switching interchange, transmission, or reception of data or information. These systems include computers, servers, ancillary equipment, software, and related services.

OMB Circular A-76—Establishes federal policy regarding the performance of commercial activities. It implements the statutory requirements of the Federal Activities Inventory Reform Act of 1998, *Public Law* 105-270.

Operations Management—The concepts, techniques and practices used in managing the operations of an organization.

Organization—The administrative and personnel structure of a business or government that reflects the organizational patterns, procurement authority and scope of activities or its various elements. It may include boards, commissions, or committees and may reflect a delegation's exemptions, as well as full or limited authority to act.

Organizational Behavior—Human behavior as it influences organizational efficiency and effectiveness.

Organizational Communication—Focuses on the processes of communication ranging from that between two persons to that of the total organization.

Organizational/Industrial Marketing—Activities of marketing directed toward organizations rather than individual consumers and includes research, product planning and development, distribution, promotion, and pricing.

Other Types—Miscellaneous contracts that use a form of pricing arrangement (such as time-and-materials, labor-hour and letter contracts) or are described by the terms governing ordering (indefinite-delivery contracts).

Outsourcing—A version of the make-or-buy decision, commonly used for services, in which a firm elects to purchase an item/service that previously, was made/performed in-house.

Overhead—Indirect costs other than those related to general and administrative expense and selling expenses; a general term often used to identify an indirect cost.

Patents—A government grant of exclusive rights to an inventor that prohibits others from making, using, or selling an invention.

Payments—The amount payable under the contract, supporting data required to be submitted with invoices, and other payment terms such as time for payment and retention.

Performance Incentives—May be considered in connection with specific product characteristics (e.g., a missile range, an aircraft speed, an engine thrust, or a vehicle maneuverability) or other specific elements of the contractor's performance. These incentives should be designed to relate profit or fee to results achieved the contractor compared with specified targets.

Personal Services—A contact that by its express terms or as administered, makes the contractor personnel appear, in effect, as government employees.

Physical Completion—When the contractor has completed required deliveries and/or performed all services, all options have expired, or the contractor has given a notice that the contract has been terminated.

Pre-award Surveys—An evaluation of a prospective contractor's ability to perform a specific contract, performed by the contract administration office or the purchasing office, with assistance from an audit organization, at the request of either office. The evaluation addresses the physical, technical, managerial, and financial capability of the prospective contractor. The adequacy of the contractor's systems and procedures, and past performance record, are also addressed.

Pricing—Concerned with strategies for pricing products such as market-based pricing, or cost-based pricing.

Principles—The explanation of the methods and operation of the processes of management.

Privity of Contract—The legal relationship between two parties to the same contract. The buyer has "privity of contract" with the prime contractor. Therefore, the buyer's relationship with subcontractors is indirect in nature.

Procurement—Acquiring the goods and services supporting the missions of the organization including the development and maintenance of relationships with suppliers and internal customers.

Product/Service Planning—Defining the product or service that satisfies the needs of clients and customers.

Program Management—The process whereby a single leader and team are responsible for planning, organizing, coordinating, directing and controlling the combined efforts of participating and assigned personnel and organizations in accomplishment of program objectives. This special management approach provides centralized authority and responsibility for the management of a specific program.

Program Manager–Contracting Officer Relationship—The authority and responsibility of the program manager who is in charge of executing the program and the contracting officer, who has a fiduciary responsibility to ensure that all laws and regulations are complied with prior to signing the contract, requires a close working relationship.

Programming—The data structures and algorithms applied in programming solutions to problems.

Promotion—Publicizing the attributes of the product/service through media and personal contacts and presentations (e.g., technical articles or presentations, news releases, advertising, and sales calls).

Property Administration—The processes used by prime contractors to account for and manage all property, both real and personal. It includes facilities, material, special tooling, special test equipment, and agency-peculiar property.

Property Control System—Procedures that meet the requirements of government property clauses to control, protect, and maintain all government property.

Proposal Preparation—Activities and events required to submit an offer or quotation, usually in response to a customer request.

Protests—A written objection by an interested party to (1) a solicitation or other request by an agency for offers for a contract for the procurement of property or services, (2) the cancellation of the solicitation or other request, (3) an award or proposed award of the contract, or (4) a termination or cancellation of an award of the contract, if the written objection contains an allegation that the termination or cancellation is based in whole or in part on improprieties concerning the award of the contract.

R&D Contract—A contract for basic research (directed toward improving or expanding new scientific discoveries, technologies, materials, processes, or techniques), or development (directed production of, or improvements in, useful products to meet specific performance requirements through the systematic application of scientific knowledge).

Records and Reports—Procedures to maintain official records of government property and periodic reports required in accordance with contract clauses.

Records Retention—After contract closeout is completed, FAR 4.805 establishes retention periods for contract files. The record retention requirements apply to both prime contracts and subcontracts. Contractors must make books, records, documents, and other supporting evidence available to the comptroller general and contracting agencies for a certain period after final payment. The calculation of a retention period starts at the end of the contractor's fiscal year in which an entry is made that charges a cost to a government contract.

Request for Information (RFI)—Tool used for gathering information from independent vendors for the purpose of determining availability of products and services and gathering market information on capabilities to perform.

Request for Proposals (RFPs)—Solicitation document used in other-than-sealed-bid procurements. RFPs are used in negotiated procurements to communicate government requirements to prospective contractors and to solicit proposals from them.

Request for Quotations (RFQs)—Solicitation document used in other-than-sealed-bids procurements. Because an RFQ is merely a request for information, quotes submitted in response to it are not offers and consequently may not be accepted by the government to form a binding contract.

Request for Technical Proposals (RFTPs)—A solicitation document used in two-step sealed bidding. Normally in letter form, it asks only for technical information; price and cost breakdowns are forbidden.

Requirements Contract—Provides for filling all actual purchase requirements of designated government activities for supplies or services during a specified contract period, with deliveries or performance to be scheduled by placing orders with the contractor.

Research and Development (R&D)—Effort that constitutes either research or development or both.

Revenue Recognition—The process of formally recording or incorporating a revenue item in the accounts and financial statements of an entity. The revenue recognition principle provides that revenue is recognized when (1) it is realized or realizable and (2) it is earned. Revenues are realized when goods and services are exchanged for cash or claims to cash (receivables). Revenues are realizable when assets received in exchange are readily convertible to known amounts of cash or claims to cash. Revenues are earned when the entity has substantially accomplished what it must do to be entitled to the benefits represented by the revenues; that is, when the earnings process is complete or virtually complete.

Risk Management—The process for identification, analysis, and treatment of loss exposure, as well as the administration of techniques to accomplish the goal of minimizing potential financial loss from such exposure.

Royalties—Any costs or charges in the nature of royalties, license fees, patent or license amortization costs, or the like that are paid for the use of or for rights in patents and patent applications in connection with performing a contract or subcontract.

Sealed Bidding—A method involving the unrestricted solicitation of bids, a public opening, and award of a contract to the lowest responsive and responsible bidder.

Seat Management (SEAT)—A customer-selected set of desktop and networking functions that may include contractor-provided personal computers and network hardware, desktop and network software, the management of the hardware and software assets, help desk, training, and the maintenance of the hardware and software.

Service Contracts—Contracts that directly engage the time and effort of a contractor whose primary purpose is to perform an identifiable task rather than furnish an end item of supply.

Simplified Acquisitions—Methods for entering into contracts without elaborate and formal solicitation techniques (i.e., invitation for bids [IFB] and request for proposals [RFPs]). Restricted to purchases under a low dollar threshold.

Small and Disadvantaged Business Concerns—A small business that is owned (at least 51 percent) by members of socially and economically disadvantaged groups (i.e., groups that have been subjected to racial or ethnic prejudice of cultural bias).

Small Business—A small business is one that is independently owned and operated, and is not dominant in its field; a business concern meeting government size standards for its particular industry type.

Small Business Innovation Research (SBIR)—The SBIR Program is a highly competitive three-phase award system that provides qualified small business concerns with opportunities to propose innovative ideas that meet the specific research and development (R&D) needs of the federal government. Federal agencies that have R&D budgets in excess of $100 million must set aside a fixed percentage of their budgets strictly for small businesses.

Socioeconomic Programs—Programs designed to benefit particular groups. They represent a multitude of program interests and objectives unrelated to procurement objectives. Some examples of these are preferences for small business and for U.S. products, required sources for specific items, and minimum labor pay levels mandated for contractors.

Sole-Source Negotiations—The process for entering into or modifying a contract after soliciting and negotiating with only one source.

Source Selection—The process wherein the requirements, facts, recommendations, and policies relevant to an award decision in a competitive procurement of a system/project are examined and the decision made.

Source-Selection Board—Any board, team, council, or other group that evaluates bids or proposals for the purpose of selecting a contract/contractor.

Source-Selection Plan—The document that describes the selection criteria, the process, and the organization to be used in evaluating proposals for competitively awarded contracts.

Specialized Knowledge Areas—Those areas that require additional specialized knowledge that is over and above the knowledge and intelligence of a person of ordinary experience.

Specifications—A description of the technical requirements for a material, product, or service that includes the criteria for determining whether the requirements have been met. As used in the law relating to patents, manufacturing, and contracting contracts, a particular order or detailed statement, account description, or listing of various events.

Standards of Conduct—Refers to the ethical conduct of personnel involved in the acquisition of goods and services. Within the federal government, business shall be conducted in a manner above reproach and, except as authorized by law or regulation, with complete impartiality and without preferential treatment.

State and Local Government—The policies and procedures that govern the acquisition and sale of goods and services at the state and local government levels.

Statement of Work (SOW)—That portion of a contract describing the actual work to be done by means of specifications or other minimum requirements, quantities, performance or delivery date, and a statement of the requisite quality. SOW defines the scope of the overall contract in the case of task order contracts.

Statistics—Tools include descriptive statistics, probability theory, probability and sampling distribution, inference estimation, and hypothesis testing.

Stop-Work Order—Under a negotiated fixed-price supply, cost-reimbursement supply, R&D or service contract, a contract clause that permits the contracting officer to order the contractor to stop work if a work stoppage is required for reasons such as state-of-the-art advancements, production or engineering breakthroughs, or realignment of programs.

Strategic Sourcing—is a systematic corporate or institutional procurement process that continuously improves and re-evaluates the purchasing activities of an organization. While most organizations implement strategic sourcing for the purposes of saving money, other reasons include improving supplier performance and minimizing risk.

Strategy and Tactics—Specific methods used during negotiations to reach agreement.

Subcontract Management—A concept that addresses subcontracting issues and the buyer's role in ensuring successful prime contractor interaction with subcontractors in order to satisfy prime contract requirements.

Supplemental Agreements—Contract modifications that are accomplished by the mutual consent of the parties.

Supply Chain—Sum total of all functions, operations, and facilities that are involved in the procurement and delivery of goods to a customer; includes manufacturers, warehouses, transportation, distribution centers, retail outlets, and inventory at stages from raw materials to finished package that flows between and among facilities.

Supply-Chain Management—Management of flows between and among all stages and facilities in a supply chain to maximize profitability.

System Acquisition Process (life cycle)—The sequence of acquisition activities starting with the agency's reconciliation of its mission needs with its capabilities, priorities and resources, and extending through the introduction of a system into operational use or the otherwise successful achievement of program objectives.

Systems and Processes—The arrangement of things so connected or related to form a whole, generally involving a number of steps or operations.

Task-Order Contract—A services contract that does not procure or specify a firm quantity of services (other than a minimum or maximum quantity) and that provides for the issuance of orders for the performance of tasks during the period of the contract.

Teaming—Agreement among two or more prospective offerors to participate jointly in a business venture.

Technical/Management Proposal—That part of the offer that describes the seller's approach to meeting the buyer's requirement.

Telecommunications—Equipment used for such modes of transmission as telephone, data, facsimile, video, radio, and audio, and such corollary items as switches, wire, cable, access arrangements, and communications security facilities and related services.

Time-and-Materials Contract—Provides for acquiring supplies or services on the basis of direct lab or hours as specified fixed hourly rates that include wages, over-head, general and administrative expenses, profit, and materials cost, including, if appropriate, material handling costs as part of material costs.

Trademark—Distinctive mark of authenticity. Words, symbols, devices, or designs affixed to or placed on an article or its container to identify an article offered for sale. Also includes "service marks," which designate particular manners or modes of service delivery protected as intellectual property.

Transportation—Applying transportation and traffic management considerations in the acquisition of supplies and acquiring transportation-related services.

Transportation-Related Services—Procedures for the acquisition of related services such as stevedoring, storage, packing, marking, and ocean freight forwarding.

Two-Step Sealed Bidding—A combination of competitive procedures designed to obtain the benefits of sealed bidding when adequate specifications are not available. Step one consists of the request for the submission of technical proposals, evaluation, and discussion without pricing. Step two involves the submission of sealed-priced bids by those who submitted acceptable technical proposals in step one.

Uniform Commercial Code—Uniform law governing commercial transactions, developed by the National conference of Commissioners on Uniform State Laws and the American Law Institute, which has been adopted by all states in the U.S. except Louisiana, and is sometimes used to aid in the interpretation and enforcement of government subcontracts.

Unsolicited Proposal—A research or developmental proposal that is made by a prospective contractor without prior formal or informal solicitation from a purchasing activity.

Warranty—A promise or affirmation given by a seller to a buyer regarding the nature, usefulness, or condition of the supplies or performance of services furnished under the contract. Generally, a warranty's purpose is to delineate the rights and obligations for defective items and services, and to foster quality performance.

Woman-Owned, Native-American-Owned, Veteran-Owned Business—A firm that is at least 51 percent owned by a woman, Native American, or veteran. In the case of a publicly owned business, at least 51 percent of the stock must be controlled by a woman, Native American, or veteran, and its management and daily business must be controlled by one or more woman, Native Americans, or veterans.

Working Capital—The excess of current assets over current liabilities that represents a company's financial liquid resources to meet demands of the operating cycle.

The CMBOK Lexicon for Commercial Contracting

(For a more extensive listing of contracting terms, please refer to NCMA's *Desktop Guide to Basic Contracting Terms, Sixth Edition*)

Acceptance—The act by which an authorized buyer representative assents to ownership of existing and identified supplies, or approves specific services rendered, as partial or complete performance of a contract.

Accessibility—The availability of public conveyances, facilities, utilities, technologies, and other designated resources to all persons. In the United States, accessibility considerations are the purview of the Access Board, an independent federal agency devoted to accessibility for people with disabilities. The Access Board develops and maintains accessibility requirements for the built environment, transit vehicles, telecommunications equipment, and electronic and information technology; provides technical assistance and training on these guidelines and standards; and enforces accessibility standards for federally funded facilities.

Accounting—The principles and practices of systematically recording, presenting, and interpreting financial data.

Acquisition Methodology—Requesting or inviting offerors to submit offers, usually by issuing a solicitation. Solicitations consist of (1) a draft contract, and (2) provisions on preparing and submitting offers.

Acquisition Planning—Activities and events required for both buyers and sellers to prepare for, negotiate, and form a binding contractual arrangement.

Adequacy of Offer or Conformance to Requirements—Purchasing techniques that enable buyers to solicit input from multiple suppliers and create a solicitation document, taking the best from each. Accordingly, sellers are able to develop a compliance matrix that lists all solicitation and functional requirements, along with an assessment of the firm's competitive strengths and weaknesses.

Administrative Changes—Unilateral contract changes, in writing, that do not affect the substantive rights of the parties.

Agreements and Restrictions—Agreements between and among nations regarding international procurement. These include the General Agreement on Tariffs and Trade (GATT), the GATT Government Procurement Code, the North American Free Trade Agreement (NAFTA), as well as bilateral agreements that have been negotiated between and among nations.

Alternate Dispute Resolution (ADR)—Any procedure that is used, in lieu of litigation, to resolve issues in controversy, including but not limited to settlement negotiations, conciliation, facilitation, mediation, fact finding, mini-trials, and arbitration.

Applications Software—Software applications relevant to contract management, including enterprise resource planning (ERP), customer relationship management (CRM), supply chain automation, sales force automation, and electronic contract management (eCM).

Arbitration—The use of an impartial third party to whom the parties to an agreement refer their disputes for resolution. Some contracts contain provisions that provide for binding arbitration of unsettled grievances.

Architect and Design Services—Professional services of an architectural or engineering nature that are required to be performed or approved by a person licensed, registered, or certified to provide such services or are associated with research, planning, development, design, construction, alteration, or repair of real property, or other related professional services such as studies and surveys.
Architect and Engineer (A&E) Services and Construction.

Auditing—The examination and review of operations for compliance with corporate policies.

Authority—The sources from which S&L government entities derive empowerment to engage in procurement activities, and that set forth the framework, parameters, and extent of their empowerment. Such authority includes state statutes, state and local regulations, charters, local ordinances, and administrative resolutions, policies, or edicts.
Bid or No-Bid Decision—Determination made by seller's management regarding whether to submit an offer, usually in response to a customer request.

Bilateral/Notice—Termination of a contract by mutual consent. Typically initiated by one party by notice of the exercise of a contractual right to termination based on particular circumstances. Generally, both the circumstances permitting the termination and the process for termination are predetermined in the contract.

Break-even Analysis—A means of determining the number of goods or services that must be sold at a given price to generate sufficient revenue to cover costs.

Budgeting—The planning, scheduling, and budgeting of organizational expenses for the fiscal period.

Buyer–Seller Relationship—Encompasses more than just the procurement process, because relationships are developed throughout the supply chain. The buyer-seller relationship affects quality of materials and parts, customer satisfaction, and competitive advantages of both parties.

Capital Budgeting—The process of planning for the best selection and financing of long-term investment proposals, taking into account the time value of money.

Cardinal Change—Change that is not within the contract's general scope. When a contractor is faced with an out-of-scope change to its contract, it generally will not refuse the effort but, rather, will seek additional compensation. Generally, if the work performed is reasonably "within the contemplation of the parties when the contract was entered into," it is considered to be within the scope of the contract.

Cash Budgeting—A schedule of expected cash receipts and disbursements for a designated period. The primary reason for a cash budget is to forecast a company's future financing needs. A cash budget is also used to avoid either unnecessary idle cash or possible cash shortages. In the case of cash shortage, it indicates whether the shortage is temporary or permanent (i.e., whether short-term or long-term borrowing is needed).

Change Orders—Written orders signed by the buyer, authorized by contract clause, to modify contractual requirements within the scope of the contract.

Commodity Warehousing, Just in Time—The physical holding of raw materials and commodities units against the time of use. Although the storage of materials for use in the production process is basically the same as storing finished products, raw-materials storage and finished-goods storage differ in terms of the type of facility each requires, the value of the stored items, and product perishability.

Common Law—A body of law common to the whole population, produced primarily by the efforts of the judiciary to harmonize their decisions with precedent decisions and changes in law or regulation.

Competitive Bidding/Negotiation—A method of contracting involving a request for proposal that states the buyer's requirements and criteria for evaluation; submission of timely proposals by a maximum number of offerors; discussions with those offerors found to be within the competitive range; and award of a contract to the one offeror whose offer, price, and other consideration factors are most advantageous to the buyer.

Compliance System—Information technology system that translates contract requirements (such as pricing, warranty, service requirements, and product changes) into executable instructions to internal systems. It includes connectivity to enterprise resource planning (ERP) tools and other customer-resource management tools that the organization uses to communicate internally and externally.

Conflict of Interest—Concerns officials and fiduciaries and their relationship to matters of private interest or gain to themselves. Ethical problems connected therewith are covered by statutes in most jurisdictions and by federal statutes on the federal level. A conflict of interest arises when an employee's personal or financial interest conflicts or appears to conflict with his or her official responsibility.

Construction Contracts—Construction means alteration of the landscape, assembly and fitting out of structures, installation of furnishings and fixtures, decoration, or repair of real property.

Constructive Changes—Verbal or written acts or omissions by employees or agents of the buyer that are of such a nature that they have the same effect as written change orders.

Consulting—The process of providing subject matter expertise to one who needs such knowledge. The knowledge may be provided in the form of either verbal or written advice. In addition, the consulting may provide the customer with some form of deliverable (e.g., written report, project plans, or—in the case of information technology consulting—a program that addresses a particular need of the client). Consulting services may be paid for in a number of ways. Two common means for determining a consultant's fee are (1) time and materials, and (2) fixed fee.

Contract Administration—The management of issues that arise during the performance of a contract.

Contract Changes or Modifications—Include any written alteration in the specification, delivery point, rate of delivery, contract period, price, quantity, or other provision of an existing contract, accomplished in accordance with a contract clause; may be unilateral or bilateral.

Contract Closeout—The process of declaring that the obligations under a contract have been satisfied and that a procurement file is both physically and administratively complete.

Contract Financing—Methods for obtaining the funds necessary for performing the contract, including payment methods, loan guarantees, advanced payments, progress payments, and contract funding.

Contract Formation—The elements of offer, acceptance, mutuality of consideration, competent parties, legal subject matter, and mutuality of agreement.

Contract Performance or Quality Assurance—A planned and systematic pattern of actions necessary to provide adequate confidence that material, data, supplies, and services conform to established technical requirements, and to achieve satisfactory performance.

Contract Principles—Fundamentals of contract management that all contracting professionals must comprehend.

Contract Structures—Specific business arrangements that govern the buyer-seller relationship; types of promises or sets of promises that courts will enforce.

Contract Termination—Actions taken pursuant to a contract clause in which either party exercises a legal right to terminate the contract.

Cooperative Agreement—Legal instrument used principally for transferring money, property, or services between or among the parties to accomplish a specific purpose of support or stimulation where substantial involvement and cooperation are expected between or among the parties.

Copyright—Royalty-free, nonexclusive, and irrevocable license to reproduce, translate, publish, use, and dispose of written or recorded material and to authorize others to do so.

Corporate Responsibility and Personal Conduct—Laws and standards governing both corporate and individual behavior, including standards of ethics and conduct, social responsibility, law, regulation, and public policy.

Cost—Includes the accounting system design for recording, accumulating, and reporting costs for specific products and services.

Cost-Based Contracts—Implementation of cost-based methods in commercial contracts, including time-and-materials contracts, indexed pricing, and any other arrangements subject to audit or independent verification.

Cost or Price Analysis—Factors to be considered in determining pricing and financial impact of a procurement, including commodity markets, price lists, price quotations, negotiated pricing, input costs, transaction costs, relational costs, and landed costs.

Customer Service—Interaction with the designated end users of the contracted products and services; includes actions to resolve customer complaints and facilitates use of products or access to services.

Data Management—Use of commercially available software tools to manage contract information, including repositories for contract documents, reporting systems, contracting process management, and portfolio management.

Database Management—Includes data modeling, query languages, and transaction processing.

Debriefing—An explanation given by the buyer to an offeror detailing the reasons the offeror's proposal was unsuccessful.

Defining Requirements—Process for defining and expressing requirements that meet the needs of the purchaser and representing those needs through measurable criteria.

Delays—Late delivery of products and services and implications to contract management; includes time requirements of obligations, impracticability, and other standards of delivery performance.

Design or Build—A method of construction contracting that combines the architectural, engineering, and construction services required for a project into a single agreement.

Discussions—Any oral or written communications between the buyer and the seller, other than communications conducted for the purpose of minor clarification, that (1) involve information essential for determining the acceptability of the proposals or (2) provide the offeror an opportunity to revise or modify its proposal.

Disputes—Disagreements between the parties regarding their rights under a contract.

Diversity—Multicultural issues in the conduct of business and trade that include cultural diversity, workplace diversity, and supplier diversity.

Documenting Requirements—Process for documenting requirements, validating requirements, and communicating to prospective suppliers; includes make-or-buy decisions and creation of solicitations.

Economics—The study of the problems arising when goods and services are scarce, relative to human desires for those goods and services.

Electronic Commerce—Marketing goods and services over the Internet by exchanging information between buyers and sellers, while in the process minimizing paperwork and simplifying payment procedures; includes both business-to-consumer (B2C) and business-to-business (B2B) transactions.

Electronic, Web-based, Clickware—Contracts for sale accomplished electronically using the Internet, where the offer is displayed via an Internet site and the acceptance is accomplished electronically. Terms are sellers' terms associated with the Web site, and obligations of the parties with regard to disclosure of terms and acceptance of liabilities are governed by law and regulation.

Employment Agreement—A contract by which one person, called the employer, engages another person, called the employee, to do something for the benefit of the employer or a third person for which the employee receives compensation. The contract may be oral or written.

Enterprise Resource Planning (ERP) System—Any software system designed to support and automate the business processes of medium and large businesses. This may include manufacturing, distribution, personnel, project management, payroll, and financials. ERP systems are accounting-oriented information systems for identifying and planning the enterprise-wide resources needed to take, make, distribute, and account for customer orders.

E-Procurement—Use of IT and systems in the procurement process. Focuses on the four basic types of e-commerce business models used in procurement: sell-side system, electronic marketplace, buy-side system, and on-line trading community.

Ethics—Of or relating to moral action, conduct, motive, or character, as ethical emotion; treating of moral feelings, duties, or conduct; containing precepts of morality; moral, professionally right, or benefiting; conforming to professional standards of conduct.

Evaluation Factors—Criteria used to evaluate offers that may include technical capability, price, past performance, and other factors. Evaluation may involve trade-offs, discretion, and examination of the products offered.

Evaluation Process—The activities and procedures used to evaluate offers against established selection criteria in accordance with the source selection plan.

Export Controls—The comprehensive set of controls that have been established to protect national security interests and foster foreign policy initiatives. The Department of State monitors and controls the export and re-export of goods and services in accordance with the *International Traffic in Arms Regulations (ITAR)*, and the Department of Commerce *Export Administration Regulation (EAR)* enforces the Export Administration Act.

Export Financing—Financing of international transactions in the exporting or importing of products and services. Addresses factors such as transit times, customs regulations, banking rules and regulations, buyer and seller credit, exchange rates, and political risk.

Fair Value—Examines product or service features that enhance profits for the final product and the ability of a commercial firm to maintain a competitive advantage in the marketplace.

Finance—Managing the money matters of the organization.

Financial Analysis—Includes international financial analysis, return on assets, return or investment, asset turnover, and variance analysis.

Financial Reporting—Includes financial statements, sales forecasting, planning, and control.

Forecasting—An estimate of financial position, results of operations, and changes in cash flows for one or more future periods based on a set of assumptions representing the most probable outcomes. If the assumptions are not necessarily the most likely outcomes, the estimate is called a "projection."

Formal and Informal Contracts—A formal contract is one to which the law gives special effect because of the form used in creating it (e.g., negotiable instruments). An informal contract is one for which the law does not require a particular set of formalities.

Forums—Administrative and judicial bodies that adjudicate disputes.

Framework Pricing Arrangement—A contract that is definitive in all respects except pricing. The agreement or contract specifies a predetermined index, formula, or algorithm (i.e., the "framework") for the calculation of price at the point of sale.

Fraud—Unethical conduct in the creation of the contract. Includes offer and acceptance: conduct that communicates a promise on the part of one party and a manifestation to the terms of the offer by the other party. Conduct of both parties represents capacity to contract, good faith dealings (honesty in fact and reasonable standard of fair dealing), and legality of purpose. Includes apparent authority: the authority that, although not actually granted, the principal knowingly permits an agent to exercise or the principal holds the agent out as possessing.

Free on Board (FOB)—Domestic transportation of goods in the United States, including documentation necessary to govern, direct control of, and provide information about a shipment; includes bill of lading, freight bills, claims, and FOB terms of sale.

Gap Fillers—Interim agreements that define the rights and obligations of the parties and establish the basis for the conduct of business prior to the establishment of a long-term contractual relationship. Includes memorandums of understanding (MOUs), letter contracts, teaming agreements, and other short-term agreements.

General and Administrative (G&A)—A subcategory of overhead; includes costs necessary for overall management and operations but not directly associated with a specific cost objective or business segment. Typical G&A costs include sales staff salaries, insurance, executive compensation, and central office expenses.

General Business—Includes those portions of other disciplines relevant to contract management (see also 1.5 and subsequent, General Business).

Generally Accepted Accounting Principles (GAAP)—A technical term encompassing conventions, rules, and procedures of accounting that are "generally accepted" and have "substantial authoritative support." The GAAP have been developed by agreement on the basis of experience, reason, custom, usage, and, to a certain extent, practical necessity rather than from a formal set of theories.

Global Issues—A corporate framework for conducting international business, including evaluation of objectives, strengths, and weaknesses as well as development of strategies for product development and marketing.

Grant—Legal instrument for transferring money, property, or services to the recipient to accomplish a specific purpose of support or stimulation where there is no substantial involvement between the grantor and the recipient during performance.

Implied, Express, Quasi Contracts—An implied contract (sometimes called "implied in fact") is one in which the terms of the contract are wholly or partly inferred from conduct or surrounding circumstance. An express contract is one in which the terms of the contract are stated in words, either written or spoken. Quasi contracts (sometimes called "implied in law") are obligations imposed by law to prevent the unjust enrichment of one person at another's expense.

Improper Practices—A broad range of activities forbidden or limited by the law or regulation with regard to the award and performance of contracts.

INCO Terms—Internationally recognized terms of sale that define responsibilities of both the buyer and the seller in any international transaction, codified into 13 distinct categories.

Indemnification—Contract provision whereby one party engages to secure another against an anticipated loss resulting from an act or forbearance on the part of one of the parties or some third party.

Independent Research and Development (IR&D)—Effort that is neither sponsored by a grant nor required in performing a contract and which falls within any of the following four areas: (1) basic research, (2) applied research, (3) development, and (4) systems and other concept formulation studies that are pursued independently by an organization to further a specific business purpose.

Information Management—Includes activities associated with applications of information science to the practical aspects of specifying, designing, implementing, and managing information systems.

Information Science—Focuses on the technical, managerial, and policy issues associated with computer-based information systems in modern organizations.

Information Technology (IT)—Includes the acquisition of IT hardware, software, telecommunications, and related resources.

Inspection—The examination (including testing) of supplies and services (including, when appropriate, raw materials, components, and intermediate assemblies) to determine whether the supplies and services conform to the contract requirements.

Insurance Law—Law governing the transfer of risk from one person (either the insured person or the policy owner) to another (the insurer). This transfer of risk is accomplished by a two-party contract called an "insurance policy."

Intellectual Property—Property that results from the fruits of mental labor.

Intergovernmental Relations—Cooperative activities among governments, including various forms of intergovernmental cooperative purchasing, joint or shared use of facilities and supplies, and procurements made by one government from another.

International Contracting—Includes the policies and procedures that govern the acquisition and sale of goods and services on a global basis.

International Organization for Standardization (ISO) Standards—The families of standards consisting of standards and guidelines relating to management systems and related supporting standards on terminology and specific tools, such as auditing (the process of checking that the management system conforms to the standard).

Invitation for Bids (IFBs)—A solicitation used in the sealed-bid method of procurement.

Labor Laws—Policies and procedures for implementing labor laws, including the National Labor Relations Act (NLRA) and state statutes in the United States.

Laws and Regulations—The statutes and regulations that provide the legal and regulatory framework for the purchase or sale of goods and services.

Leases—Rental agreements in which the lessor conveys to the lessee the right to use the lessor's personal or real property, usually in exchange for a payment of money.

Liability Costs, Warranty, Service Life, Protection, Risk—Remedies and recourse in resolution of contract performance issues, including limitations of remedies, liquidated damages, limitation of liability, breach, and damages.

Logistics—Inventory management, transportation and traffic, and distribution supporting the product or service mission of the organization.

Major Systems—A combination of elements that function together to produce the capabilities required to fulfill a mission need, including hardware, equipment, software, or any combination of these.

Management—The art and science of the processes of planning, organizing, staffing, directing, and controlling the affairs of the organization.

Market Price—The exchange value of a good or service, calculated with due consideration to market conditions, legal constraints, competitive pressures, and changes in market factors.

Market Research—The process used for collecting and analyzing information about the entire market sufficient to determine the most suitable approach to acquiring, distributing, and supporting supplies and services.

Market Strategy—The action plan of how a company will sell its services or products. The strategy must consider the company's business environment, its abilities and competencies, the desires of top management, and overall mission objectives. Market strategy consists of four basic concepts: market segmentation, market positioning, market entry, and marketing mix.

Marketing—The activity that directs the flow of goods and services from the producer to the user.

Master Agreements—Business arrangements in which the parties determine the underlying commercial arrangement governing the relationship (e.g., terms and conditions) but defer specific negotiation of elements of the contract to specific events or transactions (e.g., price).

Modes of Transportation—Means of moving freight traffic using transportation methods such as bills of lading, parcel post, bus service, air cargo, rail freight, carload and less than carload, motor freight, freight forwarder, and pipeline.

NCMA CMBOK—Definitive descriptions of the elements making up the body of professional knowledge that applies to contract management. The following terms comprise some of the terminology for the commercial contract manager. Some of the terms are common to those just outlined for the federal contract manager and some are specific to the commercial contract manager. Where definitions included in the federal lexicon are different, the corresponding federal definition is noted as "see also."

Negotiation—The process by which two or more competent parties reach an agreement to buy or sell products or services. Contract negotiations may be conducted formally or informally and may involve many people or just two—a representative for the buyer and a representative for the seller. Contract negotiation may take a few minutes or may involve lengthy discussions.

Negotiation Objectives—Strategies that provide the overall framework that will guide the conduct of the negotiation; includes both win–lose and win–win strategies and all tactics and counter-tactics necessary to achieve the desired result.

Network Systems—Systems that transmit any combination of voice, video, and/or data between users. The network includes the network operating system in the client and server machines, the cables connecting them, and all the supporting hardware in between, such as bridges, routers, and switches. In wireless systems, antennas and towers are also part of the network. In general, the network is a collection of terminals, computers, servers, and components that function in relation to each other to allow for the easy flow of data and use of resources among the interrelated entities.

Nondisclosure Agreement—A legally binding document setting forth the conditions under which proprietary information is offered and received between the parties.

Operations Management—Includes the concepts, techniques, and practices used in managing the operations of an organization.

Organization—The administrative and personnel structure that reflects the organizational patterns, procurement authority, and scope of activities of its various elements. It may include boards, commissions, or committees and may reflect a delegation's exemptions, as well as full or limited authority to act.

Organizational Behavior—Human behavior as it influences organizational efficiency and effectiveness.

Organizational Communication—Focuses on the processes of communication ranging from that between two persons to that of the total organization.)

Organizational or Industrial Marketing—The activity of marketing directed toward organizations rather than individual consumers; includes research, product planning and development, distribution, promotion, and pricing.

Outsourcing—A specialized form of consulting. When a client elects to outsource, the client generally turns a specific task over to a consultant. In the computer industry, this task might be to run a data center. The client is concerned with "what" is outsourced (in this example, running a data center). The client is typically not concerned with "how" the operation occurs. The client is hiring the consultant to provide this service based on the consultant's expertise in the following areas: process, people, and technology to perform the outsourced task. This type of service is normally contracted for on a fixed-fee basis, in which the client pays a flat fee per month for a given service. Therefore, the vast majority of the financial risk is shifted from the client to the consultant. If the consultant can effectively and efficiently provide the service, the consultant will realize a profit. Conversely, if the consultant is either ineffective or inefficient, the consultant still has to deliver the contracted deliverable for service—however, the consultant will be doing so at the consultant's loss.

Outsourcing of Contract Management—Contract administration and other business processes through long-term agreements; includes business process outsourcing (BPO) of functional responsibilities for human resources, finance and accounting, procurement, and information technology (IT).

Overhead—Any necessary cost not directly associated with the production or sale of identifiable goods or services.

Ownership, Royalties, Escrow Agreement—Legal title or right to something. Mere possession is not ownership. With ownership comes the potential of royalties for use. Royalties and rights delegated (as to an individual or corporation) by a sovereign party, including a share of the profit or product reserved by the grantor. Also includes payments made to an author or composer for each copy of a work sold or to an inventor for each article sold under a patent. Owner: may also escrow assets, creating an instrument and especially a deed of money or property held by a third party to be turned over to the grantee and become effective only upon the fulfillment of some condition; a fund or deposit designed to serve as an escrow. Includes source code escrow agreements, which allow the licensee to obtain access to the software's source code under certain circumstances, as when the licensor goes out of business or fails to make required modifications to the software.

Past Performance—Evaluating how well offerors performed in the past in the performance of similar contracts.

Patent—Government grant of exclusive rights to an inventor that prohibits others from making, using, or selling an invention.

Payment—Fulfillment of financial obligations of the contract; includes consideration, exchanges, compromise and release of claims, part-payment, and forbearance.

Performance-Based Contract—A contract that is structured around the purpose of the work to be performed as opposed to either the manner in which the work is to be performed or a broad statement of work (SOW).

Point of Sale Transactions—Business arrangements in which the entire business arrangement between the parties is executed in a single event.

Pre-award Process: Buyer—Process by which buyers develop a comprehensive plan for fulfilling requirements for products or services in a timely manner at a reasonable price; includes developing an overall strategy for the purchase, which is accomplished through market research, strategy development, initiating the procurement, and selecting a suppler.

Pre-award Process: Seller—Process by which sellers develop and execute a strategy for obtaining the award of a contract, including market strategies, pricing strategies, and responding to the procurement.

Prequalification—Buyer's announcement of interest, including criteria for selecting proposals and soliciting the participation of all offerors capable of meeting requirements.

Pricing—Strategies for pricing products such as market-based pricing or cost-based pricing.

Process and Results Management—Joint buyer-seller actions taken to successfully perform and administer a contractual agreement, including effective change management and timely contract closeout. It also includes maintaining open and effective communication, timely delivery of quality products and services, responsive corrective actions to problems, compliance with all agreed-on terms, and management of conditions and effective changes.

Procurement—Acquiring the goods and services supporting the missions of the organization includes developing and maintaining relationships with suppliers and internal customers.

Production Planning and Control—Coordination of product supply with product demand. The manufacturer must forecast customer demand and provide the finished product supply either from available inventory or by producing additional product.

Product or Service Planning—The process of defining the product or service that satisfies the needs of clients and customers.

Program Manager–Contracting Officer Relationship—The respective authority and responsibilities of the program manager, who is in overall charge of executing a program or project, and the contracts manager, who has fiduciary responsibilities for the negotiation and formation of the contract and for compliance and conformance to contractual obligations.

Program Management—The process whereby a single leader and team are responsible for planning, organizing, coordinating, directing, and controlling the combined efforts of participating and assigned personnel and organizations in accomplishment of program objectives. It is a special management approach used to provide centralized authority and responsibility for the management of a specific program.

Programming—Concerned with data structures and algorithms applied in programming solutions to problems.

Promotion—The process of publicizing the attributes of the product or service through media and personal contacts and presentations (e.g., technical articles and presentations, news releases, advertising, and sales calls).

Proposal Preparation—Activities and events required to submit an offer or quotation, usually in response to a customer request.

Protest—A written objection by an interested party to (1) a solicitation or other request by an agency for offers for a contract for the procurement of property or services, (2) the cancellation of the solicitation or other request, (3) an award or proposed award of the contract, or (4) a termination or cancellation of an award of the contract, if the written objection contains an allegation that the termination or cancellation is based in whole or in part on improprieties concerning the award of the contract.

R&D Contract—A contract for basic research (directed toward improving or expanding new scientific discoveries, technologies, materials, processes, or techniques), or development (directed production of, or improvements in, useful products to meet specific performance requirements through the systematic application of scientific knowledge).

Records Retention—Controls over the creation, maintenance, and use of records relating to a contract; includes determining a period of active access and procedures for disposition of records at the end of that period, either by destruction or by retirement to archives.

Relationship Management—Actions of the contracting parties to mutually resolve disagreements about the correct interpretation of terms and conditions without recourse to litigations or arbitration.

Reporting—Contractually required reports provided by the seller during contract fulfillment to observe performance, collect information, and measure actual contract achievement.

Request for Proposals (RFPs)—A solicitation document used in negotiated procurements to communicate the buyer's requirements to prospective contractors and to solicit proposals.

Request for Quotations (RFQs)—A solicitation document used to request information; quotes submitted in response are typically counteroffers on seller's terms.

Request for Technical Proposal (RFTP)—A solicitation document used in multiple-step bidding. Asks for technical information only; price and cost breakdowns are either budgetary or omitted at the RFTP stage. Used to pre-qualify bidders.

Research and Development (R&D)—Effort that constitutes either research or development or both.

Revenue Recognition—The process of formally recording or incorporating a revenue item in the accounts and financial statements of an entity. The revenue recognition principle provides that revenue is recognized when (1) it is realized or realizable, and (2) it is earned. Revenues are realized when goods and services are exchanged for cash or claims to cash (receivables). Revenues are realizable when assets received in exchange are readily convertible to known amounts of cash or claims to cash. Revenues are earned when the entity has substantially accomplished what it must do to be entitled to the benefits represented by the revenues; that is, when the earnings process is complete or virtually complete.

Risk Analysis—Management of factors that create the possibility of loss or injury in the performance of a contract; includes all activities necessary to identify, analyze, plan, track, or control risk management activities. It also includes communication of risks and risk management internally and externally.

Risk Management—The methodical process used to enhance opportunities and reduce risks by identifying potential opportunities and risks, assessing associated probabilities of occurrence and impacts, and determining courses of action.

Sales Contracts—Business arrangements in which all elements of the transaction are determined and defined between the parties at the time of contract formation, including mutual assent, exchange of consideration, capacity to contract, and legal purpose.

Seat Management (SEAT)—An integrated approach to delivering end user computing services under a single offering. It is a method of coordinating all of the workstations in an enterprise network and includes the installation, operation, and maintenance of hardware and software at each workstation. It offers desktop computers, servers, peripherals, networking, and support services for general purpose and scientific and engineering environments. Seat management is typically provided on a fixed monthly fee per user or "per seat" basis for the equipment and services selected. A "seat" is a workstation or terminal that can be operated by one user at a time. The service also creates efficiencies and mitigates risk through standardization and unification of procedures.

Service Contracts—Contracts that directly engage the time and effort of a contractor whose primary purpose is to perform identifiable tasks rather than furnish an end item of supply.

Shop Rights—The right of an employer to use, without payment of royalties, an invention conceived by an employee in the course of employment or through the use of the employer's facilities, the employee not having been hired to perform such work.

Single-Source Negotiation—Negotiation with a single provider, because either (1) the provider is the sole supplier of the product or service or (2) the relationship with the provider is of strategic importance, based on long-term relationships, and built on mutual trust.

Socioeconomic Programs—Institutional and government programs designed to benefit particular groups that include diversity, accessibility, and other social impacts to the business world.

Source Selection—The process wherein the requirements, facts, recommendations, and policies relevant to an award decision in a competitive procurement of a system or project are examined and the decision made.

Source-Selection Team—Multidisciplinary team responsible for evaluating offers and identifying the most advantageous offer through proposal evaluation, to include an assessment of both the proposal and the offeror's ability to successfully accomplish the prospective contract.

Specialized Knowledge Areas—Additional professional skills that are necessary for contracts managers to either (1) perform efficiently and effectively in a specific industry or work environment (e.g., construction), or (2) interact productively with other specialized professionals (e.g., finance).

Specialized, Long Lead Items—Lead time management of critical materials and deliverables. Procurement lead time starts when a material requirement is identified and spans the time until a significant portion of the material is delivered. Procurement lead time has two components: administrative lead time and production lead time. Administrative lead time begins with the identification of a material requirement and continues until a contract is awarded for the creation of the material. Production lead time is the time from contract award until material delivery. Lead time risk, therefore, is the program impact associated with the failure of material to arrive when required.

Standards of Conduct—Refer to the ethical conduct of personnel involved in the purchase or sale of goods and services. Include personal conduct and also compliance with laws, regulations, and corporate standards.

State and Local Government (S&L)—Includes the policies and procedures that govern the purchase and sale of goods and services at the state and local government levels.

State Differences and Jurisdictional Issues—Differences and distinctions between state laws and factors in determining appropriate law and regulation governing business dealings, including law of the forum, conflicts of laws, domicile, and center of gravity.

Statistics—Tools that include descriptive statistics, probability theory, probability and sampling distribution, inference estimation, and hypothesis testing.

Stop-Work Order—Instruction served on the seller by the buyer requiring that the seller cease to perform the contract and take alternative steps to limit the risk and liabilities of the parties. This is usually governed by predetermined protocols set forth in the contract. In the event of such termination, the contractor must immediately stop all work and immediately cause any and all of its suppliers and subcontractors to stop all work.

Strategy and Tactics—Specific methods used during negotiations to reach agreement.

Subcontract Management—This includes subcontracting issues and the buyer's role in ensuring successful prime contractor interaction with subcontractors to satisfy prime contract requirements.

Supplemental Agreements—Contract modifications that are accomplished by the mutual consent of the parties.

Supplier Goods, Services—Management of any contract, agreement, or purchase order (and any preliminary contractual instrument other than a prime contract) calling for the performance of any work or the making or furnishing of any material required for the performance of a prime contract; includes managing the purchase of supplies that are consumed in use or become incorporated in other property, thus losing their identity.

Supply-Chain Function—Management of the flow and storage of materials (raw materials, semi-finished goods, and finished products) from vendor sources through to the ultimate customer. It includes both inbound logistics (materials management and procurement) and outbound logistics (customer service and channels of distribution).

Supply Chain—Sum total of all functions, operations, and facilities that are involved in the procurement and delivery of goods to a customer; includes manufacturers, warehouses, transportation, distribution centers, retail outlets, and inventory at stages from raw materials to finished package that flows between and among facilities.

Supply-Chain Management—Management of flows between and among all stages and facilities in a supply chain to maximize profitability.

System Acquisition Process (life cycle)—The sequence of acquisition activities starting from the agency's reconciliation of its mission needs with its capabilities, priorities and resources, and extending through the introduction of a system into operational use or the otherwise successful achievement of program objectives.

Systems and Processes—The arrangement of things so connected or related as to form a whole, generally involving a number of steps or operations.

Teaming—Agreement among two or more prospective offerors to participate jointly in a business venture.

Technical or Management Proposal—The part of the offer that describes the seller's approach to meeting the buyer's requirement.

Telecommunications—The branch of electrical engineering concerned with the technology of electronic communication at a distance. It includes systems of hardware and software used to carry voice, video, and/or data; includes telephone wires, satellite signals, cellular links, coaxial cable, and so on, and related devices.

Time-and-Materials—One common way to pay for consulting services. When using this method of calculating payment, the consultant is paid for any time he devotes to the needs of a client. The consultant is typically paid for each hour he logs to a client's project. In addition, the consultant is generally paid for any expenses he incurs on behalf of the client (e.g., travel, engagement-specific tools or materials, copy services, etc.). All of the aforementioned items may either be limited or expanded (e.g., authorization of air travel in first class versus coach) by the specific contract entered into between the consultant and the client. This form of consulting places virtually all the risk on the client (as opposed to the consultant). That is to say, the client typically has a budget for a specific task. The client is betting that the consultant can complete the assigned work within that budget. However, the consultant is typically under no such obligation, and the bill for the consultant's time may well exceed the client's projected budget.

Trade—Law in the United States, including the Robinson-Patman Act, unfair trade laws, fair-trade laws, and other legal and regulatory restrictions on the conduct of business, especially with respect to pricing.

Trade Secrets—Any information, process, or procedure used in business that may give the owner some advantage over its competitors.

Trademark—Words, symbols, devices, or designs affixed to or placed on an article or its container to identify an article offered for sale. Also includes "service marks," which designate particular manners or modes of service delivery protected as intellectual property.

Transportation—Application of transportation and traffic management considerations in the acquisition of supplies and transportation-related services.

Transportation-Related Services—Procedures for the acquisition of related services such as stevedoring, storage, packing, marking, and ocean freight forwarding.

Uniform Commercial Code—The uniform law in the United States governing commercial transactions, developed by the National Conference of Commissioners on Uniform States Laws and the American Law Institute. It has been adopted by all states in the United States except Louisiana and is sometimes used to aid in the interpretation and enforcement of government subcontracts.

Unilateral and Bilateral Contracts—A unilateral contract is one in which only one party (promissor) makes a promise; in contrast, a bilateral contract is one in which both parties make promises.

Unilateral or Nonperformance—Termination of a contract by one of the parties. Right to terminate, notice required, and procedures for termination are typically specified in the contract. Most commonly, this is available as a remedy for nonperformance by the seller or failure to pay by the buyer.

Unsolicited Proposal—A proposal that is made by a prospective seller without prior formal or informal solicitation from the buyer.

U.S. Securities and Exchange Commission (SEC)—The SEC regulates securities markets. The SEC requires public companies to disclose meaningful financial and other information to the public, which provides a common pool of knowledge for all investors. The SEC also oversees other key participants in the securities world, including stock exchanges, broker–dealers, investment advisors, mutual funds, and public utility holding companies. The SEC is concerned primarily with promoting disclosure of important information, enforcing the securities laws, and protecting investors who interact with these various organizations and individuals. As a regulatory agency, the SEC frequently exercises its enforcement authority. Each year the SEC brings between 400 and 500 civil enforcement actions against individuals and companies that break the securities laws. Typical infractions include insider trading, accounting fraud, and providing false or misleading information about securities and the companies that issue them.

Use of Trade or Course of Dealing—Any practice or method of dealing having such regularity of observance in a place, vocation, or trade as to justify an expectation that it will be observed with respect to the transaction in question; a pattern of prior business transactions that can establish a background for the interpretation of the immediate transaction.

Warranty—A promise or affirmation given by a seller to a buyer regarding the nature, usefulness, or condition of the supplies or performance of services furnished under the contract. Generally, a warranty's purpose is to delineate the rights and obligations for defective items and services, and to foster quality performance.

Working Capital—The excess of current assets over current liabilities that represents a company's financial liquid resources to meet demands of the operating cycle.

bibliography

American Intellectual Property Association. *An Overview of Intellectual Property*. Arlington, VA: American Intellectual Property Association, 1995.

Campbell, Kelsey, editor, and Regina Mickells Bova, compiler. *Desktop Guide to Basic Contracting Terms 5th ed.* Vienna, VA: NCMA, 1994.

Diamond, Jay and Gerald Pintel. *Principles of Marketing*. Englewood Cliffs, NJ: Prentice-Hall, 1986.

Drucker, Peter F. *An Introductory View of Management*. NY: Harper and Row, 1977.

Harris, Seymore, and Richard Gill. *Vocabulary for Economics*. Flushing, NY: Data-Guide, Inc.

Nash, Jr. Ralph C., and Steven L. Schooner. *The Government Contracts Reference Book*. Washington, DC: The George Washington University, 1992.

Sikula, Andrew F. *Management and Administration*. Columbus: Charles E. Merrill Publishing Co., 1973.

Thornton, Connie L. "Contracting: A Systematic Body of Knowledge." Masters Degree Thesis, Naval Postgraduate School, 1987.

U.S. Department of Defense. *Department of Defense FAR Supplement*. Washington, DC: Government Printing Office, 1995.

Webster's *New World Dictionary of American English*, 1988.

Chapter 1

Kaliski, Burton S., *Encyclopedia of Busine$$ and Finance, Volumes 1 and 2*, Macmillian Reference USA, 2001.
Ibid., 553–556.
Ibid., 660–661.
Ibid., 1, 4, 13, 48–49.
Ibid., 70–73, 208–210, 365.
Ibid., 257–262, 267–270, 551–552.
Ibid., 13, 365–370, 393–397.
Ibid., 252, 458, 465–469, 721.
Ibid., 576–580.

Chapter 2

www.libsci.sc.edu, "Uniform Commercial Code."

www.nccusi.org, "Uniform Law Commissioners."

www.ali.org, "American Law Institute."

www.bambooweb.com, "Uniform Commercial Code."

www.law.cornell.edu, "Uniform Commercial Code."

www.acqnet.gov, FAR, para.1.101 and para.1.201

www.acqnet.gov, FAR, General Structure and Subparts.

International Commercial Contracting, FPI Inc., 1996, Section II. A. 1.

Kaliski, Burton S., *Encyclopedia of Busine$$ and Finance, Volumes 1 and 2*, Macmillian Reference USA, 2001, 776–780.

Chapter 3

www.acqnet.gov, FAR, paras 7.102-7.104, paras. 10.001 and 10.002, para. 7.105, Subchapter C, Parts 14–17.

Garrett, Gregory A., *World Class Contracting*, Riverwoods, IL: CCH, Inc, 2001.

www.acqnet.gov, FAR, para 32.703, paras 32.001, 32.102, 32.106, 32.202, and para 27.104

Parmet, Jeff C., et al., "Protecting Intellectual Property During the Internet Age." *Contract Management* (July 2003): 8–15.

Gabbard, Ernest. "Intellectual Property Rights for Commercial Contracting." *Contract Management* (June 1999): 39–40.

Thibodeaux, Lynette M. "What Everyone Should Know About Copyright, Patent and Trademarks." *Contract Management* (March 1996): 12–15.

Chapter 4

Garrett, Gregory A., *World Class Contracting*, Riverwoods, IL: CCH, Inc, 2001, pgs 84–85.
Ibid., at pages 132–142.

Jacobs, Daniel M., et al, *Building a Contract: Solicitations/Bids and Proposals; A team Effort*, Vienna, VA: NCMA, 1990, 74–80.
Ibid., 86.
Ibid., 90–92.
Ibid., 96–97.

Worthington, Margaret M. and Louis P. Goldsman, *Contracting with the Federal Government, 4th ed.*, John Wiley & Sons, Inc., 1998, 49–56.

www.acqnet.gov, FAR, Subpart 12.2, Subpart 12.6, Subpart 14.1, Subpart 14.2, Subpart 15.1, and Subpart 15.3.

Chapter 5

www.acqnet.gov, FAR, Subpart 42.5, Subpart 15.5, para. 14.407, and para. 15.507.

Clancy, Michael W. *A Guide to Procurement Debriefings and Federal Bid Protest Litigation*, Journal of Contract Management, 29, Issue 2 (1999): 30–32.

Chapter 6

Garrett, Gregory A., *World Class Contracting*, Riverwoods, IL: CCH, Inc., 2001, 158–187.

Bauman, Christine M., Lt. Col., et al., *Program and Contract Changes*, Vienna,VA: NCMA, 1996, 41–49.

Using ADR to Improve Contract Performance; Seminar on Alternate Dispute Resolution. Vienna, VA: NCMA, 2–45 through 2–55.

Chapter 7

www.acqnet.gov, FAR, Part 35, Part 36, Part 39, Part 34, Part 37, Part 19, Part 22, Part 23, Part 24, Part 25, and Part 26.

Harris, George L. "Global Sourcing: Look Before You Leap." *Contract Management* (August 2000): 6–11.

Hett-Dobricky, William P., "Doing Business with State and Local Governments." *Contract Management* (September 2000): 48–50.

Patterson, Shirley, "Supply Base Optimization and Integrated Supply Chain Management." *Contract Management* (January 2005): 24–35.

The *UCC* Table of Contents

appendix a

Article 1—General Provisions

Part 1—General Provisions

1-101 Short Titles
1-102 Scope of Article
1-103 Construction of (Uniform Commercial Code) to Promote its Purposes and Policies; Applicability of Supplemental Principles of Law
1-104 Construction Against Implied Repeal
1-105 Severability
1-106 Use of Singular and Plural; Gender
1-107 Section Captions
1-108 Relation to Electronic Signatures in Global and National Commerce Act

Part 2—General Definitions and Principles of Interpretation

1-201 General Definitions
1-202 Notice; Knowledge
1-203 Lease Distinguished from Security Interest
1-204 Value
1-205 Reasonable time; Seasonableness
1-206 Presumptions

Part 3—Territorial Applicability and General Rules

1-301 Territorial Applicability; Parties' Power to Choose Applicable Law
1-302 Variation by Agreement
1-303 Course of Performance, Course of Dealing, and Usage of Trade
1-304 Obligation of Good Faith
1-305 Remedies to be Liberally Administered
1-306 Waiver or Renunciation of Claim or Right After Breach
1-307 Prima Facie Evidence by Third-Party Documents
1-308 Performance or Acceptance Under Reservation of Rights
1-309 Option to Accelerate at Will
1-310 Subordinated Obligations

Article 2—Sales

Part 1—Short Title, General Construction and Subject Matter

2-101 Short Title
2-102 Scope; Certain Security and Other Transactions Excluded From This Article
2-103 Definitions and Index of Definitions
2-104 Definitions: "Merchant;" "Between Merchants;" "Financing Agency"
2-105 Definitions: "Transferability;" "Goods;" "Future" Goods; "Lot;" "Commercial Unit"
2-106 Definitions: "Contract;" "Agreement;" "Contract for sale;" "Sale;" "Present sale;" "Conforming" to Contract; "Termination;" "Cancellation"
2-107 Goods to Be Severed From Realty; Recording

Part 2—Form, Formation and Readjustment of Contract

2-201 Formal Requirements; Statute of Frauds
2-202 Final Written Expression; Parol or Extrinsic Evidence
2-203 Seals Inoperative
2-204 Formation in General
2-205 Firm Offers
2-206 Offer and Acceptance in Formation of Contract
2-207 Additional Terms in Acceptance or Confirmation
2-209 Modification, Rescission and Waiver
2-210 Delegation of Performance; Assignment of Rights

Part 3—General Obligations and Construction of Contract

2-301 General Obligations of Parties
2-302 Unconscionable contract or Clause
2-303 Allocation or Division of Risks
2-304 Price Payable in Money, Goods, Realty, or Otherwise
2-305 Open Price Term
2-306 Output, Requirements and Exclusive Dealings
2-307 Delivery in Single Lot or Several Lots
2-308 Absence of Specified Place for Delivery
2-309 Absence of Specific Time Provisions; Notice of Termination
2-310 Open Time for Payment or Running of Credit; Authority to Ship Under Reservation
2-311 Options and Cooperation Respective Performance
2-312 Warranty of Title and Against Infringement; Buyer's Obligation Against Infringement
2-313 Express Warranties by Affirmation; Promise, Description, Sample
2-314 Implied Warranty; Merchantability; Usage of Trade

2-315	Implied Warranty; Fitness for Particular Purpose		2-514	When Documents Deliverable on Acceptance; When on Payment
2-316	Exclusion or Modification of Warranties		2-515	Preserving Evidence of Goods in Dispute
2-317	Cumulation and Conflict of Warranties Express or Implied			

Part 6—Breach, Repudiation, and Excuse

2-318	Third Party Beneficiaries of Warranties Express or Implied
2-319	F.O.B. and F.A.S. Terms
2-320	C.I.F. and C.& F. Terms
2-321	C.I.F. or C. & F.: "Net Landed Weights;" "Payment on Arrival;" Warranty of Condition on Arrival
2-322	Delivery "Ex-Ship"
2-323	From of Bill of Lading Required in Overseas Shipment; "Overseas"
2-324	"No Arrival, No sale" Term
2-325	"Letter of Credit" Term; "Confirmed Credit"
2-326	Sale on Approval and Sale or Return; Consignment Sales and Rights of Creditors
2-327	Special Incidents of Sale on Approval and Sale or Return
2-328	Sale by Auction

2-601	Buyer's Rights on Improper Delivery
2-602	Manner and Effect of Rightful Rejection
2-603	Merchant Buyer's Duties as to Rightfully Rejected Goods
2-604	Buyer's Options as to Salvage of Rightfully Rejected Goods
2-605	Waiver of Buyer's Objections by Failure to Particularize
2-606	What Constitutes Acceptance of Goods
2-607	Effect of Acceptance; Notice of Breach; Burden of Establishing Breach After Acceptance; Notice of Claim or Litigation to Person Answerable Over
2-608	Revocation of Acceptance in Whole or in Part
2-609	Right to Adequate Assurance of Performance
2-610	Anticipatory Repudiation
2-611	Retraction of Anticipatory Repudiation
2-612	"Installment contract;" Breach
2-613	Casualty to Identified Goods
2-614	Substituted Performance
2-615	Excuse by Failure of Presupposed Conditions
2-616	Procedure on Notice Claiming Excuse

Part 4—Title, Creditors, and Good Faith Purchasers

2-401	Passing of Title; Reservation for Security; Limited Application of This Section
2-402	Rights of Seller's Creditors Against Sold Goods
2-403	Power to Transfer; Good Faith Purchase of Goods; "Entrusting"

Part 5—Performance

2-501	Insurable Interest in Goods; Manner of Identification of Goods
2-502	Buyer's Right to Goods on Seller's Repudiation, Failure to Deliver or Insolvency
2-503	Manner of Seller's Tender of Delivery
2-504	Shipment by Seller
2-505	Seller's Shipment Under Reservation
2-506	Rights of Financing agency
2-507	Effect of Seller's Tender; Delivery on Condition
2-508	Cure by Seller of Improper Tender or Delivery; Replacement
2-509	Risk of Loss in the Absence of Breach
2-510	Effect of Breach on Risk or Loss
2-511	Tender of Payment by Buyer; Payment by Check
2-512	Payment by Buyer Before Inspection
2-513	Buyer's Right to Inspection of Goods

Part 7—Remedies

2-701	Remedies for Breach of Collateral contracts Not Impaired
2-702	Seller's Remedies on Discovery of Buyer's Insolvency
2-703	Seller's Remedies in General
2-704	Seller's Right to Identify Goods to the Contract Notwithstanding Breach or to Salvage Unfinished Goods
2-705	Seller's Stoppage of Delivery in Transit or Otherwise
2-706	Seller's Resale Including Contract for Resale
2-707	"Person in the Position of a Seller"
2-708	Seller's Damages for Non-acceptance or Repudiation
2-709	Action for the Price
2-710	Seller's Incidental Damages
2-711	Buyer's Remedies in General; Buyer's Security Interest in Rejected Goods
2-712	"Cover;" Buyer's Procurement of Substitute Goods

2-713	Buyer's Damages for non-delivery or Repudiation	2A-209	Lessee Under Finance Lease as Beneficiary of Supply Contract
2-714	Buyer's Damages for Breach in Regard to Accepted Goods	2A-210	Express Warranties
2-715	Buyer's Incidental and Consequential Damages	2A-211	Warranties Against Interference and Against Infringement; Lessee's Obligation Against Infringement
2-716	Buyer's Right to Specific Performance or Replevin	2A-212	Implied Warranty of Merchantability
2-717	Deduction of Damages From the Price	2A-213	Implied Warranty of Fitness for Particular Purpose
2-718	Liquidation or Limitation of Damages; Deposits	2A-214	Exclusion or Modification of Warranties
2-719	Contractual Modification or Limitation of Remedy	2A-215	Cumulation and Conflict of Warranties Express or Implied
2-720	Effect of "Cancellation" or "Rescission" on Claims for Antecedent Breach	2A-216	Third-Party Beneficiaries of Express or Implied Warranties
2-721	Remedies for Fraud	2A-217	Identification
2-722	Who Can Sue Third Parties for Injury to Goods	2A-218	Insurance and Proceeds
2-723	Proof of Market Price; Time and Place	2A-219	Risk of Loss
2-724	Admissibility of Market Quotations	2A-220	Effect of Default on Risk or Loss
2-725	Statute of Limitations in Contracts for Sale	2A-221	Casualty to Identified Goods

Article 2A—Leases

Part 1—General Provisions

2A-101	Short Title
2A-102	Scope
2A-103	Definitions and Index of Definitions
2A-104	Leases Subject to Other Law
2A-105	Territorial Application of Article to Goods Covered by Certificate of Title
2A-106	Limitation on Power of Parties to Consumer Lease to Choose Applicable Law and Judicial Forum
2A-107	Waiver or Renunciation of Claim or Right After Default
2A-108	Unconscionability
2A-109	Option to Accelerate at Will

Part 2—Formation and Construction of Lease Contract

2A-201	Statute of Frauds
2A-202	Final Written Expression; Parol or Extrinsic Evidence
2A-203	Seals Inoperative
2A-204	Formation in General
2A-205	Firm Offers
2A-206	Offer and Acceptance in Formation of Lease Contract
2A-208	Modification, Rescission, and Waiver

Part 3—Effect of Lease Contract

2A-301	Enforceability of Lease Contract
2A-302	Title To and Possession Of Goods
2A-303	Alienability of Party's Interest Under Lease Contract or of Lessor's Residual Interest in Goods; Delegation of Performance; Transfer of Rights
2A-304	Subsequent Lease of Goods by Lessor
2A-305	Sale or Sublease of Goods by Lessee
2A-306	Priority of Certain Liens Arising by Operation of Law
2A-307	Priority of Liens Arising by Attachment or Levy on, Security Interests in, and Other Claims to Goods
2A-308	Special Rights of Creditors
2A-309	Lessor's and Lessee's Rights When Goods Become Fixtures
2A-310	Lessor's and Lessee's Rights When Goods Become Accessions
2A-311	Priority Subject to Subordination

Part 4—Performance of Lease Contract: Repudiated, Substituted, and Excused

2A-401	Insecurity; Adequate Assurance of Performance
2A-402	Anticipatory Repudiation
2A-403	Retraction of Anticipatory Repudiation
2A-404	Substituted Performance
2A-405	Excused Performance
2A-406	Procedure on Excused Performance
2A-407	Irrevocable Promises: Finance Leases

Part 5—Default

A. In General
2A-501 Default: Procedure
2A-502 Notice After Default
2A-503 Modification or Impairment of Rights and Remedies
2A-504 Liquidation of Damages
2A-505 Cancellation and Termination and Effect of Cancellation, Termination, Rescission, or Fraud on Rights and Remedies
2A-506 Statute of Limitations
2A-507 Proof of Market Rent: Time and Place

B. Default by Lessor
2A-508 Lessee's Remedies
2A-509 Lessee's Rights on Improper Delivery; Rightful Rejection
2A-510 Installment Lease Contracts: Rejection and Default
2A-511 Merchant Lessee's Duties as to Rightfully Rejected Goods
2A-512 Lessee's Duties as to Rightfully Rejected Goods
2A-513 Cure by Lessor of Improper Tender or Delivery; Replacement
2A-514 Waiver of Lessee's Objections
2A-515 Acceptance of Goods
2A-516 Effect of Acceptance of Goods; Notice of Default; Burden of Establishing Default After Acceptance; Notice of Claim or Litigation to Person Answerable Over
2A-517 Revocation of Acceptance of Goods
2A-518 Cover; Substitute Goods
2A-519 Lessee's Damages for Non-delivery, Repudiation, Default, and Breach of Warranty in Regard to Accepted Goods
2A-520 Lessee's Incidental and Consequential Damages
2A-521 Lessee's Right to Specific Performance or Replevin
2A-522 Lessee's Right to Goods on Lessor's Insolvency

C. Default by Lessee
2A-523 Lessor's Remedies
2A-524 Lessor's Right to Identify Goods to Lease Contract
2A-525 Lessor's Right to Possession of Goods
2A-526 Lessor's Stoppage of Delivery in Transit or Otherwise
2A-527 Lessor's Rights to Dispose of Goods
2A-528 Lessor's Damages for Non-acceptance, Failure to Pay, Repudiation, or Other Default
2A-529 Lessor's Action for the Rent
2A-530 Lessor's Incidental Damages
2A-531 Standing to Sue Third Parties for Injury to Goods
2A-532 Lessor's Rights to Residual Interest

Article 3—Negotiable Instruments

Part 1—General Provisions and Definitions
3-101 Short Title
3-102 Subject Matter
3-103 Definitions
3-104 Negotiable Instrument
3-105 Issue of Instrument
3-106 Unconditional Promise or Order
3-107 Instrument Payable in Foreign Money
3-108 Payable on Demand or at Definite Time
3-109 Payable to Bearer or to Order
3-110 Identification of Person to Whom Instrument is Payable
3-111 Place of Payment
3-112 Interest
3-113 Date of Instrument
3-114 Contradictory Terms of Instrument
3-115 Incomplete Instrument
3-116 Joint and Several Liability; Contribution
3-117 Other Agreements Affecting Instrument
3-118 Statute of Limitations
3-119 Notice of Right to Defend Action

Part 2—Negotiation, Transfer, and Indorsement
3-201 Negotiation
3-202 Negotiation Subject to Rescission
3-203 Transfer of Instrument; Rights Acquired by Transfer
3-204 Indorsement
3-205 Special Indorsement; Blank Indorsement; Anomalous Indorsement
3-206 Restrictive Indorsement
3-207 Reacquisition

Part 3—Enforcement of Instruments
3-301 Person Entitled to Enforce Instrument
3-302 Holder in Due Course
3-303 Value and Consideration
3-304 Overdue Instrument
3-305 Defenses and Claims in Recoupment

3-306	Claims to an Instrument		3-604	Discharge by Cancellation or Renunciation
3-307	Notice of Breach of Fiduciary Duty		3-605	Discharge of Indorsers and Accommodation Parties
3-308	Proof of Signatures and Status as Holder in Due Course			
3-309	Enforcement of Lost, Destroyed, or Stolen Instrument			

Article 4—Bank Deposit

Part 1—General Provisions and Definitions

3-310	Effect of Instrument on Obligation for Which Taken
3-311	Accord and Satisfaction by Use of Instrument
3-312	Lost, Destroyed, or Stolen Cashier's Check, Teller's Check, or Certified Check

4-101	Short Title
4-102	Applicability
4-103	Variation by Agreement; Measure of Damages; Action Constituting Ordinary Care
4-104	Definitions and Index of Definitions
4-105	"Bank;" "Depositary Bank;" "Payor Bank;" "Intermediary Bank;" "Collecting Bank;" "Presenting Bank"
4-106	Payable Through or Payable at Bank; Collecting Bank
4-107	Separate Office of Bank
4-108	Time of Receipt of Items
4-109	Delays
4-110	Electronic Presentment
4-111	Statute of Limitations

Part 4—Liability of Parties

3-401	Signature
3-402	Signature by Representative
3-403	Unauthorized Signature
3-404	Impostors; Fictitious Payees
3-405	Employer's Responsibility for Fraudulent Indorsement by Employee
3-406	Negligence Contributing to Forged Signature or Alteration of Instrument
3-407	Alteration
3-408	Drawee Not Liable on Unaccepted Draft
3-409	Acceptance of Draft; Certified Check
3-410	Acceptance Varying Draft
3-411	Refusal to Pay Cashier's Checks, Teller's Checks, and Certified Checks
3-412	Obligation of Issuer of Note or Cashier's Check
3-413	Obligation of Acceptor
3-414	Obligation of Drawer
3-415	Obligation of Indorser
3-416	Transfer Warranties
3-417	Presentment Warranties
3-418	Payment or Acceptance by Mistake
3-419	Instruments Signed for Accommodation
3-420	Conversion of Instrument

Part 2—Collection of Items: Depository and Collecting Banks

4-201	Status of Collecting Bank as Agent and Provisional Status of Credits; Applicability of Article; Item Indorsed "Pay Any Bank"
4-202	Responsibility for Collection or Return; When Action Timely
4-203	Effect of Instructions
4-204	Methods of Sending and Presenting; Sending Directly to Payor Bank
4-205	Depositary Bank Holder of Unindorsed Item
4-206	Transfer Between Banks
4-207	Transfer Warranties
4-208	Presentment Warranties
4-209	Encoding and Retention Warranties
4-210	Security Interest of Collecting Bank in Items, Accompanying Documents and Proceeds
4-211	When Bank Gives Value for Purposes of Holder in Due Course
4-212	Presentment by Notice of Item Not Payable By, Through, or At Bank; Liability of Drawer or Indorser
4-213	Medium and Time of Settlement by Bank
4-214	Right of Charge-Back or Refund; Liability of Collecting Bank; Return of Item

Part 5—Dishonor

3-501	Presentment
3-502	Dishonor
3-503	Notice of Dishonor
3-504	Excused Presentment and Notice of Dishonor
3-505	Evidence of Dishonor

Part 6—Discharge and Payment

3-601	Discharge and Effect of Discharge
3-602	Payment
3-603	Tender for Payment

4-215	Final Payment of Item by Payor Bank; When Provisional Debits and Credits Become Final; When Certain Credits Become Available for Withdrawal	
4-216	Insolvency and Preference	

Part 3—Collection of Items: Payor Banks

4-301	Deferred Posting; Recovery of Payment by Return of Items; Time of Dishonor; Return of Items by Payor Bank
4-302	Payor Bank's Responsibility for Late Return of Item
4-303	When Items Subject to Notice, Stop-Payment Order, Legal Process, or Setoff; Order in Which Items May Be Charged or Certified

Part 4—Relationship Between Payor Bank and Its Customer

4-401	When Bank May Charge Customer's Account
4-402	Bank's Liability to Customer for Wrongful Dishonor; Time of Determining Insufficiency of Account
4-403	Customer's Right to Stop Payment; Burden of Proof of Loss
4-404	Bank Not Obliged to Pay Check More Than Six Months Old
4-405	Death or Incompetence of Customer
4-406	Customer's Duty to Discover and Report Unauthorized Signature or Alteration
4-407	Payor Bank's Right to Subrogation on Improper Payment

Part 5—Collection of Documentary Drafts

4-501	Handling of Documentary Drafts; Duty to Send for Presentment And to Notify Customer of Dishonor
4-502	Presentment of "On Arrival" Drafts
4-503	Responsibility of Presenting Bank for Documents and Goods; Report of Reasons for Dishonor; Referee in Case of Need
4-504	Privilege of Presenting Bank to Deal With Goods; Security Interest for Expenses

Article 4A—Funds Transfers

Part 1—Subject Matter and Definitions

4A-101 Short Title
4A-102 Subject Matter
4A-103 Payment Order-Definitions
4A-104 Funds Transfer-Definitions
4A-105 Other Definitions
4A-106 Time Payment Order is Received
4A-107 Federal Reserve Regulations and Operating Circulars
4A-108 Exclusion of Consumer Transactions Governed by Federal Law

Part 2—Issue and Acceptance of Payment Order

4A-201 Security Procedure
4A-202 Authorized and Verified Payment Orders
4A-203 Unenforceability of Certain Verified Payment Orders
4A-204 Refund of Payment and Duty of Customer to Report with Respect to Unauthorized Payment Order
4A-205 Erroneous Payment Orders
4A-206 Transmission of Payment Order Through Funds-Transfer or Other Communication System
4A-207 Misdescription of Beneficiary
4A-208 Misdescription of Intermediary Bank or Beneficiary's Bank
4A-209 Acceptance of Payment Order
4A-210 Rejection of Payment Order
4A-211 Cancellation and Amendment of Payment Order
4A-212 Liability and Duty of Receiving Bank Regarding Unaccepted Payment Order

Part 3—Execution of Sender's Payment Order by Receiving Bank

4A-301 Execution and Execution Date
4A-302 Obligations of Receiving Bank in Execution of Payment Order
4A-303 Erroneous Execution of Payment Order
4A-304 Duty of Sender to Report Erroneously Executed Payment Order
4A-305 Liability for Late or Improper Execution or Failure to Execute Payment Order

Part 4—Payment

4A-401 Payment Date
4A-402 Obligation of Sender to Pay Receiving Bank
4A-403 Payment by Sender to Receiving Bank
4A-404 Obligation of Beneficiary's Bank to Pay and Give Notice to Beneficiary
4A-405 Payment by Beneficiary's Bank to Beneficiary
4A-406 Payment by Originator to Beneficiary; Discharge of Underlying Obligation

Part 5—Miscellaneous Provisions

4A-501 Variation by Agreement and Effect of Funds-Transfer System Rule
4A-502 Creditor Process Served on Receiving Bank; Setoff by Beneficiary's Bank
4A-503 Injunction or Restraining Order with Respect to Funds Transfer
4A-504 Order in Which Items and Payment Orders may be Charged to Account; Order of Withdrawals from Account
4A-505 Preclusion of Objection to Debit of Customer's Account
4A-506 Rate of Interest
4A-507 Choice of Law

Article 5—Letters of Credit

5-101 Short Title
5-102 Definitions
5-103 Scope
5-104 Formal Requirements
5-105 Consideration
5-106 Issuance, Amendment, Cancellation, and Duration
5-107 Confirmer, Nominated Person, and Adviser
5-108 Issuer's Rights and Obligations
5-109 Fraud and Forgery
5-110 Warranties
5-111 Remedies
5-112 Transfer of Letter of Credit
5-113 Transfer by Operation of Law
5-114 Assignment of Proceeds
5-115 Statute of Limitations
5-116 Choice of Law and Forum
5-117 Subrogation of Issuer, Applicant, and Nominated Person
5-118 Security Interest of Issuer or Nominated Person

Article 6—Bulk Transfers and Bulk Sales

Alternative A

1 Repeal
2 Amendment
3 Amendment
4 Savings Clause

Alternative B

Part 1—Subject Matter and Definitions

6-101 Short Title
6-102 Definitions and Index of Definitions
6-103 Applicability of Article
6-104 Obligations of Buyer
6-105 Notice to Claimants
6-106 Schedule of Distribution
6-107 Liability for Noncompliance
6-108 Bulk Sales by Auction; Bulk Sales Conducted by Liquidator
6-109 What Constitutes Filing; Duties of Filing Officer; Information from Filing Officer
6-110 Limitation of Actions

Article 7—Warehouse Receipts, Bills of Lading, and Other Documents of Title

Part 1—General

7-101 Short Title
7-102 Definitions and Index of Definitions
7-103 Relation of Article to Treaty, Statute, Tariff, Classification or Regulation
7-104 Negotiable and Non-negotiable Warehouse Receipt, Bill of Lading or Other Document of Title
7-105 Construction Against Negative Implication

Part 2—Warehouse Receipts: Special Provisions

7-201 Who May Issue a Warehouse Receipt; Storage Under Government Bond
7-202 Form of Warehouse Receipt; Essential Terms; Optional Terms
7-203 Liability for Non-receipt of Misdescription
7-204 Duty of Care; Contractual Limitation of Warehouseman's Liability
7-205 Title Under Warehouse Receipt Defeated in Certain Cases
7-206 Termination of Storage at Warehouseman's Option
7-207 Goods Must be Kept Separate; Fungible Goods
7-208 Altered Warehouse Receipts
7-209 Lien of Warehouseman
7-210 Enforcement of Warehouseman's Lien

Part 3—Bills of Lading; Special Provisions

7-301 Liability for Non-receipt or Misdescription; "Said to Contain;" "Shipper's Load and Count;" Improper Handling
7-302 Through Bills of Lading and Similar Documents
7-303 Diversion; Reconsignment; Change of Instructions

7-304	Bills of Lading in a Set		8-103	Rules for Determining Whether Certain Obligations and Interests are Securities or Financial Assets
7-305	Destination Bills			
7-306	Altered Bills of Lading			
7-307	Lien of Carrier		8-104	Acquisition of Security or Financial Asset or Interest Therein
7-308	Enforcement of Carrier's Lien			
7-309	Duty of Care; Contractual Limitation of Carrier's Liability		8-105	Notice of Adverse Claim
			8-106	Control
			8-107	Whether Indorsement, Instruction, or Entitlement Order is Effective

Part 4—Warehouse Receipts and Bills of Lading; General Obligations

7-401	Irregularities in Issue of Receipt or Bill or Conduct of Issuer
7-402	Duplicate Receipt or Bill; Overissue
7-403	Obligation of Warehouseman or Carrier to Deliver; Excuse
7-404	No Liability for Good Faith Delivery Pursuant to Receipt or Bill

8-108	Warranties in Direct Holding
8-109	Warranties in Indirect Holding
8-110	Applicability; Choice of Law
8-111	Clearing Corporation Rules
8-112	Creditor's Legal Process
8-113	Statute of Frauds Inapplicable
8-114	Evidentiary Rules Concerning Certificated Securities
8-115	Securities Intermediary and Others Not Liable to Adverse Claimant
8-116	Securities Intermediary as Purchaser For Value

Part 5—Warehouse Receipts and Bills of Lading; Negotiation and Transfer

7-501	Form of Negotiation and Requirements of "Due Negotiation"
7-502	Rights Acquired by Due Negotiation
7-503	Document of Title to Goods Defeated in Certain Cases
7-504	Rights Acquired in the Absence of Due Negotiation; Effect of Diversion; Seller's Stoppage of Delivery
7-505	Indorser Not a Guarantor for Other Parties
7-506	Delivery Without Indorsement; Right to Compel Indorsement
7-507	Warranties on Negotiation or Transfer of Receipt or Bill
7-508	Warranties of Collecting Bank as to Documents
7-509	Receipt or Bill; When Adequate Compliance With Commercial Contract

Part 2—Issue and Issuer

8-201	Issuer
8-202	Issuer's Responsibility and Defenses; Notice of Defect or Defense
8-203	Staleness as Notice of Defect or Defense
8-204	Effect of Issuer's Restriction on Transfer
8-205	Effect of Unauthorized Signature on Security Certificate
8-206	Completion or Alteration of Security Certificate
8-207	Rights and Duties of Issuer with Respect to Registered Owners
8-208	Effect of Signature of Authenticating Trustee, Registrar, or Transfer Agent
8-209	Issuers Lien
8-210	Overissue

Part 6—Warehouse Receipts and Bills of Lading; Miscellaneous Provisions

7-601	Lost and Missing Documents
7-602	Attachment of Goods Covered by a Negotiable Document
7-603	Conflicting Claims; Interpleader

Part 3—Transfer of Certificated and Uncertificated Securities

8-301	Delivery
8-302	Rights of Purchaser
8-303	Protected Purchaser
8-304	Indorsement
8-305	Instruction
8-306	Effect of Guaranteeing Signature, Indorsement, or Instruction
8-307	Purchaser's Right to Requisites for Registration of Transfer

Article 8—Investment Securities

Part 1—Short Title and General Matters

8-101	Short Title
8-102	Definitions

Part 4—Registration

8-401	Duty of Issuer to Register Transfer
8-402	Assurance that Indorsement or Instruction is Effective
8-403	Demand That Issuer Not Register Transfer
8-404	Wrongful Registration
8-405	Replacement of Lost, Destroyed, or Wrongfully Taken Security Certificate
8-406	Obligation to Notify Issuer of Lost, Destroyed, or Wrongfully Taken Security Certificate
8-407	Authenticating Trustee, Transfer Agent, and Registrar

Part 5—Security Entitlements

8-501	Securities Account; Acquisition of Security Entitlement from Securities Intermediary
8-502	Assertion of Adverse Claim Against Entitlement Holder
8-503	Property Interest of Entitlement Holder in Financial Asset Held By Securities Intermediary
8-504	Duty of Securities Intermediary to Maintain Financial Asset
8-505	Duty of Securities Intermediary with Respect to Payments and Distributions
8-506	Duty of Securities Intermediary to Exercise Rights as Directed By Entitlement Holder
8-507	Duty of Securities Intermediary to Comply with Entitlement Order
8-508	Duty of Securities Intermediary to Change Entitlement Holder's Position to Other Form of Security Holding
8-509	Specification of Duties of Securities Intermediary by Other Statute or Regulation; Manner of Performance of Duties of Securities Intermediary and Exercise of Rights of Entitlement Holder
8-510	Rights of Purchaser of Security Entitlement from Entitlement Holder
8-511	Priority Among Security Interests and Entitlement Holders

Article 9—Secured Transactions

Part 1—General Provisions

Subpart 1—Short Title, Definitions, and General Concepts

9-101	Short Title
9-102	Definitions and Index of Definitions
9-103	Purchase-Money Security Interest; Application of Payments; Burden of Establishing
9-104	Control of Deposit Account
9-105	Control of Electronic Chattel Paper
9-106	Control of Investment Property
9-107	Control of Letter-of-Credit Right
9-108	Sufficiency of Description

Subpart 2—Applicability of Article

9-109	Scope
9-110	Security Interests Arising Under Article 2 or 2A

Part 2—Effectiveness of Security Agreement; Attachment of Security Interest; Rights of Parties to Security Agreement

Subpart 1—Effectiveness and Attachment

9-201	General Effectiveness of Security Agreement
9-202	Title to Collateral Immaterial
9-203	Attachment and Enforceability of Security Interest; Proceeds; Supporting Obligations; Formal Requisites
9-204	After-Acquired Property; Future Advances
9-205	Use or Disposition of Collateral Permissible
9-206	Security Interest Arising in Purchase or Delivery of Financial Asset

Subpart 2—Rights and Duties

9-207	Rights and Duties of Secured Party Having Possession or Control of Collateral
9-208	Additional Duties of Secured Party Having Control of Collateral
9-209	Duties of Secured Party if Account Debtor Has Been Notified of Assignment
9-210	Request for Accounting; Request Regarding List of Collateral or Statement of Account

Part 3—Perfection and Priority

Subpart 1—Law Governing Perfection and Priority

9-301	Law Governing Perfection and Priority of Security Interests
9-302	Law Governing Perfection and Priority of Agricultural Liens
9-303	Law Governing Perfection and Priority of Security Interests in Goods Covered by a Certificate of Title
9-304	Law Governing Perfection and Priority of Security Interests in Deposit Accounts
9-305	Law Governing Perfection and Priority of Security Interests in Investment Property

9-306	Law Governing Perfection and Priority of Security Interests in Letter-of-Credit Rights	9-327	Priority of Security Interests in Deposit Account
9-307	Location of Debtor	9-328	Priority of Security Interests in Investment Property
9-308	When Security Interest or Agricultural Lien is Perfected; Continuity of Perfection	9-329	Priority of Security Interests in Letter-of-Credit Right
9-309	Security Interest Perfected Upon Attachment	9-330	Priority of Purchaser of Chattel Paper or Instrument
9-310	When Filing Required to Perfect Security Interest or Agricultural Lien; Security Interests and Agricultural Liens to Which Filing Provisions Do Not Apply	9-331	Priority of Rights of Purchasers of Instruments, Documents, and Securities Under Other Articles; Priority of Interests in Financial Assets and Security Entitlements Under Article 8
9-311	Perfection of Security Interests in Property Subject to Certain Statutes, Regulations, and Treaties	9-332	Transfer of Money; Transfer of Funds from Deposit Account
9-312	Perfection of Security Interests in Chattel Paper, Deposit Accounts, Documents, Goods Covered by Documents, Instruments, Investment Property, Letter-of-Credit Rights, and Money; Perfection by Permissive Filing; Temporary Perfection Without Filing or Transfer or Possession	9-333	Priority of Certain Liens Arising by Operation of Law
		9-334	Priority of Security Interests in Fixtures and Crops
		9-335	Accessions
		9-336	Commingled Goods
9-313	When Possession By or Delivery To Secured Party Perfects Security Interest Without Filing	9-337	Priority of Security Interests in Goods Covered by Certificate of Title
9-314	Perfection by Control	9-338	Priority of Security Interest or Agricultural Lien Perfected by Filed Financing Statement Providing Certain Incorrect Information
9-315	Secured Party's Rights on Disposition of Collateral and in Proceeds		
9-316	Continued Perfection of Security Interest Following Change in Governing Law	9-339	Priority Subject to Subordination

Subpart 3—Priority

Subpart 4—Rights of Bank

9-317	Interests That Take Priority Over or Take Free of Unperfected Security Interest or Agricultural Lien	9-340	Effectiveness of Right of Recoupment or Set-off Against Deposit Account
		9-341	Bank's Rights and Duties With Respect To Deposit Account
9-318	No Interest Retained in Right to Payment That Is Sold; Rights and Title of Seller of Account or Chattel Paper With Respect To Creditors and Purchasers	9-342	Bank's Right to Refuse to Enter Into or Disclose Existence of Control Agreement

Part 4—Rights of Third Parties

9-319	Rights and Title of Consignee With Respect To Creditors and Purchasers	9-401	Alienability of Debtor's Rights
		9-402	Secured Party Not Obligated on Contract of Debtor or in Tort
9-320	Buyer of Goods		
9-321	Licensee of General Intangible and Lessee of Goods in Ordinary Course of Business	9-403	Agreement Not To Assert Defenses Against Assignee
9-322	Priorities Among Conflicting Security Interests In and Agricultural Liens in Same Collateral	9-404	Rights Acquired by Assignee; Claims and Defenses Against Assignee
		9-405	Modification of Assigned Contract
9-323	Future Advances	9-406	Discharge of Account Debtor; Notification of Assignment; Identification and Proof of Assignment; Restrictions on Assignment of Accounts, Chattel Paper, Payment Intangibles, and Promissory Notes Ineffective
9-324	Priority of Purchase-Money Security Interests		
9-325	Priority of Security Interests in Transferred Collateral		
9-326	Priority of Security Interests Created by New Debtor		

9-407 Restrictions on Creation or Enforcement of Security Interest in Leasehold Interest or in Lessor's Residual Interest
9-408 Restrictions on Assignment of Promissory Notes, Health Care Insurance Receivables, and Certain General Intangibles Ineffective
9-409 Restrictions on Assignment of Letter-of-Credit Rights Ineffective

Part 5—Filing

Subpart 1—Filing Office; Contents and Effectiveness of Financing Statement

9-501 Filing Office
9-502 Contents of Financing Statement; Record of Mortgage as Financing Statement; Time of Filing Financing Statement
9-503 Name of Debtor and Secured Party
9-504 Indication of Collateral
9-505 Filing and Compliance with Other Statutes and Treaties for Consignments, Leases, Other Bailments, and Other Transactions
9-506 Effect of Errors or Omissions
9-507 Effect of Certain Events on Effectiveness of Financing Statement
9-508 Effectiveness of Financing Statement if New Debtor Becomes Bound by Security Agreement
9-509 Persons Entitled to File a Record
9-510 Effectiveness of Filed Record
9-511 Secured Party of Record
9-512 Amendment of Financing Statement
9-513 Termination Statement
9-514 Assignment of Powers of Secured Party of Record
9-515 Duration and Effectiveness of Financing Statement; Effect of Lapsed Financing Statement
9-516 What Constitutes Filing; Effectiveness of Filing
9-517 Effect of Indexing Errors
9-518 Claim Concerning Inaccurate or Wrongfully Filed Record

Subpart 2—Duties and Operation of Filing Office

9-519 Numbering, Maintaining, and Indexing Records; Communicating Information Provided in Records
9-520 Acceptance and Refusal to Accept Record
9-521 Uniform Form of Written Financing Statement and Amendment
9-522 Maintenance and Destruction of Records
9-523 Information from Filing office; Sale or License of Records
9-524 Delay by Filing Office
9-525 Fees
9-526 Filing Office Rules
9-527 Duty to Report

Part 6—Default

Subpart 1—Default and Enforcement of Security Interest

9-601 Rights After Default; Judicial Enforcement; Consignor or Buyer of Accounts, Chattel Paper, Payment Intangibles or Promissory Notes
9-602 Waiver and Variance of Rights and Duties
9-603 Agreement on Standards Concerning Rights and Duties
9-604 Procedure if Security Agreement Covers Real Property or Fixtures
9-605 Unknown Debtor or Secondary Obligor
9-606 Time of Default for Agricultural Lien
9-607 Collection and Enforcement by Secured Party
9-608 Application of Proceeds of Collection or Enforcement; Liability for Deficiency and Right to Surplus
9-609 Secured Party's Right to Take Possession After Default
9-610 Disposition of Collateral After Default
9-611 Notification Before Disposition of Collateral
9-612 Timeliness of Notification Before Disposition of Collateral
9-613 Contents and Form of Notification Before Disposition if Collateral; General
9-614 Contents and Form of Notification Before Disposition if Collateral; Consumer-Goods Transaction
9-615 Application of Proceeds of Disposition; Liability for Deficiency and Right to Surplus
9-616 Explanation of Calculation of Surplus or Deficiency
9-617 Rights of Transferee of Collateral
9-618 Rights and Duties of Certain Secondary Obligors
9-619 Transfer of Record or Legal Title
9-620 Acceptance of Collateral in Full or Partial Satisfaction of Obligation; Compulsory Disposition of Collateral
9-621 Notification of Proposal to Accept Collateral
9-622 Effect of Acceptance of Collateral
9-623 Right to Redeem Collateral
9-624 Waiver

Subpart 2—Noncompliance with Article

9-625	Remedies for Secured Party's Failure to Comply with Article
9-626	Action in which Deficiency or Surplus is in Issue
9-627	Determination of Whether Conduct was Commercially Reasonable
9-628	Nonliability and Limitation on Liability of Secured Party; Liability of Secondary Obligor

Part 7—Transition

9-701	Effective Date
9-702	Savings Clause
9-703	Security Interest Perfected Before Effective Date
9-704	Security Interest Unperfected Before Effective Date
9-705	Effectiveness of Action Taken Before Effective Date
9-706	When Initial Financing Statement Suffices to Continue Effectiveness of Financing Statement
9-707	Amendment of Pre-Effective-Date Financing Statement
9-708	Persons Entitled to File Initial Financing Statement or Continuation Statement
9-709	Priority

The *FAR* Table of Contents

appendix b

Subchapter A—General

Part 1—Federal Acquisition Regulations System

1.1	Purpose, Authority, Issuance
1.2	Administration
1.3	Agency Acquisition Regulations
1.4	Deviations from the FAR
1.5	Agency and Public Participation
1.6	Career Development, Contracting Authority, and Responsibilities
1.7	Determinations and Findings

Part 2—Definitions of Words and Terms

2.1	Definitions
2.2	Definitions Clause

Part 3—Improper Business Practices and Personal Conflicts of Interest

3.1	Safeguards
3.2	Contractor Gratuities to Government Personnel
3.3	Reports of Suspected Antitrust Violations
3.4	Contingent Fees
3.5	Other Improper Business Practices
3.6	Contracts with Government Employees or Organizations Owned or Controlled by Them
3.7	Voiding and Rescinding Contracts
3.8	Limitation on the Payment of Funds to Influence Federal Transactions
3.9	Whistleblower Protections for Contractor Employees

Part 4—Administrative Matters

4.1	Contract Execution
4.2	Contract Distribution
4.3	Paper Documents
4.4	Safeguarding Classified Information Within Industry
4.5	Electronic Commerce in Contracting
4.6	Contract Reporting
4.7	Contractor Records Retention
4.8	Government Contract Files
4.9	Taxpayer Identification Number Information
4.10	Contract Line Items
4.11	Central Contractor Registration
4.12	Annual Representations and Certifications
4.13	Personal Identity Verification of Contractor Personnel

Subchapter B—Competition and Acquisition Planning

Part 5—Publicizing Contract Actions

5.1	Dissemination of Information
5.2	Synopses of Proposed Contract Actions
5.3	Synopses of Contract Awards
5.4	Release of Information
5.5	Paid Advertisements
5.6	Publicizing Multi-Agency Use Contracts

Part 6—Competition Requirements

6.1	Full and Open Competition
6.2	Full and Open Competition After Exclusion of Sources
6.3	Other Than Full and Open Competition
6.4	Sealed Bidding and Competitive Proposals
6.5	Competition Advocates
6.6	Stafford Act Preference for Local Area Contractor

Part 7—Acquisition Planning

7.1	Acquisition Plans
7.2	Planning for the Purchase of Supplies in Economic Quantities
7.3	Contractor Versus Government Performance
7.4	Equipment Lease or Purchase
7.5	Inherently Governmental Functions

Part 8—Required Sources of Supplies and Services

8.1	Excess Personal Property
8.2	[Reserved]
8.3	[Reserved]
8.4	Federal Supply Schedules
8.5	Acquisition of Helium
8.6	Acquisition from Federal Prison Industries, Inc.
8.7	Acquisition from Nonprofit Agencies Employing People Who Are Blind or Severely Disabled
8.8	Acquisition of Printing and Related Supplies
8.9	[Reserved]
8.10	[Reserved]
8.11	Leasing of Motor Vehicles

Part 9—Contractor Qualifications

9.1	Responsible Prospective Contractors
9.2	Qualifications Requirements
9.3	First Article Testing and Approval

9.4 Debarment, Suspension, and Ineligibility
9.5 Organizational and Consultant Conflicts of Interest
9.6 Contractor Team Arrangements
9.7 Defense Production Pools and Research and Development Pools

Part 10—Market Research

Part 11—Describing Agency Needs

11.1 Selecting and Developing Requirements Documents
11.2 Using and Maintaining Requirements Documents
11.3 Acceptable Material
11.4 Delivery or Performance Schedules
11.5 Liquidated Damages
11.6 Priorities and Allocations
11.7 Variation in Quantity
11.8 Testing

Part 12—Acquisition of Commercial Items

12.1 Acquisition of Commercial Items—General
12.2 Special Requirements for the Acquisition of Commercial Items
12.3 Solicitation Provisions and Contract Clauses for the Acquisition of Commercial Items
12.4 Unique Requirements Regarding Terms and Conditions for Commercial Items
12.5 Applicability of Certain Laws to the Acquisition of Commercial Items
12.6 Streamlined Procedures for Evaluation and Solicitation for Commercial Items

Subchapter C—Contracting Methods and Contract Types

Part 13—Simplified Acquisition Procedures

13.1 Procedures
13.2 Actions At or Below the Micro-Purchase Threshold
13.3 Simplified Acquisition Methods
13.4 Fast Payment Procedure
13.5 Test Program for Certain Commercial Items

Part 14—Sealed Bidding

14.1 Use of Sealed Bidding
14.2 Solicitation of Bids
14.3 Submission of Bids
14.4 Opening of Bids and Award of Contract
14.5 Two-Step Sealed Bidding

Part 15—Contracting by Negotiation

15.1 Source Selection Processes and Techniques
15.2 Solicitation and Receipt of Proposals and Information
15.3 Source Selection
15.4 Contract Pricing
15.5 Pre-award, Award, and Post-award Notifications, Protests, and Mistakes
15.6 Unsolicited Proposals

Part 16—Types of Contracts

16.1 Selecting Contract Types
16.2 Fixed-Price Contracts
16.3 Cost-Reimbursement Contracts
16.4 Incentive Contracts
16.5 Indefinite-Delivery Contracts
16.6 Time-and-Materials, Labor-Hour, and Letter Contracts
16.7 Agreements

Part 17—Special Contracting Methods

17.1 Multi-year Contracting
17.2 Options
17.3 [Reserved]
17.4 Leader Company Contracting
17.5 Interagency Acquisitions Under the Economy Act
17.6 Management and Operating Contracts

Part 18—Emergency Acquisitions

18.1 Available Acquisition Flexibilities
18.2 Emergency Acquisition Flexibilities

Subchapter D—Socioeconomic Programs

Part 19—Small Business Programs

19.1 Size Standards
19.2 Policies
19.3 Determination of Small Business Status for Small Business Programs
19.4 Cooperation with the Small Business Administration
19.5 Set-Asides for Small Business
19.6 Certificates of Competency and Determinations of Responsibility
19.7 The Small Business Subcontracting Program
19.8 Contracting with the Small Business Administration (The 8(a) Program)
19.9 [Reserved]

19.10	Small Business Competitiveness Demonstration Program
19.11	Price Evaluation Adjustment for Small Disadvantaged Business Concerns
19.12	Small Disadvantaged Business Participation Program
19.13	Historically Underutilized Business Zone (HUBZone) Program
19.14	Service-Disabled Veteran-Owned Small Business Procurement Program

Part 20—Reserved

Part 21—Reserved

Part 22—Application of Labor Laws to Government Acquisitions

22.1	Basic Labor Policies
22.2	Convict Labor
22.3	Contract Work Hours and Safety Standards Act
22.4	Labor Standards for Contracts Involving Construction
22.5	[Reserved]
22.6	Walsh-Healey Public Contracts Act
22.7	[Reserved]
22.8	Equal Employment Opportunity
22.9	Nondiscrimination Because of Age
22.10	Service Contract Act of 1965, as Amended
22.11	Professional Employee Compensation
22.12	[Reserved]
22.13	Special Disabled Veterans, Veterans of the Vietnam Era, and Other Eligible Veterans
22.14	Employment of Workers with Disabilities
22.15	Prohibition of Acquisition of Products Produced by Forced or Indentured Child Labor
22.16	Notification of Employee Rights Concerning Payment of Union Dues or Fees
22.17	Combating Trafficking in Persons

Part 23—Environment, Energy and Water Efficiency, Renewable Energy Technologies, Occupational Safety, and Drug-Free Workplace

23.1	[Reserved]
23.2	Energy and Water Efficiency and Renewable Energy
23.3	Hazardous Material Identification and Material Safety Data
23.4	Use of Recovered Materials
23.5	Drug-Free Workplace
23.6	Notice of Radioactive Material
23.7	Contracting for Environmentally Preferable Products and Services
23.8	Ozone-Depleting Substances
23.9	Contractor Compliance with Toxic Chemical Release Reporting
23.10	Federal Compliance with Right-to-Know Laws and Pollution Prevention Requirements

Part 24—Protection of Privacy and Freedom of Information

| 24.1 | Protection of Individual Privacy |
| 24.2 | Freedom of Information Act |

Part 25—Foreign Acquisition

25.1	Buy American Act—Supplies
25.2	Buy American Act—Construction Materials
25.3	[Reserved]
25.4	Trade Agreements
25.5	Evaluating Foreign Offers—Supply Contracts
25.6	[Reserved]
25.7	Prohibited Sources
25.8	Other International Agreements and Coordination
25.9	Customs and Duties
25.10	Additional Foreign Acquisition Regulations
25.11	Solicitation Provisions and Contract Clauses

Part 26—Other Socioeconomic Programs

26.1	Indian Incentive Program
26.2	Disaster or Emergency Assistance Activities
26.3	Historically Black Colleges and Universities and Minority Institutions

Subchapter E—General Contracting Requirements

Part 27—Patents, Data, and Copyrights

27.1	General
27.2	Patents
27.3	Patent Rights under Government Contracts
27.4	Rights in Data and Copyrights
27.5	[Reserved]
27.6	Foreign License and Technical Assistance Agreements

Part 28—Bonds and Insurance

28.1	Bonds and Other Financial Protections
28.2	Sureties and Other Security for Bonds
28.3	Insurance

Part 29—Taxes

29.1 General
29.2 Federal Excise Taxes
29.3 State and Local Taxes
29.4 Contract Clauses

Part 30—Cost Accounting Standards Administration

30.1 General
30.2 CAS Program Requirements
30.3 CAS Rules and Regulations [Reserved]
30.4 Cost Accounting Standards [Reserved]
30.5 Cost Accounting Standards for Educational Institutions [Reserved]
30.6 CAS Administration

Part 31—Contract Cost Principles and Procedures

31.1 Applicability
31.2 Contracts with Commercial Organizations
31.3 Contracts with Educational Institutions
31.4 [Reserved]
31.5 [Reserved]
31.6 Contracts with State, Local, and Federally Recognized Indian Tribal Governments
31.7 Contracts with Nonprofit Organizations

Part 32—Contract Financing

32.1 Non-Commercial Item Purchase Financing
32.2 Commercial Item Purchase Financing
32.3 Loan Guarantees for Defense Production
32.4 Advance Payments for Non-Commercial Items
32.5 Progress Payments Based on Costs
32.6 Contract Debts
32.7 Contract Funding
32.8 Assignment of Claims
32.9 Prompt Payment
32.10 Performance-Based Payments
32.11 Electronic Funds Transfer

Part 33—Protests, Disputes, and Appeals

33.1 Protests
33.2 Disputes and Appeals

Subchapter F—Special Categories of Contracting

Part 34—Major System Acquisition

34.0 General
34.1 Testing, Qualification and Use of Industrial Resources Developed Under Title III, Defense Production Act
34.2 Earned Value Management System

Part 35—Research and Development Contracting

Part 36—Construction and Architect–Engineer Contracts

36.1 General
36.2 Special Aspects of Contracting for Construction
36.3 Two-Phase Design-Build Selection Procedures
36.4 [Reserved]
36.5 Contract Clauses
36.6 Architect-Engineer Services
36.7 Standard and Optional Forms for Contracting for Construction, Architect-Engineer Services, and Dismantling, Demolition, or Removal of Improvements

Part 37—Service Contracting

37.1 Service Contracts—General
37.2 Advisory and Assistance Services
37.3 Dismantling, Demolition, or Removal of Improvements
37.4 Nonpersonal Health Care Services
37.5 Management Oversight of Service Contracts
37.6 Performance-Based Acquisition

Part 38—Federal Supply Schedule Contracting

38.1 Federal Supply Schedule Program
38.2 Establishing and Administering Federal Supply Schedules

Part 39—Acquisition of Information Technology

39.1 General
39.2 Electronic and Information Technology

Part 40—Reserved

Part 41—Acquisition of Utility Services

41.1 General
41.2 Acquiring Utility Services
41.3 Requests for Assistance
41.4 Administration
41.5 Solicitation Provision and Contract Clauses

41.6 Forms
41.7 Formats

Subchapter G—Contract Management

Part 42—Contract Administration and Audit Services

42.1 Contract Audit Services
42.2 Contract Administration Services
42.3 Contract Administration Office Functions
42.4 Correspondence and Visits
42.5 Post-award Orientation
42.6 Corporate Administrative Contracting Officer
42.7 Indirect Cost Rates
42.8 Disallowance of Costs
42.9 Bankruptcy
42.10 [Reserved]
42.11 Production Surveillance and Reporting
42.12 Novation and Change-of-Name Agreements
42.13 Suspension of Work, Stop-Work Orders, and Government Delay of Work
42.14 [Reserved]
42.15 Contractor Performance Information
42.16 Small Business Contract Administration
42.17 Forward Pricing Rate Agreements

Part 43—Contract Modifications

43.1 General
43.2 Change Orders
43.3 Forms

Part 44—Subcontracting Policies and Procedures

44.1 General
44.2 Consent to Subcontracts
44.3 Contractors' Purchasing Systems Reviews
44.4 Subcontracts for Commercial Items and Commercial Components

Part 45—Government Property

45.1 General
45.2 Competitive Advantage
45.3 Providing Government Property to Contractors
45.4 Contractor Use and Rental of Government Property
45.5 Management of Government Property in the Possession of Contractors
45.6 Reporting, Reutilization, and Disposal

Part 46—Quality Assurance

46.1 General
46.2 Contract Quality Requirements
46.3 Contract Clauses
46.4 Government Contract Quality Assurance
46.5 Acceptance
46.6 Material Inspection and Receiving Reports
46.7 Warranties
46.8 Contractor Liability for Loss of or Damage to Property of the Government

Part 47—Transportation

47.1 General
47.2 Contracts for Transportation or for Transportation-Related Services
47.3 Transportation in Supply Contracts
47.4 Air Transportation by U.S.-Flag Carriers
47.5 Ocean Transportation by U.S.-Flag Vessels

Part 48—Value Engineering

48.1 Policies and Procedures
48.2 Contract Clauses

Part 49—Termination of Contracts

49.1 General Principles
49.2 Additional Principles for Fixed-Price Contracts Terminated for Convenience
49.3 Additional Principles for Cost-Reimbursement Contracts Terminated for Convenience
49.4 Termination for Default
49.5 Contract Termination Clauses
49.6 Contract Termination Forms and Formats

Part 50—Extraordinary Contractual Actions

50.1 General
50.2 Delegation of and Limitations on Exercise of Authority
50.3 Contract Adjustments
50.4 Residual Powers

Part 51—Use of Government Sources by Contractors

51.1 Contractor Use of Government Supply Sources
51.2 Contractor Use of Interagency Fleet Management System (IFMS) Vehicles

Subchapter H—Clauses and Forms

Part 52—Solicitation Provisions and Contract Clauses

52.1 Instructions for Using Provisions and Clauses
52.2 Text of Provisions and Clauses
52.3 Provision and Clause Matrix

Part 53—Forms

53.1 General
53.2 Prescription of Forms
53.3 Illustration of Forms

Appendix

Index